How It Works®

Science and Technology

Third Edition

Marshall Cavendish
99 White Plains Road
Tarrytown, NY 10591

Website: www.marshallcavendish.com

Third edition updated by Brown Reference Group plc.

Library of Congress Cataloging-in-Publication Data
How it works: science and technology.—3rd ed.
p. cm.
Includes index.
ISBN 0-7614-7314-9 (set)   ISBN 0-7614-7319-X (Vol. 5)
1. Technology—Encyclopedias. 2. Science—Encyclopedias.
[1. Technology—Encyclopedias. 2. Science—Encyclopedias.]
T9 .H738 2003
603—dc21   2001028771

Consultant: Donald R. Franceschetti, Ph.D., University of Memphis

Brown Reference Group
Editor: Wendy Horobin
Associate Editors: Paul Thompson, Martin Clowes, Lis Stedman
Managing Editor: Tim Cooke
Design: Alison Gardner
Picture Research: Becky Cox
Illustrations: Mark Walker

Marshall Cavendish
Project Editor: Peter Mavrikis
Production Manager: Alan Tsai
Editorial Director: Paul Bernabeo

Printed in Malaysia
Bound in the United States of America
08 07 06 05 04   6 5 4 3 2

Title picture: A Galileo thermometer, see *Density*

How It Works®

Science and Technology

Volume 5

Cotton

Electrical Engineering

Marshall Cavendish

New York • London • Toronto • Sydney

Contents

Volume 5

Cotton

Archaeologists date the earliest use of cotton to about 3000 B.C.E. in Pakistan. Its antiquity is also established in the New World with a similar prehistory dating in Peru. The name cotton is attributed to the Arabic *qutun* (or *kutun*). It can be argued that despite strong competition from synthetic fibers, cotton remains the world's most versatile fiber. Certainly it is the most important vegetable fiber, produced by various species of the genus *Gossypium* in the Malvaceae family, and it still accounts for more than half of all fibers supplied to the textile industry. Of the many cotton species, only two are of major significance. These are *Gossypium hirsutum*, comprising the bulk of the world's commercial cottons, and *Gossypium barbadense*, which includes the fine, world-famous Sea Island and Egyptian cottons.

About 70 nations grow cotton, most of them classified as developing countries. Some 80 percent of the crop comes from these developing countries with the remainder supplied almost entirely by the United States.

During the growing period, cotton needs the warm, sunny climate associated with tropical and subtropical regions, such as the southern United States, though varieties have been adapted to widely differing cultural conditions. It is usually grown as an annual. Rainfall is important at certain stages, often supplemented by irrigation.

Cotton manufacture

After picking, cotton bolls are fed into machines called gins, which separate the fiber from the seed and remove impurities before the cotton is compressed into large bales. Each bale is graded for quality. When it reaches the spinning mill, the

process of cleaning continues through a series of machines that also open up and draw the fibers parallel. Following a number of drawing-out operations, the cotton is finally twisted into yarn. Blending is carried on throughout the operation to maintain uniformity. Cotton yarn is supplied to weaving and knitting mills, and the manufactured fabric can be bleached, dyed, printed, and finished. End uses range from all types of apparel and household materials, carpets, and industrial textiles to tenting and umbrella fabrics.

It was the Industrial Revolution that elevated the status of cotton to King Cotton. Toward the end of the 18th century, cotton provided less than 5 percent of the world's textile raw materials. By 1890, cotton accounted for nearly 80 percent of total textile consumption. The emergent factory system coincided with a number of remarkable inventions, including the steam engine, the cotton gin for stripping the lint from cottonseed mechanically, multispindle spinning with the mule and the spinning jenny, and the appearance in the weaving industry of the flying shuttle.

During the 20th century, the industry entered a constant state of development, sustained by the

◄ Cotton is an extremely versatile fiber that can be woven, knitted, dyed, or printed into a wide variety of finished materials. It is a very durable fabric—fragments of cotton cloth have been dated to 3000 B.C.E.

pressures of commercial competition. The mule gave way to the ring-spinning frame; now the so-called open-end, or break-spinning, machine, in which separated fibers are formed into a yarn on the inside surface of a rapidly rotating turbine, has become an important commercial method of yarn production. In weaving, automatic machinery has achieved dominance, using large yarn packages. In knitting, where yarn uniformity is more critical, processes for improving cotton yarn regularity and garment stability in wash-and-wear situations are of significance. In finishing, attention has been concentrated on improving easy-care performance to add to cotton's natural attributes, which include good absorbency, washability and resistance to abrasion, high strength (cotton is actually 25 percent stronger wet than dry), and an adaptability for all types of weather conditions.

The cotton plant also supports a large cotton-seed industry, providing animal foodstuffs and other byproducts for pharmaceuticals, cosmetics, and plastics. Short cotton fibers unsuited for spinning have a wide range of industrial uses. Very short fibers are used in papermaking to make disposable clothing, tissues, and similar products. The short fibers left on the seed after ginning (linters) are mostly cellulose and are used in making mattresses, high-quality writing paper, plastics, explosives, and many other products. The part of the cotton plant to be harvested is the seed pod, or cotton boll, which contains seed cotton, that is, seeds covered with fibers (lint). On ripening, the boll splits and exposes several locks of white fluffy seed cotton. In many parts of the world, this is removed from the dry capsule (burr) by hand, but where labor costs are high, machines are used.

Five varieties of cotton-harvesting machines have been developed. The most common types, however, are the picker and the stripper. The picker, also called spindle picker, is self-propelled. One, two, and four row models are available. The picking mechanism consists essentially of revolving drums, one on each side of each row, and a barbed spindle that plucks the boll out of the burr. The cotton is brushed off the spindle by a rubber doffer, which conveys it to the hopper.

The stripper removes the seed cotton together with the burr. Strippers are less complicated machines than pickers. They are usually self-propelled, but some are tractor mounted. The plants enter a gatherer that lifts the twigs bearing the bolls, which are broken from the plant and transported mechanically or pneumatically to the hopper, where the bolls are separated from the twigs. Modern machines may have a burr extractor, with or without a cotton cleaner, to remove burrs and other trash. Strippers are used for short- and medium-fiber-length varieties of cotton and are once-over machines.

Strippers are available that can pull up to six rows of plants at a time. In the United States, cotton is normally planted in rows 38 or 40 in. (1 m) apart; in some places where cotton is all hand picked, a common row spacing is 20 in. (50 cm).

Owing to a high moisture content, which will promote fungus growth, the cotton must be dried before it can be conveyed to the cotton gin. It may be stored for this purpose in a silo under controlled conditions of temperature and humidity. From these silos, the cotton may be blown through ducts to the gin. The duct may have a trap in it to separate the green (immature) bolls, which are heavier and will fall to the bottom of the duct.

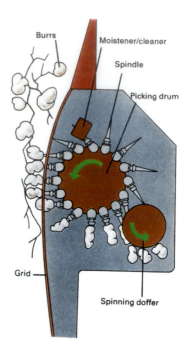

▲ Part of a cotton-harvesting machine. Spindles penetrate the cotton bolls as the picking drum rotates. Spinning doffers remove the cotton, which is blown into a basket. The spindles are then cleaned by moisteners.

FACT FILE

- Dacca muslin, a cotton fabric spun by 17th-century Indian craftsmen, was so fine that 73 sq. yds. (61 m²) of the material weighed only 16 oz. (454 g). This is less than a quarter of the weight of modern machine-made muslins. All yarn for Dacca muslin was spun by hand with a simple drop spindle.

- A law passed in Britain in 1700, owing to pressure from wool manufacturers, prohibited the sale of cotton goods. The Manchester Act of 1736, which replaced it, led to the world domination of the Lancashire cotton industry. In 1913, Lancashire exported 7 billion yards (6.4 billion m) of cotton fabric.

- A single cottonseed can produce up to 20,000 seed-hair fibers on its surface. An ounce (28 g) of ginned cotton contains about 100 million fibers, and the fibers in an 800 lbs. (363 kg) bale would stretch 12½ million miles.

SEE ALSO: CLOTHING MANUFACTURE • EXPLOSIVE • FABRIC PRINTING • FIBER, NATURAL • PAPER MANUFACTURE • PLASTICS • TEXTILE

Counterfeiting and Forgery

Forgery is the criminal act of making false copies of objects of value with the intention to deceive. The term *counterfeiting* refers specifically to the forgery of currency—banknotes and coins.

Counterfeiting and other types of forgery have been practiced for many centuries. Since ancient times, coins have been struck from solid metal using dies rather than cast from molten metal, as die-struck coins are harder to copy. Michelangelo allegedly gained fame when he sculpted a small statue, buried it for a while to make it look old, and then stepped forward as the responsible artist when the statue was discovered. More recently, early U.S. currency was printed with the legend "Tis Death to Counterfeit" as a warning to potential infractors.

Counterfeiting of banknotes

Until the 20th century, banknotes were easy to copy, and counterfeiting was widespread. The first notes of the Bank of England—issued from 1694—were handwritten, for example. In the United States, individual banks printed their own notes until the 1860s. These notes were easy to copy, and counterfeiters would start to produce successful fakes soon after each new issue.

Counterfeiting gained new significance when World War I interrupted international gold shipments and drove gold coins out of circulation in many countries, thus increasing the dependence on notes for transactions. An increase in international counterfeiting in the 1920s was one of the chief motives for the formation in 1923 of Interpol, an international police organization. In 1929, a conference in Geneva led to 32 major powers signing an international convention against counterfeiting. Its signatories agreed to punish counterfeiters of any country's money and to extradite accused counterfeiters on request.

In the United States, the Secret Service was set up in 1865 as the division of the Treasury with responsibility for tracking down counterfeiters. However, for many years, it was government policy to conceal the extent of counterfeiting from the public. This secrecy was intended to preserve public and commercial confidence in the currency. Not until the late 1930s did the secretary of the treasury initiate a program that used leaflets and motion pictures to teach the public how to spot fake currency. Even now, many millions of dollars' worth of counterfeit notes are seized by U.S. authorities each year. Much of this bogus currency is in circulation by the time it is traced, and the bearer carries the loss personally.

Anticounterfeit measures

The materials, designs, and printing process of banknotes are all chosen with a view to deterring counterfeiters. In most countries, the paper for notes is made under licence by a single company from a unique blend of cotton and linen. Such paper is more durable than that made from wood pulp. (A few countries, notably Australia, Brazil, and Singapore, now have some plastic notes.) The paper may bear a translucent watermark or incorporate metal strips as proof of authenticity; the positions of these features relative to the printed design may also help check for fake notes.

Most notes are printed using plates engraved by the printing company. During printing, the paper is forced into grooves in the plate to receive the viscous ink. This process leaves raised lines of ink, distinguishing real notes from photocopied notes, which look and feel flat by comparison.

The designs of banknotes are deliberately complicated, typically featuring portraits of famous people or historic texts and scenes. Plates are engraved by several people working separately, and a machine tool called a geometric lathe engraves complex background patterns. Fine details in the images and background of a note increase the likelihood of blurring in counterfeit notes, and some combinations of front and reverse designs have elements that unite to form an image when the note is viewed against a light.

The inks used to print banknotes are usually manufactured by the printing companies themselves according to secret formulas. Thus exact color matches are difficult for counterfeiters to achieve, particularly when three or more unusual inks are used in a single design.

▲ This French 50 franc note features a number of anticounterfeiting devices. As well as a metal foil strip, a watermark figure appears on the left-hand side. Under fluorescent light, a small white lamb appears (bottom left), which is invisible in daylight. This note goes to even more stringent precautions with another watermark of an airplane.

In addition to the printed design, some notes are inlaid with metal foil in which holographic designs have been etched. Such foils are easy to recognize when genuine and are difficult to forge.

Counterfeit-detecting tests

A number of devices are designed to provide quick and easy tests for counterfeit banknotes at points of sale and bank counters. One such device uses an ultraviolet lamp to reveal paper that has been treated with chemical brighteners. Ultraviolet light causes such paper to glow bluish white, while genuine notes do not. The U.S. First National Bank estimates that this test is effective for around 50 percent of all counterfeit notes.

Another machine depends on the iron (III) oxide inks used on U.S. banknotes or the metal strips used in British banknotes. They give the note magnetic qualities that can be read by a magnetic head similar to those in tape recorders.

Quick chemical tests include felt pens whose ink fades rapidly owing to chemicals in genuine notes but darkens permanently on fake notes. Once detected, a counterfeit note remains permanently marked as such, alerting retailers who might not have their own tester pens.

Counterfeit coins

Coin counterfeiting is much rarer than note counterfeiting, since the face values of coins tend to be less than those of notes. While genuine coins are struck between engraved dies in a machine press, counterfeit coins are usually cast from molten metal in a mold because die presses are expensive, and counterfeiters rarely have the skills to make dies. The casting process leaves its mark on counterfeit coins: because cast coins shrink in the mold as they cool, they are smaller than the genuine coins used to make the mold; the definition of the design is poor; and the coins often have a greasy feel.

Counterfeit coins can also be identified by the poor reproduction of the security design, called reeding or milling, on the edge of many coins. Furthermore, the cheap alloys used to make fake coins give a gray appearance, and their electromagnetic properties cause the coins to be rejected by the coin detectors of vending machines.

Forgery

Common acts of forgery include the faking or illegal alteration of documents. Some documents are printed on paper that carries intricate designs, characteristic watermarks, or holographic foils of the types used for banknotes. Tickets for concerts and sporting events are typically protected from forgery by these features.

◀ This statuette was thought to be an Egyptian antiquity until X-ray studies (background) revealed it as a fake. The body consists of resin weighted with brass filings, which appear as dark areas in the X ray.

Checks and other valuable documents tend to be forged by making handwritten alterations to genuine originals in order to increase their value. In such cases, the alterations can be revealed by viewing them under specific wavelengths of light. Inks that appear to be the same color in daylight can reflect different colors under alternative light sources, revealing the false additions.

Objects of art and valuable antiquities can be forged using a variety of techniques. Statues can be cast from resins, surface treated, and weighted to resemble bronze originals, for example. X-ray images and chemical analysis soon reveal fakes.

Modern copies of antique paintings can be painted over old paintings of lesser value, whose cracks then appear through the new paint. New paintings may also be cracked by rolling the canvas around a stick and then aged by filling the cracks with a dark powder that resembles dirt.

Fluorescence, infrared, and X-ray photography are often used to determine the authenticity of a piece. Flakes of paint can also be analyzed chemically for consistency with an artist's known mixing habits and with the availability of pigments at the supposed time of painting.

SEE ALSO: ARCHAEOLOGICAL TECHNOLOGIES • COINS AND MINTING • INK • METALWORKING • PAPER MANUFACTURE • PRINTING

Crane

◄ Construction sites often use a number of different cranes depending on the load to be lifted. This site features a number of single-jib crawler cranes in the background, used for lighter loads. Toward the front are two guy derricks, which are used to move loads from side to side and have a counterbalancing mast secured by guy ropes. On the far left, the first sections of a tower crane are being built.

In modern industry and commerce, the necessity of lifting and moving heavy loads takes so many different forms that a variety of cranes have been designed to deal with them. Cranes can mostly be divided into two types, with numerous variants of each: bridge cranes and jib cranes.

Any type of crane may be fitted with one of a number of lifting attachments. Webs, nets, ropes, or cables (wire rope) may be attached to the hook. For lifting bulk materials, such as ore, gravel, earth, and so on, a clam (or grab) is used, consisting of two jaws on a hinge that can be opened and shut by the operator. The operator is often responsible for the safety of the lifting operation. There is a mathematical relationship between the available strength of a cable or a rope and the angle at which it is wrapped around the article to be lifted, and the operator may be charged with the responsibility of not lifting the load until it is safely attached.

Bridge cranes

For indoor applications, such as in machine tool works, steel mills, and other types of factories, a traveling electric bridge crane is used. The hoisting apparatus travels back and forth across the width of the working area on an overhead bridge made of steel girders, while the bridge itself can travel the length of the building on trolley wheels along an elevated framework (gantry) that supports it at each end. The gantry is built against the walls of the room, or alternatively is a structural part of the building's framework. Thus, the crane can pick up a load and put it down any-

A giant container crane, which spans three rail tracks and a roadway. It is capable of five operating motions, including tilt and slew. It can also lift when the jib is level.

where in the room without taking up any floor space itself. An overhead bridge crane may be operated by means of pendants—cables and switches hanging down from the bridge—or by an operator in an overhead cab that travels along one side of the bridge. A bridge crane may be used almost continuously on a work shift, for example, to carry ladles of molten metal in a foundry, or it may be used only intermittently to move large objects, as in the erection of heavy machinery. Rotary bridge cranes can be used in circular spaces. In this type of crane, one end of the overhead beam is supported by a central pivot, while the other end sweeps round a circular rail on the periphery.

Gantries for bridge cranes may be built out of doors, as in a stockyard, but more usually, the outdoor bridge crane is mounted on legs with wheels that run on rails. In this case, it is called a goliath crane. Goliath cranes are often designed so that the bridge extends between and beyond the legs, extending the useful operating area—and requiring cantilever weights or supports on the legs or on the end of the bridge.

Another development is the free-path goliath crane, in which the legs are mounted on large pneumatic rubber tires so that it can be driven around the work area. The wheels can be turned through 90 degrees (with power-assisted steering) to make the greatest possible use of the crane through maneuverability.

Jib cranes

Jib cranes, also known as derrick cranes, are the most familiar type because they are often mobile and widely used outdoors. The jib is the long boom, nearly always of a lattice construction (to save weight), that is derricked (raised upward and lowered outward to alter the working radius of the machine) and slewed (turned) in a circle along with the superstructure. On any crane, most of the lifting is done by a pulley connected to a cable that is wound on a drum inside the superstructure. On a jib crane, while the jib can be derricked with the load on it, its main purpose is to make the lifting function available over the work area.

The jib crane, if fully mobile, is usually powered by a diesel engine. The lattice construction of the jib has great strength, and the weight saving is important because the lighter the weight of the jib itself, the more the machine can lift. The jib consists of an upper and lower section, and most jibs are designed so that extra sections can be added in the middle. The sections are 20 ft. (6 m) long, and the assembly, which requires a lot of room, must be done with the jib on the ground.

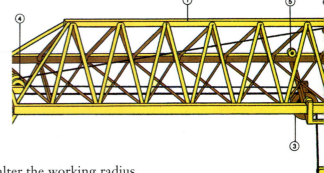

Jib cranes are mounted on rubber-tired wheels for use on outdoor sites where the ground is flat and firm. Where the surface is soft or irregular, the crane is mounted on a track similar to that of a military tank. Tracks spread the weight of the machine over a wider area than wheels so that the pressure per square inch is much less.

Telescoping boom cranes

Self-propelled cranes are usually too slow to be driven on the street, so they are usually hauled to the site on flatbed trailers. In the last decade, the telescoping boom crane mounted on its own vehicle has been developed. It is designed to be driven to the site; on arrival, the boom is extended hydraulically to its full length in a minute or so. This type of extremely mobile crane is convenient and economical for use on a site where there are only a few lifting jobs to be done and where they can all be accomplished within a short period of time. (A construction company has such a large investment in heavy equipment that the more versatile the machine is, the lower the actual operating costs.)

The disadvantages of the telescoping boom crane are that the boom is relatively heavier than the lattice jib and the whole machine is smaller. Thus, its effective operation is somewhat restricted. To extend its operating range to the maximum, it has hydraulically operated outrigger supports with hydraulic jacks on their tips. When these are fully extended, the crane can reach a calculated distance from its center of gravity for a load without tipping itself over.

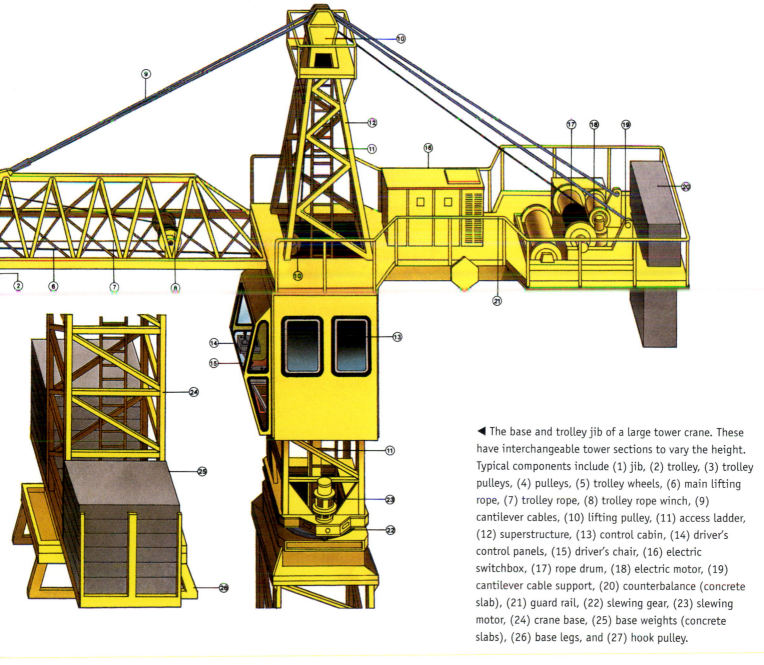

◀ The base and trolley jib of a large tower crane. These have interchangeable tower sections to vary the height. Typical components include (1) jib, (2) trolley, (3) trolley pulleys, (4) pulleys, (5) trolley wheels, (6) main lifting rope, (7) trolley rope, (8) trolley rope winch, (9) cantilever cables, (10) lifting pulley, (11) access ladder, (12) superstructure, (13) control cabin, (14) driver's control panels, (15) driver's chair, (16) electric switchbox, (17) rope drum, (18) electric motor, (19) cantilever cable support, (20) counterbalance (concrete slab), (21) guard rail, (22) slewing gear, (23) slewing motor, (24) crane base, (25) base weights (concrete slabs), (26) base legs, and (27) hook pulley.

Tower cranes

In the construction of tall buildings, tower cranes are used. The lattice tower supports a horizontal boom, which extends on both sides of it in opposite directions. On one end of the boom, which is usually shorter than the other, a counterweight may be suspended. On the other end, the hoisting mechanism runs back and forth on a trolley. The maximum load can be lifted when the trolley is close to the tower, and it diminishes as the trolley moves away from the tower along the boom.

Up to a height of about 200 ft. (61 m), the tower can be free-standing, mounted in a concrete block or on a ballasted base, but above that height, it is fastened to the building at one or more points. An alternative is the climbing tower crane, which is built in what will be a stairwell or an elevator shaft in the finished building. As the building goes higher, extra sections are inserted into the tower, and the crane is raised along with it. Today, for greater mobility, tower cranes are being mounted on ballasted trolleys that run on rails and even on crawlers and trucks.

Scotch derrick cranes have a rotating mast that is held vertical by two inclined rigid structural backstays attached to the top. Also attached to the top of the mast are the suspension ropes for the low-pivoting derricking jib. The advantage of this type of crane is that the maximum weight can be handled in a wide radius because the legs are secured or weighted far behind the mast. The scotch derrick crane may be fastened to the steel structure of the building and moved higher as the building goes up. Alternatively, it may be mounted on structural steel towers called gabbards, which may be either static or mounted on a track and powered.

Cranes on wharfs and docks

For the rapid loading and unloading of ships, the most familiar type of crane used is the level-luffing dockside crane. Level-luffing means that the load is neither lifted nor lowered by the jib when the jib is derricked (luffed) in or out. The dockside crane may be mounted on a structure that straddles a railway or a road; in this case, it is called a portal crane. If it is mounted with one side on the quay and the other side on a gantry at a higher level, it is called a semiportal crane.

For unloading bulk materials from ships, the transporter grab crane may be used. The load is supported by a trolley that runs on a bridge. This type of bridge crane is sometimes designed to move the load over a considerable distance.

More and more cargo is now being transported, especially by sea, in standard-sized containers. Special cranes are installed on the

▶ Tower cranes being used to construct a tall building. The top section of the crane is mounted on powerful hydraulic rams that can push it up high enough for a new section of tower to be inserted underneath. In this way, the crane always remains higher than the structure being built. The top of the crane is then dismantled when the building is finished, though sometimes the tower remains as part of the building's structure.

dockside that are similar in design to the transport grab crane and are capable of very rapid and precise handling of these uniform containers.

Modern cranes

Under the pressure of increasing trade and advanced technology in building and industrial processes, cranes are being built today with substantially enhanced capabilities. A goliath crane used in the building of power stations can lift several hundred tons. A crane used to unload ore from bulk carriers can weigh 850 tons (770 tonnes) and unload 2,000 tons (1,820 tonnes) per hour; the grab weighs over 20 tons (18.2 tonnes), and its contents may weigh up to 24 tons (22 tonnes). A floating crane built by the Japanese on a converted tanker can lift over 3,000 tons (2,700 tonnes).

SEE ALSO: BUILDING TECHNIQUES • DOCK • FREIGHT HANDLING • PULLEY • SKYSCRAPER

Cryogenics

Cryogenics is the study of the behavior of matter at low temperature, and specifically it deals with temperatures from −58 to −459.6°F (−50 to −273.1°C), or from 223 K to 0 K. Temperatures from ambient to −58°F are generally studied under the heading refrigeration. The science divides itself into two areas. There are situations where the normal physical laws apply, and there are situations where matter adopts peculiar properties at low temperature.

An example of the first is the cooling of something that is normally gaseous, such as nitrogen, to a low temperature so that it becomes liquid and then, on further cooling, solid. A significant example of the second category is the way in which certain metals lose all electrical resistance as their temperatures approach absolute zero. This phenomenon is known as superconductivity. A basic property of superconductors, apart from the lack of resistance, is that external magnetic fields cannot penetrate their interior: they are perfect diamagnets for very high magnetic fields.

Cryogenics is exploited industrially as an integral part of many manufacturing processes. A host of ferrous and nonferrous metals, chemicals, petrochemicals, and other goods depend on the product of a cryogenic process at some point in their manufacturing cycle. Oxygen and nitrogen are easily the most important cryogenic products.

Cold production

If high-pressure gas is expanded to a lower pressure, there is a drop in temperature, and almost all methods of producing low temperatures depend on this principle. The simplest embodiment of the principle is expansion across a valve, but cooling by this so-called Joule–Thompson effect is not a very efficient technique. A more efficient way is expansion in a reciprocating engine or turbine.

Air separation

The production of oxygen, nitrogen, and argon is effected by separating air at cryogenic temperatures. The air, after removal of dust, water, and carbon dioxide, is cooled to liquefaction temperature and separated by fractional distillation. The basis for distillation is the fact that when a mixture of liquids of different boiling points is heated, the vapor driven off is richer in the component with the lower boiling point (nitrogen), while the liquid remaining contains more of the component with the higher boiling point (oxygen).

In a typical plant, air is drawn into the unit through a filter and compressed to about 88 psi

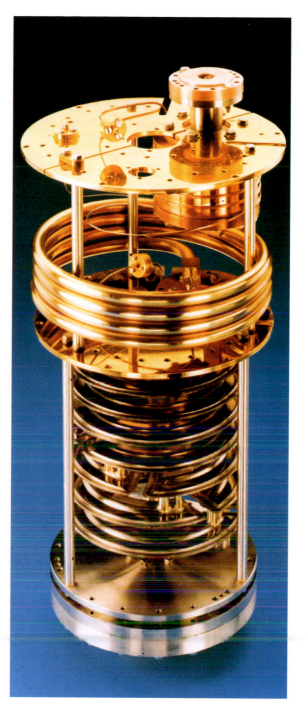

◀ The heart of a cryostat. This dilution refrigerator uses a mixture of helium-3 (He-3) and helium-4 (He-4) and an electromagnetic effect to achieve temperatures approaching −459.6°F (−273.1°C), which is absolute zero, at the bottom of the flask.

(6 bar) by a turbo compressor. The air is cooled and washed and delivered to the main exchanger, where it is cooled to −274°F (−170°C) by continuous heat exchange with outgoing waste nitrogen and gaseous products. Carbon dioxide and water vapor are either removed by molecular sieves before heat exchange or are deposited on the surface of the air passages of the plate-fin type heat exchanger and resublimed by reversing the waste nitrogen and air streams. Product gases flow in separate passes of the exchanger and are not contaminated.

Part of the cold compressed air is returned through a balancing stream in the main exchanger and taken from there to the expansion turbine used for the production of refrigeration. This expanded air then enters the upper (low-

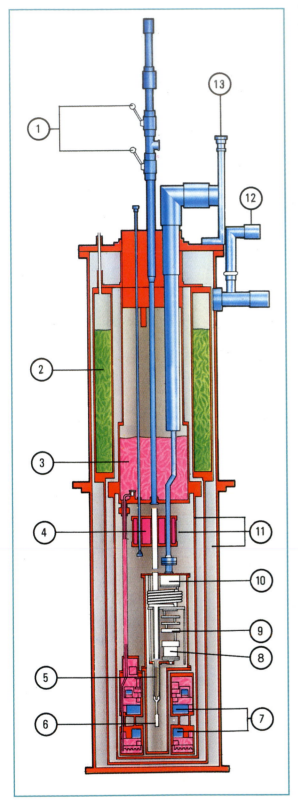

The interior of a cryostat. The sample to be cooled lies between a set of superconducting magnets where the scientist can work on it.
(1) Sample access ports
(2) Liquid nitrogen
(3) Liquid helium
(4) Liquid helium at −457.6°F (−272°C)
(5) Copper cold points
(6) Cooled sample
(7) Superconducting magnets
(8) He-3/He-4 at −459.6°F (−273.1°C)
(9) Heat exchangers
(10) He-3/He-4 at −457.6°F (−272°C)
(11) Vacuum chamber
(12) High-vacuum pumping lines
(13) He-3 pumping line to keep He-3 in circulation

the poor liquid serves as reflux for the lower column, and part is subcooled before being expanded into the top of the upper column to provide reflux. The rich liquid is passed through an absorber to remove residual carbon dioxide and hydrocarbons and fed to the upper column.

Air is finally separated in the upper column into gaseous oxygen and waste nitrogen. Oxygen collects as liquid in the condenser and is pumped through an absorber to remove any residual hydrocarbons before being returned to the condenser. Some of the liquid may be withdrawn as product. Gaseous oxygen is taken off at a point immediately above the condenser and leaves the system through the main exchanger. Waste nitrogen is withdrawn as vapor from the upper column and is then passed through the poor liquid/rich liquid subcooler before leaving the plant through the main exchanger.

Argon containing about 2 percent oxygen and nitrogen impurity can be produced by additional rectification in a separate side column fitted to the main rectification system. This crude argon can be refined to 99.999 percent in a purification unit.

Gas liquefaction

Air-separation plants can provide either gas or liquid products, and where large quantities of liquid are required, gas can be liquefied in separate liquefiers. The reason for providing oxygen, nitrogen, and other products in liquid form are, first, to make storage and transportation convenient and, second, to provide a means of refrigeration. Liquefied gases are usually stored and transported in vacuum-insulated tanks and road or rail tankers. The vessels employed for storing and transporting liquids have inner and outer shells, and the space between the shells is packed with an insulating powder and evacuated.

Product gaseous nitrogen is compressed and water cooled before being fed through a warm exchanger, where it is further cooled in a heat exchanger with low-pressure recycled nitrogen. A freon refrigeration unit reduces the temperature still more, and the product nitrogen then passes through the intermediate exchanger, where cooling is again carried out with recycled nitrogen.

Part of the product stream leaving the intermediate exchanger is expanded in the expansion turbine, returning as a recycled low-pressure, low-temperature stream through the liquefier and exchangers to the suction side of the compressor. The remainder of the product stream passes through the liquefier and is taken off as a liquid. Variations of this cycle are employed, including, for example, the use of a second turbine instead of the freon unit.

pressure) column. The balancing stream is necessary because of the different specific heats of the air at a pressure of 6 bar and the outgoing low-pressure streams.

The main flow of air leaving the exchanger is taken to the lower (high-pressure) column, where it is separated into an oxygen-rich fraction at the base of the column and a fraction containing very little oxygen (known as poor liquid) at the top of the column in the condenser-reboiler. Some of

Applications

A large number of industrial processes from engineering to food manufacturing can be undertaken more efficiently, more rapidly, or more cheaply under conditions of extreme cold using liquid nitrogen. Liquid nitrogen boils at a temperature of –320°F (–196°C), and at this level, it can modify the characteristics of several types of products. Beside acting as a conventional freezing agent, it can shrink metals, embrittle normally flexible materials, and solidify oils with a low freezing point.

Liquid nitrogen is extensively used in the food industry and in several areas has replaced other means of refrigeration. Quick freezing of fruit, vegetables, and meat is now common practice, resulting in significant benefits for the consumer in terms of improved quality and flavor retention. After freezing, goods can be delivered by refrigerated container vehicles, which are kept cold by injecting liquid nitrogen into the container base.

An interesting engineering application is shrink fitting, which is a method of assembling components where the inner part has to be inserted into a hole or cavity in the outer part. Examples include inserting axles on the wheels of locomotives, impellers on pump shafts, and rings on cylinder blocks. The fitting is achieved by immersing the inner component in a bath of liquid nitrogen, causing it to shrink. The contraction for mild steel is 0.0022 in. for each inch of diameter. This contraction gives the necessary clearance for correct fitting and avoids the problems associated with the use of mechanical force or distortion by heating.

Liquid nitrogen is used for rigidifying plastics and rubbers as part of certain manufacturing processes and also in scrap recovery systems. Old vehicle tires, first precut into sections, can be embrittled and then ground into crumb rubber. The recovered rubber, free of metal and other contaminants, is recycled into other products, such as roofing materials. Another form of scrap recovery involves chilling insulated copper wire and then passing it through rollers to crack off the insulation, leaving the valuable copper intact.

An example of rigidifying rubber or plastic material in a manufacturing process is deflashing. Compression molding of plastic or rubber products results in the formation of a fin of excess material where the two pieces were forced together. This fin, or flash, can be made brittle by immersion in liquid nitrogen, which cools the thin flash more quickly than the main body of the molding. The flash is then removed by tumbling in a barrel.

Liquid nitrogen is used in many other applications ranging from bomb disposal, where a battery can be frozen to reduce the voltage to zero, to pipe freezing. The freezing of pipelines allows repairs to be carried out, new sections fitted, or valves replaced without the need to drain the line. Water, oil, gasoline, and chemical pipelines can be frozen successfully without bursting.

Outside of industry, nitrogen is used in cryosurgery to destroy cells with a fine jet of liquid, enabling delicate operations such as neurosurgery to be carried out in greater safety. The medical field also provides a variety of storage applications in conjunction with small insulated vessels. These uses include the storage of tissues, vaccines, viruses, sperm, and blood cells.

Liquid oxygen, unlike liquid nitrogen, does not have direct applications, and the reason for liquefying it is to provide an economic means of storage and distribution. In some instances, liquid oxygen is taken close to the point of consumption, as in high-altitude breathing. Modern fighter aircraft store liquid oxygen and convert it to gas.

Liquid helium

Commercial quantities of helium are separated from natural gas using a cryogenic process and liquefied exploiting similar principles to those previously outlined for nitrogen liquefaction. The helium is compressed, precooled with liquid nitrogen, expanded in two-stage expansion turbines, and then expanded across a valve.

▼ A dilution refrigerator, used for neutron-scattering experiments that analyze atomic structure. They are controlled from the unit on the left (1). A radioactive source (2) fires a stream of neutrons at a frozen sample in a cryostat (3). The temperature is measured by a nearby unit (4) that counts gamma rays emitted by a cobalt source and it is displayed on a screen (8). The beam is stopped by a shield (5). The neutrons diffracted by the sample are picked up by the neutron detector (6). The cryostat is run from the control box (7).

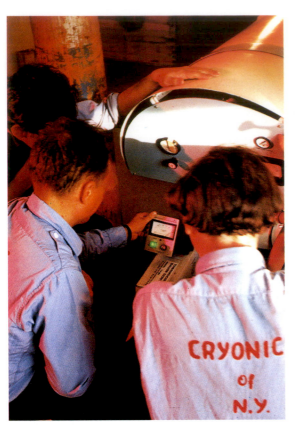

◄ The deep-frozen body of a member of the Cryonics Society, welded in a steel container, is enclosed in a vacuum cylinder. The society believes that at some future date medicine will advance to the point where these carefully preserved bodies may be revived.

The only method of obtaining temperatures approaching absolute zero is by using the physical properties of liquid helium, which boils at 4.2 K at atmospheric pressure. Use of a vacuum pump to lower pressure permits temperatures of the order of 1 K to be achieved. The temperature limit with a mechanical vacuum pump is 0.8 K. Further lowering of temperature is obtained by adiabatic demagnetization, where liquid helium temperatures within a few ten millionths of a degree above absolute zero have been reached.

Liquid helium has some remarkable properties. Even at the unattainable temperature of absolute zero it would still remain liquid at atmospheric pressure. The flow properties of liquid helium are much more marked than for normal liquids, and it is capable of high flows through very fine capillary-sized diameters. The liquid is said to be superfluid.

Liquid helium is also used to create space simulation chambers and in bubble chambers. Space simulation chambers need to reproduce near-perfect vacuum conditions and do so by following conventional pumping down by cryopumping. This technique uses liquid-helium-cooled panels that condense and solidify residual components—mainly oxygen and nitrogen.

FACT FILE

■ In 1883, a Russian scientist, Openchowski, used the evaporation of ether to produce low temperatures in a probe used for freezing the cerebral cortex of experimental animals for short periods. This technique prevented hemorrhaging and widespread tissue damage. Cold-probe surgery is now used to give relief from trembling to people suffering from Parkinson's disease.

■ Cryopumps operate by freezing out condensable gases within a gas-tight enclosure. The gases condense on the inside surface owing to the circulation of liquid helium at a temperature of 20 K through condenser plates. Cryopumps are capable of producing an almost complete vacuum at high speed. One use is the creation of simulated high-altitude test environments.

■ In order to amplify the sensitivity and accuracy of technical equipment used for navigating, mapping, and communications, refrigerators that can achieve temperatures as low as 77 K have been installed in space program flights to cool sensors and optical elements.

► Photomicrograph of human red blood cells. Freeze etching lets scientists see a cell structure with formerly impossible precision.

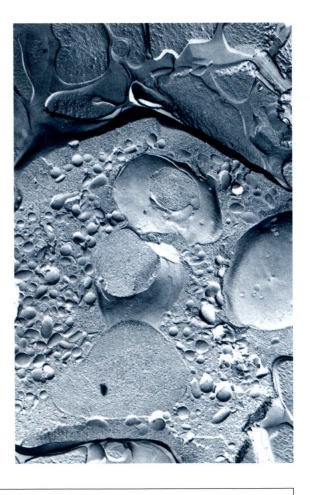

SEE ALSO: AIR • DISTILLATION AND SUBLIMATION • HEAT EXCHANGER • NITROGEN • OXYGEN • REFRIGERATION • SUPERCONDUCTIVITY

Cryptology

Ever since the written word has been used to communicate information, people have sought ways to ensure that only the intended recipient actually understands that information. Anyone passing secret messages is likely to be using a code or cipher of some sort. The complexity of the chosen method will depend upon the degree of security required.

Probably the earliest form of mechanical device was a rod of known diameter, around which was wrapped a narrow strip of parchment, barber's pole fashion. The message was written along the length of the rod, unwrapped, and delivered. The fragments of words and letters on the strip were meaningless until wrapped around a rod of the correct diameter.

Unlike a cipher, a code or code word contains no hidden message but merely refers the reader to a prearranged second meaning. Some large companies, diplomats, and the military use code books to instruct their operators and to keep them informed. Either real words or groups of random letters can be used, so that

A R T L E may mean ..... Abandon negotiations
B R T Y D ..... Contact head office
C S L G U ..... Competitors arriving soon.

Though rather inflexible, the code book system can be made secure if the code letters are transmitted in the form of a cipher. If words are used they must be chosen carefully so that no clue to the real meaning is even hinted at. For example, if the message is to be "You are fired," CAT would be reasonable as a code word, but GUN would not.

During World War II, coded messages were transmitted to Resistance groups in Europe. These could be broadcast on normal BBC channels for all the world to hear, including the Germans. They were even announced with words like, "And now some messages to our friends in Europe." Following this would be a coded message such as "The milkman will call in the morning." This piece of news would be read slowly and clearly and repeated in case reception was poor. To particular groups in France, it could mean that a prearranged target was to be bombed the next morning. They would then play their part by attacking antiaircraft positions in that area. The Germans suspected nothing.

Military operations from small to large were often given code names, such as Overlord and Torch. Companies researching new products

▲ The Enigma machine gave the Germans a significant advantage in sending secret messages during World War II, until a British warship intercepted a German submarine carrying the device. Though intelligence services had made great inroads in cracking the code, possession of an Enigma machine and understanding of how it worked enabled the Allied Forces to decipher German messages faster and thus hasten the end of the war.

code name them so that they can be discussed without giving away their true nature.

Some codes are not intended to be particularly secret, more to save time or radio space. The ten code is used by both citizens' band radio enthusiasts and by the police, particularly in the United States. The code is simply a list of numbers following the number 10. The code 10:20 to a CB user means that the caller wants to know where you live. In practice, the question would be asked as "What's your twenty?"

Probably the best-known code of all is the Morse code. It was developed for use with the electric telegraph well over 100 years ago. In those days before microphones had been invented, the only signal that could be sent by wire was a simple OFF or ON. Hence, the dots and dashes of Morse code.

The most commonly used letters are given short codings, E being a single dot, while the least used have more complex ones, X being dash dot dot dash. Morse code retains its popularity in radio transmission; using a very narrow band width, it can still be used when poor reception conditions preclude other forms of transmission.

DIGITAL ENCRYPTION

The Data Encryption Standard (DES) of the U.S. National Bureau of Standards works by dividing text into four-bit digital types and subjecting it to 18 stages of transposition and substitution. The key generator in DES applies 16 keys (derived from a 56 bit main key) in turn to the initial permutation of the text. At each stage, the digital form message (shown symbolically in letter form) is further transposed. Without knowledge of the keys involved, it is claimed, no computer can crack the cipher generated. Users have a published algorithm, and secret paired-key generators for the main 56 bit key (actually 64 bits—eight bits are used for internal coding).

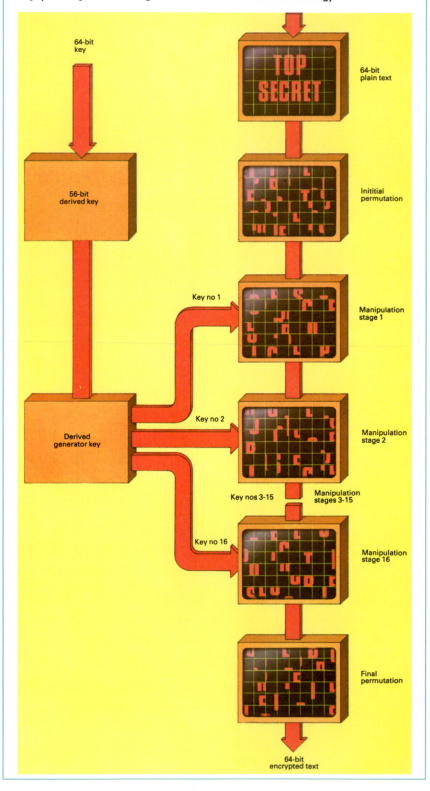

Ciphers

Unlike a code, a cipher actually contains the secret to be transmitted. Numerical ciphers can be made that are very secure indeed. Here is a very simple example of just one method.

Suppose the message to be encoded is *How It Works*. First, each letter of the alphabet has a number, as follows:

A B C D E F G H I J K L M N O P Q R S T U V W X Y Z
1 2 3 4 5 6 7 8 9 10 11 12 13 14 15 16 17 18 19 20 21 22 23 24 25 26

By substitution, the message becomes

8 15 23 9 20 23 15 18 11 19

Next, choose ten random numbers and add them in turn to the numbers from the alphabet to get ten new numbers.

8	15	23	9	20	23	15	18	11	19	
73+	22+	48+	35+	67+	4+	54+	27+	81+	59+	.....Random numbers
—	—	—	—	—	—	—	—	—	—	
81	37	71	44	87	27	69	45	92	78	..... New numbers

The new numbers would then be transmitted, probably in two blocks of five:

81 37 71 44 87 27 69 45 92 78

When these numbers are received, the agent refers to a copy of the random numbers. Subtracting them from the numbers received gives the real alphabet numbers and in turn the message.

In reality, these random numbers would be printed in the form of a booklet containing many tear-off pages. Both sender and agent would have identical copies. Having used one page of numbers, the sender would tear it out and destroy it, as would the agent. Each set of numbers is used only once, giving rise to the name "one time pad." When used with much more sophisticated ciphers than this, the system is virtually 100 percent secure.

Transposition and substitution

Two important practices in cryptology are transposition and substitution. Transposition involves changing the order of the letters of a message so as to render them unreadable. The following is just one method of many and illustrates the use of a key word. The key word will have been agreed on by sender and receiver in advance. In this example, the message is *Urgent help needed, rebels advancing*, and the key word is *cowardly*. In our key word, A is the letter nearest to the beginning of the alphabet and is given the number 1. Next to appear in the alphabet would be C, and it is numbered 2. D is next, 3; and so on, until we get:

```
C O W A R D L Y
2 5 7 1 6 3 4 8
```

A coding grid is then made with the key word and numbers at the top and the message written below.

```
C O W A R D L Y
2 5 7 1 6 3 4 8
U R G E N T H E
L P N E E D E D
R E B E L S A D
V A N C I N G
```

Now, starting at 1 and reading downward, we get the letters EEEC. Under 2, we get ULRLV, under 3 TDSN, and so on, until we have the unbroken line

EEECULRVTDSNHEAGRPEANELIGNBNEDD

For transmission, the above letters would be split into groups of five, and the final enciphered message would be:

EEECU LRVTD SNHEA GRPEA NELIG NBNED D

To reassemble the original message, it is simply a matter of redrawing the grid, key word and numbers, and finding out how many letters are going to appear in a column. By counting the number of letters appearing in the cipher (31 in this case) on the blank grid, it can be seen that each column has four letters except for the last, which has three.

Further security results from changing the letters themselves as well as their order. Substitution ciphers can involve complex mathematics and machines. In this example, one of the simplest will be used and one alphabet is simply reversed beneath the usual alphabet:

A B C D E F G H I J K L M N O P Q R S T U V W X Y Z
Z Y X W V U T S R Q P O N M L K J I H G F E D C B A

The original cipher, with its letters substituted from the reverse alphabet, would now read

VVVXF OIEGW HMSVZ TIKVZ MVORT MYMVW W

This would appear to dash the hopes of the would-be code breaker. Not so, for though the letters of the transposed message have been changed, their frequency of appearance has not.

► This alphanumeric keyboard unit has a 1,000 character electronic memory. The message is transmitted as digits and can be reconstructed at another alphanumeric terminal. Electronic encryption has replaced mechanical coding devices, as it is significantly more difficult to crack an electronic code.

Letter frequency can be of great value to the cryptanalyst. Anyone who looks at a few pages of a book and notes how often each letter appears will soon find out that E is by far the most frequently used. A check on the substitution cryptogram will show that the most frequently used letter is V. This discovery allows the code breaker to assume that V is really E and gives the key to the simple substitution. In a cipher involving only substitution, the code breaker also looks for frequently appearing pairs of letters representing sh, ch, th, and so forth.

A way had to be found of taking away the clue of letter frequency from the cryptanalyst. Though there are many ways of doing this with pen and paper, a machine was to make them all obsolete. Around the 1920s in Germany, the machine was invented that was to give British cryptanalysts of World War II more headaches than the bombs. It was aptly named Enigma.

Enigma had a keyboard similar to a typewriter and a set of three disks with the alphabet engraved around them for setting-up purposes. Each disk had edge contacts corresponding to the letters used on it and linking it with its neighbor. To encipher the message *retreat*, the letter R would be pressed on the main keyboard, sending an electric signal through the circuits of each disk. The signal was then sent back through the disks by a different pathway to illuminate a letter on the machine's second alphabet display. Thus, R could become A (or any other letter, depending on how the disks were set up).

Pressing E may result in Y being indicated; T may become B. The clever part of Enigma was that each time a key was pressed, a disk would move to its next contact point, thus altering the entire circuit. In this way each letter was given its own unique pathway through the labyrinth of Enigma.

The second R in our message will, therefore, not be another A (it may become P). The second E may become Q, and for A and T one may get L and V. The resulting cryptogram would be

A Y B P Q L V

In the word *retreat*, three letters are repeated. In the Enigma version, none are used twice.

On the front of the machine were rows of sockets with interconnecting jack plugs and leads that could be set up in hundreds of ways to add yet more variables to the machine's circuits. Add to this the fact that the disks themselves were interchangeable and that later models could use more disks, and it is clear that the chances of correctly identifying a single letter would be remote.

Messages could be decoded in the field using a second Enigma in reverse, as long as the starting positions of the disks and jack plugs were known. Enigma was eventually cracked, but only after a great deal of work.

Electronic encoding

Today's electronic technology has enabled computers to transmit and receive coded information with an extremely high degree of security. The following example outlines the principles of a typical system, code-named Spider.

The first element in the system is a computer, looking no more sinister than any to be found in large companies all over the world. The message to be sent is typed out on the keyboard in plain English. The computer then begins to encode the message, first turning it into a complex numerical format using the elements of substitution and transposition already described. The computer's ability to manipulate large, random numbers is of great importance to the security of the code.

Spider's transmitter now sends an initializing code to Spider II, which may be anywhere in the world. The code simply says, "Stop whatever you are doing and get ready to receive a message that I have encoded using program 5819."

The message is not going to be sent in a continuous string, but fragmented to ensure further security, after it has been further scrambled electronically. The speed at which computers can receive data is called the baud rate. By increasing the baud rate, the system can transmit each mes-

◀ Boris Hagelin, the inventor of a six-disk rotor machine that produces 101,405,850 different encoded letters before it repeats. Sale of the machine to the U.S. military made him a millionaire. Electronic enciphering has now replaced such devices.

sage fragment at a speed measured in microseconds. When the message has been received, the baud rate can be slowed down before it is uploaded by Spider II. If the message is to be sent piece by piece, it is important that the sender knows that each piece has arrived safely, and so Spider II sends back a verification signal every time a fragment is received.

To confuse anyone who may be trying to pick up Spider's signals, the two computers play a game of electronic hide and seek known as frequency hopping. Unless the listener knows the order of change in signal, the most he or she could expect to hear would be a few isolated words.

This order of transmission, frequency change could be given out in the initialization code so that each machine would know which of the hundreds of possible channels are to be used and in what order. The system can go one better by not putting all its eggs in one basket; it will use Spider II's verification signal to suggest the next frequency by code.

Should all the channels being used be monitored, Spider has another trick to play. This trick is simply to transmit similar but irrelevant bursts of binary code on many frequencies and to keep these hopping as well.

SEE ALSO: Computer • Electronic surveillance • Radio • Security system • Stealth technologies • Telegraph

Crystals and Crystallography

Any specimen of condensed matter—usually solid but occasionally liquid—that is arranged in an ordered structure is called a crystal. Crystallography is the study of crystal structures and the measurement of their characteristic geometries and dimensions.

For centuries, humans have been fascinated by the regular geometric forms of crystals, which reflect their regular structures, and by how they reflect and color light. The word *crystal* derives from the Greek for "clear ice."

Ionic crystals

Perhaps the most familiar crystals in everyday life are those of common salt (sodium chloride, NaCl). Salt is an example of an ionic crystalline solid: it consists of sodium ions (Na^+) and chloride ions (Cl^-) arranged in a regular structure called a lattice. The sodium ions in salt are positively charged spheres that have radii of 1.16 Å (0.116 nm). Each sodium ion is surrounded by six chloride ions, which are negatively charged spheres with radii of 1.67 Å (0.167 nm). The chloride ions form the points of an octahedron centered on a sodium ion, and each chloride ion is surrounded by an octahedron of six sodium ions.

The forces that hold ionic crystals together are the electrostatic attractions between ions of opposite charge. The spacing of the ions is determined by several factors: a balance between the attractive forces; the repulsive forces of like charged ions; and a short range repulsion that arises when the electron clouds of the ions begin to overlap.

Covalent crystals

The atoms in covalent crystal are held together by covalent bonds, in which pairs of electrons are shared by pairs of atoms. The angles between the bonds that an atom forms are determined by the electronic structure of the atom, and those bond angles determine the geometry of the lattice.

Diamond is a good example of a covalent crystal. It consists of carbon atoms that are each bonded to four other carbon atoms. When a carbon atom forms four single covalent bonds with four other atoms, those four bonds point to the vertices of a tetrahedron. Thus, the four carbon atoms that surround each carbon atom in diamond form the points of a perfect tetrahedron. Each of those four carbon atoms is surrounded by its own tetrahedron of carbon atoms, and so on throughout the whole of a crystal. In fact, all the atoms in a diamond form a single molecule that

is held together by extremely strong covalent bonds, thus helping to explain why diamond is the hardest of all known substances.

Metallic crystals

The lattices in metallic crystals have the same geometries as those in ionic crystals. A major difference between metals and ionic solids is that all the sites of a metal lattice are occupied by positively charged metal ions whereas those of an ionic lattice are occupied by ions of alternating charges. The electrostatic repulsions between the positive ions are overcome by a "sea" of electrons that swarm around the metal ions and "glue" them together. These electrons are what give metals their characteristic electrical and thermal conductivities and their typical luster.

Forces in other types of crystals

Sugar is an example of a crystalline solid in which the particles that occupy the lattice sites are attracted to one another by forces other than covalent, ionic, or metallic bonds. The strongest forces at work between molecules of sugar (sucrose, $C_{12}H_{22}O_{11}$) are hydrogen bonds—attractions that form between the hydrogen atoms of hydroxyl groups (–OH) in one molecule and the unbonded electron pairs of oxygen atoms in a hydroxy group in another molecule.

Other forces that act between molecules are caused by attractions between electric dipoles. Polar molecules have permanent dipoles caused by uneven distributions of electrons. Nonpolar molecules and noble gas atoms have temporary

▲ Crystals of methanol illuminated by polarized light and viewed through a polarizing filter. This viewing system emphasizes the boundaries between crystalline regions. The orientation of the crystal structure changes abruptly at these boundaries.

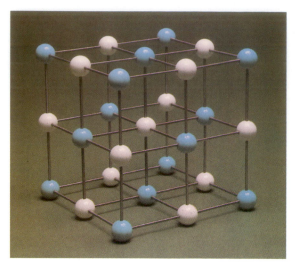

◄ This ball-and-stick model illustrates a cubic structure, such as that formed by sodium chloride. The two types of ions are represented by two colors of balls. In general, the negative ions in such a crystal are larger than the positive ions. In sodium chloride, for example, Cl⁻ has a radius slightly more than 1.4 times that of Na⁺.

dipoles caused by oscillations of their electron clouds. These cause attractions, called van der Waals forces, that are much weaker than hydrogen bonds and dipole–dipole attractions.

Periodic structures and unit cells

The basic grouping of atoms, ions, or molecules within a crystal is called a unit cell. The crystal structure itself can be thought of as an array of unit cells that are repeated in three directions. Crystals are thus periodic structures, since the pattern of unit cells repeats after a fixed distance in each direction. Crystal lattices can be divided into 14 basic types, called *Bravais lattices*, based on the symmetry of the unit cells.

In perfect crystals, the shape of a crystal resembles that of the unit cell, so the cubic unit cell of sodium chloride underlies the cuboid shapes of crystals of common salt. When a perfect crystal fragments, it has a strong tendency to do

▼ This magnified view of Epsom salt crystals reveals a largely uniform crystal geometry despite the presence of numerous irregularities in each crystal. Epsom salt is hydrated magnesium sulfate ($MgSO_4 \cdot 7H_2O$).

so along certain planes of the unit cell called cleavage planes. Jewelers use cleavage planes to cut crystals of gemstones that have well-defined, flat faces that correspond to cleavage planes.

X-ray crystallography

Distinguishing between crystals is often difficult as their external structure may be irregular, belying the internal symmetry. To probe deeper into the crystal, a crystallographer will use X rays.

In 1912, the German physicist Max von Laue predicted that crystals should diffract X rays and produce characteristic interference patterns in the same way that fine gratings diffract visible light, because diffraction depends on the slits of a grating having a similar width to the wavelength of light that is to be diffracted, and X-ray wavelengths are similar to the spacings between particles in crystals. Two colleagues of Laue soon demonstrated the effect by producing a pattern of dark spots on a photographic plate behind a crystal of copper sulfate through which an X-ray beam had been shone.

Within a few years of Laue's prediction, the English physicist William Bragg had developed an equation for measuring the geometries of unit cells from the locations of spots in X-ray diffraction patterns. Bragg reasoned that diffraction patterns form as a result of interference between X rays that are scattered by adjacent planes in a crystal. The dark spots appear at scattering angles where the peaks of X-ray photons scattered by the one layer coincide with the peaks of photons from the next layer. Where this happens, there must be a difference between the distances traveled by the two photons that corresponds to a whole number of

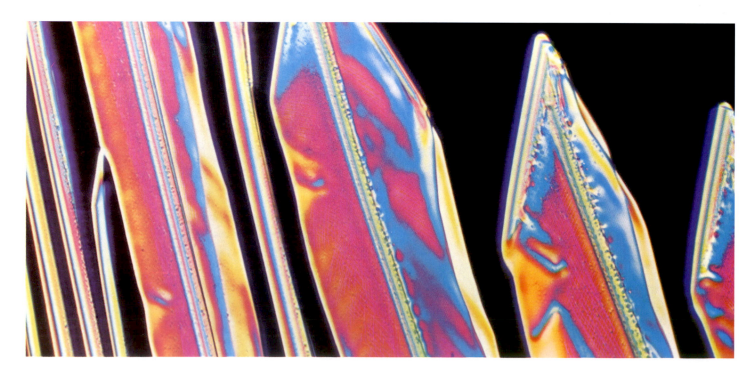

wavelengths of the X-ray photons. Using this reasoning, Bragg developed an equation that enabled him and subsequent crystallographers to determine the structures of crystalline substances and calculate the spacings of the atoms within them.

Advanced crystallography

Modern crystallographic techniques can reveal an amazing amount of information about crystalline solids and even about materials that do not form perfect crystals. Such information includes the bond lengths and angles in molecules, the natures of crystalline regions in synthetic polymers, the three-dimensional folding of protein chains, the shapes of virus molecules, and the characteristics of the active sites of natural enzymes.

The introduction of computers for the analysis of diffraction patterns drastically reduced the time taken to perform a crystallographic study. The use of cooling improves the sharpness of diffraction patterns by reducing the amount of vibration in crystals and extends the scope of crystallography to materials that are liquids or gases at normal room temperature.

Crystal formation

Crystals can form from a liquid at its melting point, from a saturated solution as it cools, or from a saturated vapor. The starting point for a crystal may be a speck of dust that acts as a platform for the deposition of solid or a small "seed" crystal deliberately added to start crystallization.

Some substances have more than one crystalline form. Titanium dioxide (TiO_2), for example, exists in three distinct forms in nature: anatase, brookite, and rutile. Synthetic titanium dioxide, which is manufactured for use as a pigment, may be anatase or rutile, depending on the manufacturing process.

Impurities

Traces of impurities can have profound effects on the properties of crystals. While completely pure aluminum oxide (Al_2O_3) is colorless, the presence of minute traces of chromium and iron oxides forms ruby, a red gemstone; traces of titanium dioxide—itself colorless—give sapphire, a blue gemstone. In these substances, chromium, iron, or titanium ions take the positions of aluminum ions in the aluminum oxide lattice. The colors arise because the trace ions modify the covalent bonding system of the whole crystal—not just the bonds around the trace ions—and create an energy level to which electrons jump as they absorb photons of visible light.

Impurities play an important role in semiconductors. Silicon, for example, can be "doped" by adding small amounts of aluminum or phosphorus. The trace impurities sit in the host silicon lattice and modify its ability to conduct electricity.

Crystals in industry

Crystals have a variety of unusual properties that stem from their uniformity of composition and their completely integral structures. Many crystals are manufactured for commercial use, since they may not exist in nature or they may be too rare and expensive to extract by mining.

Diamond's extreme hardness is a direct result of its integral crystal structure and the strength of the bonds that hold it together. Industrial diamonds are made by subjecting graphite to extremely high temperatures and pressures.

Silicon crystals are manufactured by slowly drawing a shaft of silicon crystal from a bath of molten silicon. The operation requires ultrapure silicon and an extremely clean environment in order to produce silicon that is acceptable for the manufacture of semiconductor devices.

Crystals of quartz (silicon dioxide, SiO_2) and lithium tantalate ($LiTaO_3$) are piezoelectric—their surfaces develop electric charges when placed under pressure, and their dimensions change when charged electrodes are connected to their surfaces. Such crystals vibrate at a precise frequency when accurately cut and placed in an appropriate electrical circuit, making them useful frequency filters for timing devices.

The interaction of crystals of ruby with light and microwave radiation makes them ideal for use in lasers and masers. Synthetic crystals called phosphors form the images on computer monitors and television screens by glowing red, green, or blue when struck by a beam of electrons.

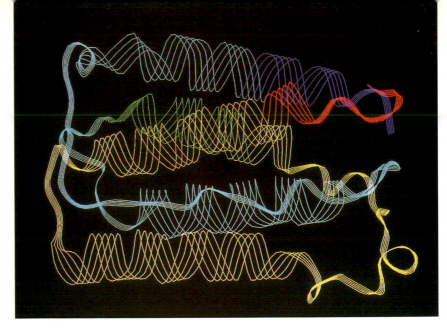

▲ Biological materials can also form crystalline structures, but their complicated chemical formulas mean that their crystal structure has to be modeled using a computer graphics program. This example is the protein interferon, which is released by the immune system in response to a viral infection.

SEE ALSO:
CARBON • CATHODE-RAY TUBE • CHEMICAL BONDING AND VALENCY • CONDENSED-MATTER PHYSICS • DIAMOND • LASER AND MASER • LIQUID CRYSTAL • PIEZOELECTRIC MATERIAL

Dairy Industry

Dairy production goes back to 3000 B.C.E., when milk and butter were supplied to the city states of Mesopotamia from the flocks of sheep herded on the outlying plains.

The development of the dairy industry in Europe was preceded by the advent of livestock-improvement methods based on selection of cattle. One of the reasons for the English Enclosure Acts of the 18th century was that selective breeding could not take place as long as animals grazed in common. Town herds were a common feature of the big cities of England during the first half of the 19th century; in London alone, there were estimated to be about 24,000 cows in 1850. In the surrounding counties, farmhouse industries made butter by the traditional method of churning cream, and cheese was made in oak tubs or brass cheese kettles. Part of the wealth generated during the Industrial Revolution was diverted to agriculture. Flying herds became common in the 19th century. They were cows, just calved, bought by town cowkeepers from country farmers, milked until dry, and then sold for beef.

The expansion of the railway played a key part in widening the distribution and increasing the amount of milk supplied in Britain and the United States. It has been estimated that the milk carried to London by rail doubled between 1866 and 1868.

A cheese factory was opened in Koshkonong, Wisconsin, as early as 1831, and butter factories were opened in the United States in the 1860s. Further advances in milk preservation were made with Gail Borden's patent for a condensed milk process in 1856 and the introduction of the refrigerated railroad car in 1867. By 1895, pasteurization, a mild heat treatment, was being used to extend the keeping life of fresh milk.

Today, the dairy industries of the world are huge enterprises. In the European Union alone, the dairy herd numbers around 20.8 million cows, and there are around 9.25 million in the United States dairy herd. Advances in technology and farming practice are increasing milk yield each year and widening the range of products available to the consumer.

Milk as a food

Although the dairy industries of the technologically advanced countries use the cow as their milk source, all mammals from goats and reindeer to whales and porpoises use milk as a source of protein, fat, carbohydrate, mineral matter, and vitamins for feeding their young. The main protein in cow's milk is casein, which constitutes about

◀ The design of milking parlors is changing radically. Many farmers use computers to record milk yield, matings and calvings, and to predict milk output and feeding requirements.

2.6 percent by weight of the milk. The average fat content of milk is about 3.8 percent, though some breeds of cow, such as the Jersey or South Devon, yield a high proportion of cream and give milk with a 5 percent or more fat content. The carbohydrates are in the form of the milk sugar lactose, which not only provides energy but aids the absorption of calcium by the body. Milk is a good source of high-quality protein, easily absorbed calcium, and riboflavin (vitamin B2). Riboflavin helps to prevent disorders such as angular stomatitis, which results in the cracking of skin at the corners of the mouth.

One pint (0.5 l) per day should supply about one-quarter of the protein required and all the calcium recommended for the diets of most people. The energy value of 8 pints (4 l) has been estimated as being sufficient to supply the 3,000 kilocalories (often referred to simply as calories) needed daily by a moderately active man.

Milking

Mechanical milking machines use a cup that fits around the udder and withdraws milk by intermittent suction. It is vital to cool the raw milk to below 50°F (10°C) at once to prevent the growth of naturally occurring bacteria, which can amount to as many as 500 per milliliter in a healthy cow. The control of infection is very highly developed. In Britain, for example, a tuberculosis-free and brucellosis-free herd has been maintained by a national program of testing over 40 years.

Hygienic practice in handling is essential in controlling the quality of milk. For example, the milking cups should be washed with a disinfectant formulated with chlorine or iodine, and all milk processing equipment should be washed with a detergent at a temperature of 140 to 170°F

(60–77°C) to remove fat and mineral deposits. The bacteria are eliminated by using either steam or one of the proprietary chemical agents that are known collectively as biocides.

Milk is delivered to the dairy in insulated bulk tankers. On arrival, the milk in each tanker is mixed and a sample taken for testing. Apart from testing for compositional quality, the milk is subjected to the Resazurin test. A mauve dye called Resazurin is added to a milk sample, and the extent to which the sample turns pink is the measure of the bacteriological quality.

To give a more accurate assessment of the hygienic quality of milk, a bacterial count method is used. Samples of milk are collected regularly from dairy farms and taken to central testing laboratories. Here they are analyzed for compositional and hygienic quality and for the presence of antibiotics or other inhibitory substances. The results of these tests partly determine the amount of money a farmer receives for the milk supply.

Milk processing

Pasteurization is a heat treatment process that destroys any disease-producing bacteria present in the milk and eliminates the vast majority of harmless bacteria that would otherwise cause spoilage. Most dairies use the high-temperature short-time (HTST) process for continuous pasteurization of milk. The milk is heated to 161°F (71°C) and held at that temperature for 15 seconds. The temperature is measured with a thermocouple, and if the required temperature has not been reached, a flow-diversion valve recycles the milk for further heating. Immediate cooling of the milk is essential after pasteurization, and it is accomplished by using the hot milk to partly heat the incoming cold milk, thus saving energy. The bottles are filled automatically with the milk at a temperature of 38°F (3°C).

Pasteurized milk has a life of about four days in a refrigerator, whereas sterilized milk can be stored for at least seven days without refrigeration, as it is put through more severe heat treatment. To sterilize milk, it is first of all homogenized. This is a process in which milk is forced through small openings to break up the fat globules so that the cream is thoroughly mixed in and will no longer separate. (In the United States, most milk sold in stores is homogenized.) Then it is steam heated at 22°F (104°C) for at least 20 minutes. In Britain, milk is steamed in long-necked glass bottles or in high-density polyethylene bottles. Sterilized milk may develop a cooked flavor owing to slight caramelization of the lactose.

A comparatively recent innovation is the ultra-high temperature (UHT) process, also known as Uperization, in which milk is heated to a temperature of at least 270°F (132°C) for not less than one second. The method of heating may be indirect, by passing the milk through a heat exchanger prior to packaging, or direct, in which steam is injected into the milk and then removed again by evaporation. UHT milk will keep for several months unrefrigerated, unless opened to the air.

Cream

Cream is rich in milk fat and vitamin A, but most of the calcium stays in the skim milk left after cream separation. To separate the cream, whole milk is warmed to about 120°F (49°C) and passed through a centrifuge, where it passes over a stack of rapidly rotating disks. The disks throw the heavier skim milk to the walls of the centrifuge from which it leaves by a separate outlet pipe. The machine is adjustable for the weight of the cream desired. Light cream and heavy cream should have a fat content of 18 percent and 48 percent, respectively; both creams are pasteurized at 175°F (79.5°C) to give a storage life of four days in a refrigerator. Cream may also be homogenized to thicken it and ensure even distribution of fat. A grade of cream with 35 percent fat is ideal for making whipped cream for cake and dessert decoration.

Whey is the liquid residue from cheese making, and it contains a small amount of fat, which can be separated to make whey cream. Soured cream is made from light cream by treating it with a strain of bacteria to develop the piquancy.

Butter processing

Cream for the manufacture of butter may be used directly (sweet cream) or ripened by cultures such as *Cremoris streptococcus*, thus producing the conditions for flavor development and the elimination of undesirable taints.

▼ Cheese making at the Kristianstad dairy in Sweden. These Casomatic units handle a large part of the process automatically.

▲ The production of English farmhouse cheese makes use of mass production methods. After rennet has been added to the milk, the resulting curd is cut to assist in draining the whey. These workers are milling and salting the curd before it is pressed into molds.

The cream is first kept overnight at 41°F (5°C). This aging process ensures that the butter-fat globules in the cream reach the correct structure for churning. The cream, whether ripened or sweet, is brought to a temperature of between 45°F (7°C) and 54°F (12°C) before it is fed into a continuous butter maker that incorporates three stages of manufacture: churning, separating, and working. Butter globules coalesce to form butter grains during churning, the watery buttermilk is then drained off and the butter grains are worked or kneaded until it achieves the correct consistency and moisture content for popular taste.

Salt, in the form of a slurry, is frequently added in the working section to improve flavor and prolong shelf life. Salt levels vary, but the most usual amount is 2 percent.

The natural color of the butter is due to the pigment carotene, and since the cream of Jersey and Guernsey cows is rich in this pigment, it gives a deeply colored butter. Grass and green vegetables are the best sources of carotene, but cereal-fed cows tend to give a pale butter because of the lower carotene content in the cereal. The color, however, may be supplemented by adding the pigment annatto, which is also used frequently in margarine manufacture.

Cheese

In the manufacture of a hard cheese, such as Cheddar, pasteurized whole milk is soured by converting some of the lactose into lactic acid with a culture—a carefully prepared growth—of lactic acid bacteria. Rennet, a coagulant, is added to turn the milk proteins into a curd, which is subsequently cut into ½ in. (13 mm) cubes to allow the liquid residue, or whey, to separate.

The curd is shrunk and hardened by slowly raising the temperature to 100°F (38°C), after which the curd particles settle into a matted mass at the bottom of the cheese vat. The whey is drained off and the curd cut into blocks, which are piled on top of one another to remove more whey under pressure. The method of treatment during piling, or cheddaring, varies from place to place but always involves further cutting, turning, and piling to a greater height. Often a weight is placed on top of the pile to assist drainage.

The blocks are then milled (cut) into small pieces and salted to preserve and flavor the final cheese. After the curd has been pressed in molds for up to 48 hours, it is removed to the ripening room in which it is held at a temperature of 41 to 50°F (5–10°C) and controlled humidity. The cheese matures over a period of three to six months as a result of the action of bacteria and enzymes in the cheese.

A high moisture content is obtained in the manufacture of the soft cheese Camembert by omitting the pressure and heating stages. Also, the surface of the cheese is inoculated with the mold *Penicillium camemberti*, which excretes enzymes into the cheese, resulting in the characteristic flavor. Blue-veined cheese, such as Stilton, uses the mold *Penicillium roqueforti*, but in this case, mold growth is encouraged in the interior of the cheese by piercing it with metal wires to provide the air supply required by the mold.

Cottage cheese, made from pasteurized fat-free milk, is an example of the lactic type that relies upon acidity to coagulate the milk protein. A culture of lactic acid bacteria is added to the milk to develop acidity, and rennet is used in very small quantities. The particular texture of the cheese is achieved by the cutting of the curd and subsequent slow heating to ensure that particles are kept separate. The curd particles are then washed and drained and blended with a salted cream dressing. Cottage cheese has a moisture content of between 70 and 80 percent, a low calorie value, and a short keeping time.

Processed cheese is a combination of cheese with additives for consistency and flavor that is melted and poured into retail containers.

Condensed and evaporated milk

Both of these products involve concentration by evaporation at temperatures in the range 130 to 145°F (54–63°C) under a vacuum. Condensed milk is a sweetened product relying on a sugar concentration of about 43 percent to preserve the canned product. Evaporated milk is preserved by sterilizing the cans of milk in an autoclave at 240°F (115°C) for about 20 minutes.

The texture of condensed milk is achieved by seeding with a small quantity of lactose crystals and by slow cooling of the concentrated product to 75°F (24°C), followed by further cooling with agitation to about 60°F (16°C). Since canned condensed milk is not heat treated, it is vital that hygienic operation should apply at all stages of processing, and it is customary to steam sterilize the cans and lids before filling. Evaporated milk should keep for about two years provided the temperature is kept below 60°F (16°C). At storage temperatures above about 70°F (21°C) there is the possibility of browning or oxidation occurring, which, though harmless, does not appeal to the consumer.

Dried milk

Two techniques are used for drying: roller drying and spray drying, the latter being more common. Before skim milk can be spray dried, the milk solids content must be increased to about 40 percent by vacuum evaporation. After this, the concentrated milk is preheated to about 150°F (66°C) and sprayed into an air-heated drying chamber by using a nozzle or a spinning wheel. The milk droplets are dried by the air at a temperature of about 380°F (190°C) and pneumatically conveyed from the bottom of the drying chamber to the packaging room. The final product has less than 5 percent moisture.

One of the problems with early spray-dried milk powders was their poor reconstitution properties when added to beverages. This is solved by passing the milk powder through a turbulent air stream before it is dry. The milk particles collide with one another and form clusters of milk powder, which are dried and packaged. This process is known as agglomeration and results in instant milk powder.

Yogurt

The unique flavor and texture of yogurt is obtained by treating milk with a culture of *Lactobacillus bulgaricus* and *Streptococcus thermophilus*. The milk should be pasteurized at 194°F (90°C) before inoculation to kill its natural organisms, some of which taint the yogurt.

After the milk has been cooled to 100°F (38°C), it is inoculated with the culture and incubated in bulk or in sterile retail cartons and the culture allowed to develop at that temperature for several hours. The finished product must be cooled to below 41°F (5°C); otherwise the culture will remain active and the yogurt will become increasingly acidic to taste.

◀ Instantizers, used to improve the solubility of dried milk. These machines, also called fluid bed driers, remove the residual moisture from dried milk and crystallize the lactose.

The milk is frequently fortified with up to 3 percent skim milk powder to supplement the protein content and give a means of controlling the viscosity of the yogurt. A low fat natural yogurt will contain just over 1 percent and have about 18 calories per ounce. In the case of fruit yogurts, fruit is added after cooling and stirred in before the yogurt is packaged.

Future trends

Research is continuing in the development of new products based on milk. Powdered yogurt mixtures that would require only the addition of water may become available. In Germany, the shelf life of conventional yogurt has been greatly extended by a pasteurizing process. High-temperature processes make possible products such as canned pudding. The latest trend is in healthful foods, with yogurts enriched with added vitamins, soluble fiber, and micronutrients becoming popular. Other additives are claimed to alleviate menopausal symptoms in women, and a new Swedish yogurt is claimed to be an appetite suppressor.

Cheese whey used to be a troublesome by-product because it depleted the oxygen supply of rivers into which it was discharged. Now, however, valuable nutrients such as protein, mineral salt, and lactose are extracted by filtration, leaving a much cleaner effluent. The United States alone produces over 10 million tons (9 million tonnes) of whey, of which only a third is utilized; there is believed to be great scope for the further development of new products and novel processes.

▼ Milk pasteurizing equipment. All milk for public consumption has to undergo some form of heat treatment to kill disease-causing bacteria.

SEE ALSO: AGRICULTURAL SCIENCE • FAT • FERMENTATION • FOOD PROCESSING • MICROBIOLOGY • MILKING MACHINE • NUTRITION AND FOOD SCIENCE • PROTEIN

Dam

Many people have dammed small streams using mud, sticks, and stones. The basic principles involved in keeping these small structures from collapsing or failing to contain water are the same as those facing the engineers of our largest dams. Indeed, an accepted method in helping to design dams is to build realistic small-scale models and test them to destruction.

A dam must be able to prevent water from being passed through it. It must not be pushed downstream or lifted up by the pressure of water behind it. If too much water backs up behind the dam, there must be adequate means of diverting it around the dam and downstream in a controlled manner. These diversions are called spillways, and if they do not have sufficient capacity at times of flood, then overflow passing over the crest of the dam may cause irreparable damage, especially on earth-fill constructions.

There are basically two mechanisms with which a dam resists the loads imposed upon it. The first type, the gravity dam, has been used since antiquity and relies upon weight of material. The other type, the arch dam, relies upon the principle of the arch to take the loads in a horizontal direction into the sides of the structure and the abutments they bear upon. Some dams may rely on both principles.

The earliest dams were probably constructed of earth banking—there is some evidence in India and Sri Lanka of their use for water storage in ancient times. The Romans learned their engineering from the Greeks, using concrete and hydraulic mortar, which led to the success of their innumerable masonry dams built in Europe and North Africa. Near Rome, three dams were built to provide lakes as recreation facilities for the villa of the emperor Nero. In Spain, there are still examples left of Roman dams and aqueduct systems built to provide water for nearby towns. The Moors did not continue the tradition of reservoirs in Spain, preferring underground storage.

From the expulsion of the Moors until the 19th century, the Spanish led the world in dam building for irrigation. They exported the technology to the Americas, where at Potosi in Bolivia, for example, dammed reservoirs were used to power ore-crushing mills to provide silver for export back to Spain. Spanish expansion into Mexico and California included the introduction of damming and irrigation projects. In New England, timber dams made from the abundant supplies of local wood stored water and powered sawmills around which whole communities grew up.

In Europe, the Austrians built dam reservoirs to help increase their fish stocks because they were a landlocked country. In the Dolomites, Austrian engineers built dams to control flooding in northern Italy. France had been a center for hydropower ever since the Romans built a mill near Arles in 300 C.E. The Industrial Revolution brought demands for better transportation, and in both France and England, projects were introduced to provide dams that would add to the navigability of rivers or provide water for canals. In England, a widespread and standardized earth-fill

TYPES OF DAM

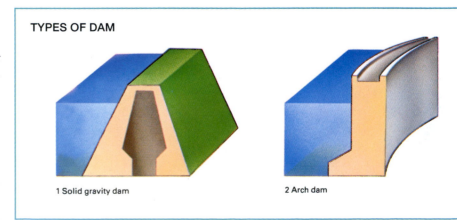

1 Solid gravity dam

2 Arch dam

dam system was evolved to create the reservoirs that were to supply the growing industrial towns of the northern counties.

Hydropower dams

During the 19th century, the United States steadily developed its hydropower resources, mainly in California and New England. By the end of the 19th century, the turbine had been developed, and its use to create electricity from hydropower was developed in both the United States and in France. In the 1890s, the Niagara Falls were the site for the first hydroelectric power (HEP) project, providing electricity for Buffalo. HEP has become such an important source of energy to some countries that, for example, in Norway virtually 100 percent of the country's electricity is produced this way. From the beginning of this century in the western states of the United States, multiuse projects for water supply, irrigation, and HEP were introduced. To create a unified approach and encourage cooperation between states, the Bureau of Reclamation was set up to finance, plan, and construct all United States irrigation and HEP projects.

Modern multiuse plans are typified by the Columbia Basin Project. Started in 1933 with the Grand Coulee Dam (the largest concrete structure ever built), 640 miles (1,660 km) of river up to the Canadian border were dammed virtually headwater to tailwater in a cascade system. The system revitalized the area, providing irrigation, HEP, navigation right up into Canada, flood and soil control, increased fishing, and improved public health by controlling malaria.

Today it is not just rivers but the sea as well that can be dammed behind barriers to control the flow of the tides. In France on the Rance estuary and in several places in Russia, such systems are being used to provide tidal electric power. On the river Thames in England, the Thames Barrier at Woolwich lies ready to dam up spring tides that may threaten to flood London.

Earth-fill construction

Dams made from banking up earth are probably the first type to have been constructed. These early dams were made from one sort of material, chosen for its watertightness and availability. These are known as homogeneous dams, and many are still in use. It is likely that there were many failures of these early dams, and it was not until thorough research into soil mechanics had been accomplished in the 1940s that their behaviour was understood.

It is essential that there is ample spillway capacity to divert floodwaters around these dams since any significant quantity of water passing over the crest may seriously erode them and often leads to failure; for instance, in 1889, the South Fork Dam in Pennsylvania failed in this manner. Any water percolating through the structure or underneath it must be controlled so that it cannot move the material from which the dam and its foundation are constructed.

There have been a number of refinements that have evolved through time that help maintain earth-fill dams in a stable condition. When the

▲ The Hoover Dam, one of the largest in the world, supplies water for irrigation projects in California, Arizona, and Nevada.

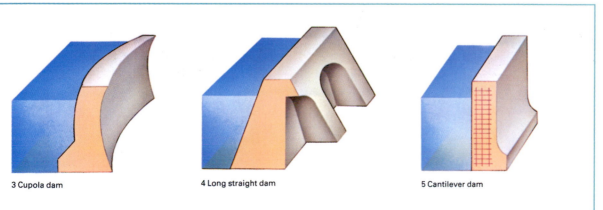

3 Cupola dam

4 Long straight dam

5 Cantilever dam

◄ Dams are built in a number of basic shapes or a combination of structures to suit the amount of water being dammed, the location of the dam, and the rock structure underneath the dam. Curved dams have great strength and can be built in awkward spaces; straight dams rely on gravity to anchor them.

adequate compaction of the construction material. A technique known as hydraulic fill, for sluicing the large quantities of material into place, was developed in the United States. Unfortunately, a number of failures during construction, such as at the Fort Peck Dam, have led to this technique being neglected in recent years.

Rock-fill dams

The first extensive use of rock-fill dams was in California at the time of the Gold Rush in 1849. These earliest examples consisted of loose hand-dumped rock cores faced on the waterface with compacted turfs to act as a waterproof membrane. As machinery took over from labor as the cheapest way of building, so the core of loose rubble became larger and its slopes flatter. The waterface was now faced in timber or more commonly in concrete to form the waterproof layer.

By 1931, the technique was advanced enough to build the 328 ft. (100 m) high Salt Springs Dam in California. Modern methods of compaction introduced in the 1950s mean that previous problems caused by inadequate compaction have been virtually eliminated. In some instances, the available quarried rock fill may be too small to be dumped, and in these cases, a system of rolled rock fill has been introduced to create dams that are virtually indistinguishable from the more refined types of earth- or gravel-fill dams. The Round Butte Dam on the Deschutes River in Oregon is one such example. The safety record of rock-fill dams is exemplary.

Solid-masonry gravity dams

A solid masonry gravity dam is one made of concrete or stone and is, in general, a straight wall resisting pressure of water trying to push the dam along and overturn it. Its sheer weight transfers loads to the foundations by vertical compressive forces and horizontal shearing forces. The stability of the dam therefore depends upon its weight and the strength of its base.

The earliest remains of a masonry dam are in Egypt, near Cairo, where the Sadd el-Kafara was built in approximately 2750 B.C.E. to store water for men and animals working a nearby quarry. It consists of two 78 ft. (24 m) wide walls of solid masonry with a gravel infill between. The total width of the dam is therefore something like 275 ft. (84 m) at the base. Even this great mass of materials did not hold back the waters for long. Throughflow and overflow seem to have taken their toll early on, stripping out the infill section and pushing aside the central masonry sections, letting the waters through. The Romans built many fine masonry dams, especially in

dam is of the homogeneous type, a gravel drain set into the foundation on the "airface" side of the dam pulls water (which inevitably saturates the dam) away from the airface, discharging it from the base of the dam. This keeps the airface dry and therefore stable. Paving the waterface and letting grass grow on the airface protects the structure from wave action and rainwash, respectively. Flattening of the slopes of the dam also adds to its stability by reducing its tendency to creep over a period of time.

Modern earth-fill dams are composites using an impervious core extending into an impervious foundation. In England in the 19th century, a standardized construction using puddled clay evolved as the core material. This core ran through the center of the dam and extended into a trench dug down into the bedrock. An impervious layer is created in this way, and the trench (which is used in most dams) helps lock the dam into its valley and prevents it from sliding.

The United States has had a particularly bad failure record for these dams, especially in the 19th century, but an improved grasp of soil mechanics has led to a number of successful high dams being built in this manner—for example, the Swift Dam on the Lewis River in Washington, which is 400 ft. (122 m) above streambed, and the New Don Pedro Dam on the Tuolomne River in California, which is some 550 ft. (168 m) high.

Some of the techniques introduced in the 20th century include the use of machinery to ensure

▲ A dam is not necessarily built of thick concrete—the shape of the dam wall gives it its strength. Dams are usually placed in harsh, bleak surroundings. Today's technology makes it possible to erect dams in previously impossible construction sites.

Spain and North Africa. The Spanish continued the tradition, building a number of large solid-masonry gravity dams, such as Almonacid de la Cuba, built in the 13th century south of the city of Saragossa.

By the end of the 19th century, there had been a large amount of written theory accumulated in Europe about the construction of gravity dams. Certain basic principles of design had been noted. First, a dam must resist overturning. There must be no tension loads imposed at any point upon the masonry. All loads applied to the structure taken down vertically into its base must act on this base within the middle third of the wall. This principle of the middle third is a basic concept of engineering practice. Second, the dam must resist being slid downstream, and the shearing strength of the masonry with which it is constructed must therefore exceed the horizontal loads imposed upon it. Third, compressive stresses in the masonry must be less than crushing strength by some margin. Above a certain height, this rule supersedes that of the middle third. Forces in the foundation must also not exceed its crushing strength. Finally, the dam must be provided with adequate spillway capacity to protect the fabric in times of flood.

Solid-masonry gravity constructions are more costly in terms of materials than modern structural dams. They still have their uses where the stability of the valley they sit in is questionable and it is desired that the dam itself must take all the imposed loads. An outstanding example of the solid-masonry gravity design is the Grand Coulee Dam on the Columbia River in Washington.

Solid-masonry arch dams

Arch action was known to the Romans, who used it in most of their building programs. The one exception appears to be in their dams. The advantage of the arch in dam construction is that for the same quantities of material as used in a gravity dam a considerably stronger structure can be built. In an arch dam, loads are carried principally in a horizontal direction into the sides of the structure and thence into the abutments it rests on.

One of the earliest arch dams was built in Spain in the 17th century at Elche. Here, the dam was built with a height of 76 ft. (23 m) and thickness of 34 ft. (10 m), making a height-to-thickness ratio of just over 2, which is too slender to be considered a gravity structure. The Spanish had realized by now that an arch or arched dam was best used in narrow rocky gorges because of the limited spanning potential of a single arch and the need for strong bearings. Gravity dams were best employed on wide valley floors where strength

▶ The spillway of Llyn Brianne Dam in Wales. The wide concrete channel carries excess water to guard against overspills. The water may leave the dam at 100 mph (160 km/h).

was needed from within the dam's weight itself. In the United States, the first arch dams were the Pathfinder and Buffalo Bill, built in Wyoming in the early 1900s. They stand 214 ft. (65 m) and 315 ft. (96 m) high, respectively.

The arch dam has a very good safety record with no failures of the wall itself ever recorded. In France, however, in 1959 the failure of the Malpasset Dam because of a slip in the rock abutment highlighted the main problem of arch dams.

Early-20th-century development led to the trial-load method of analysis favored in the United States and the modeling method of design preferred in Europe. Arch-gravity dams rely for their strength on a combination of sheer weight and arch action. When an arch dam has thicker arches at the base than at the crest, arch action will take the loads horizontally at the top, while toward the bottom, the loads are increasingly taken vertically by gravity. Modern arch design now includes double-curve structures like the Ithaca dam in New York, which is only 8ft. (2.4 m) thick at its base.

Multiple-arch dams

An arch structure is stronger the smaller the radius of the arch curve. Because of this fact, it is difficult for strong, small-radius arch dams to span very wide valleys. To overcome this, in Spain in the 18th century, Don Pedro introduced a number of small dams using multiple small-radius arches that bore onto buttresses secured to the valley floor. These systems were very successful and are used today, for example, in the 287 ft. (87 m) high Bartlett Dam on the Verde River in Arizona.

Steel and timber dams

Timber dams were first built in New England, where they were used to store water and to power sawmills around which whole communities developed. A timber dam will not last more than 50 years, which is why there are few remains of the earliest examples in the United States. In fact, such a dam will seldom remain watertight for more than a few years. They are useful, though, as coffer dams to hold back water during construction work and as temporary dams for use while a more permanent structure is being constructed.

Steel dams, with a steel-plate deck and steel frame buttresses, were built around the turn of the 20th century. The cost and need for regular maintenance meant they were never widely introduced.

Dam records

The current tallest dam is the 1985 Rogun Dam in Tajikistan, which stands 1,099 ft. (335m) high. The heaviest dam is the Syncrude Tailings Dam in Canada, weighing in at 706,320 cu. yds. (540,000 m³) in volume.

Current considerations

Despite the long history of dam building, there are still problems that have not been satisfactorily overcome. Furthermore, it is only in recent years that we have come to realize the far-reaching environmental effects that dams can cause.

The massive Three Gorges Dam on the Yangtse River in China, for instance, has experienced major protests over the environmental damage that its construction has caused and the amount of people that will be displaced—between 1.2 and 1.9 million people are expected to be forced to leave their homes, and 620,000 acres (250,000 ha) of farmland will be lost. The Aswan High Dam in Egypt has proved contentious because it controls the amount of water available to states downstream and also because it prevents the Nile from flooding annually. In Britain, the construction of dams has been halted and the water companies are required to focus instead on ways of saving water.

The problem of siltation of reservoirs has also still not been successfully solved. For example, Lake Mead behind the Hoover Dam lost 3 percent of its water capacity to silt in the first 14 years of its existence. And in Egypt, the silts that once fertilized the land around the river Nile are now being stored up behind the Aswan High Dam. Water standing in a reservoir will also be subject to evaporation, and thus, the remaining water will become increasingly saline.

As the number of dams all over the world goes up, they are increasingly being located in previ-

▲ Behind a dam lies an immense reservoir of potential energy readily convertible into power as the water is released to drive turbines and generate electricity. When a dam bursts, the results are usually catastrophic.

ously unacceptable sites. Many of these are in earthquake zones, thus adding to the problems of designing safe structures. It has even been suggested that the pressure imposed on Earth's surface by the weight of these unnatural lakes can lead to minor earthquakes, and there is evidence of minor quakes occurring in areas where before damming this phenomenon was unheard of.

The flooding of huge areas of land behind dams also creates problems. Whole communities are wiped out and have to be resettled. Agricultural land may be lost, and in the case of the Nile dams, ancient monuments and part of a nation's culture were partly lost to the waters. In Tasmania, the Australian government was under strong pressure to abandon the Franklin River project, which would lose some 540 sq. miles (1,400 km²) of land listed on the UN World Heritage register.

However, it is in Surinam and in the plans for the development of the Amazon Basin in Brazil that the enormous problems and side effects that can result from dam-building projects can be seen most clearly. In Surinam, to the north of Brazil, Lake Brokopondo was created in 1964 on some 580 sq. miles (1,500 km²) of virgin rainforest. The trees that it swamped began to decompose, producing foul-smelling hydrogen sulfide gas. Decomposition has turned the waters acidic, and they have attacked the steel turbine casings. Furthermore, the decaying nutrients have created ideal conditions for water weeds and especially water hyacinths to grow on the surface. These weeds have formed a dense mat that both poisons the fish and prevents sun from penetrating into the depths of the lake, where the plants that the fish feed on are found. Worse still, the water-weeds provide ideal breeding grounds for malaria and schistosomiasis—two of the most deadly diseases known to man.

SEE ALSO: ENERGY RESOURCES • HYDROELECTRIC POWER • TURBINE • WATER SUPPLY

Data Storage

The outstanding feature of modern computer systems is their ability to handle very large quantities of data. This feature involves the use of equally large quantities of memory, both to hold the data during processing and to hold the programs or instructions that control the processing operations. Digital computers have two main data storage areas, the main memory and the backing store, which can be compared to a filing center for storing papers. Storage can be divided into two types according to its ability to retain information. With a volatile memory device, the data is retained only as long as power is supplied to it. Nonvolatile memories are able to retain the stored data without a power supply, and this type is often used to hold program instructions and other nonchanging data.

Another important distinction lies in the way memory can be used, with random access memory, or RAM, allowing data to be written into or read from any section of the memory. With read-only memory (ROM) the contents of the memory are fixed and can only be read, though this can be done from any part of the memory. A typical use for ROM is to hold the language instructions for a computer, whereas RAM temporarily holds the data that is being worked on. As both use microchips, the storage capacity is limited.

The term *backup storage* is applied to devices linked directly to the computer processor and using magnetic tape or disks coated with a magnetic iron oxide film or optical devices such as CD-ROMs (compact disc read-only memory). Tapes and disks are the most common forms of backup storage, but many computers use more than one type of store, as each has certain inherent advantages and limitations that make it better suited to particular applications.

Development of storage devices

Data input to calculators and similar machines began as long ago as the mid-19th century in the form of punched cards. This method was followed by ticker tape, a paper ribbon with holes punched into it in binary sequences. Both methods were used until the early 1950s, which heralded the arrival of the first magnetic tape drives. The first hard disk drive was introduced in 1957 as part of IBM's RAMAC 350 computer and had what was then considered to be a massive storage capacity of 5 MB (megabytes), stored on fifty 24 in. (60 cm) disks.

Initially, hard disk drives were confined to mainframe and minicomputer operations because

of their large size and the expense of installing them—each disk cost tens of thousands of dollars, and they were stacked in towers several feet high. It was not until the idea of personal computers began to take off in the early 1980s that hard disk drives began to shrink to the size of a small shoebox. Even then, their storage capacity of 10 MB was considered too large for a personal computer.

As a result, the first personal computers used floppy disks to store programs needed by the hardware for it to run and for writing data. The first "floppies" were 8 in. or 5.25 in. (20 or 13.5 cm) disks of mylar plastic coated with a magnetic oxide and housed inside a soft plastic cover. Modern floppy disks are smaller at 3.5 in. (9 cm) and are enclosed in a more durable plastic case.

Hard disk drives finally became a standard component of the personal computer in 1983, when IBM incorporated them into their PC/XT model. The size of the disks inside the drive had gone down to 5.25 in. and could be housed in a box 3 in. (7.5 cm) high. The memory capacity of these devices was 20 MB. Increasing miniaturization continued to push drives to even smaller sizes, the 3.5 in. arriving in 1987 and the 2.5 in. (6.5 cm) a few years later for use in portable computers. These are now the standard sizes found in personal and laptop computers. Storage capacity also increased significantly—most personal computers now come equipped with many gigabytes (GB) of memory, and the cost of a hard disk drive has dropped to less than one dollar per megabyte.

▲ Hard disk drives are a standard feature of modern computers. They are capable of storing the vast amounts of data needed for running computer programs and files produced by running software applications. By the end of the 1990s, the storage capacity of hard disks was doubling every nine months as technology found new ways to increase the density of magnetic material on the platters.

Inside a hard disk drive

A hard disk drive consists of a sealed aluminum box with an entry point for the power supply and an electronic control board on one side. Inside the box are two or more platters stacked on a central spindle. The platters are made from an aluminum alloy coated with a magnetic iron oxide and polished to a mirror finish. On both sides of the platter is an arm mechanism that holds the read-write head. When the drive is operating, the platters spin at between 3,600 and 7,200 rpm in a counterclockwise direction. The actuator arm responds to commands received from the keyboard or mouse and moves the read-write head to the correct place on the platter. It retrieves the data requested and transfers it to the central processing unit. From here, it can be con- verted into visual form on-screen, sent down a telephone line as a fax or internet connection, or directed to a printer.

The movement of the actuator arm is very fast and precise. Powered by a linear motor, the arm can move from the hub to the edge of the platter and back nearly 50 times a second. The read-write heads are carried on the tip of the arm but do not actually touch the surface of the platter. The slipstream created by the rapidly rotating disks is sufficient to keep the head floating about one micron (one-millionth of a meter) above the surface of the disk. When the system is turned off, the platters stop spinning and the heads touch down in a specified landing zone, away from where the data is stored. A speck of dust or severe knock to the drive could cause the heads to crash

HARD DISK DRIVE

Hard disk drives typically consist of two or more platters, with a read-write head positioned on both sides of the platter. The actuator arms are all synchronized so that the read-write heads all move to the same place on each side of the platter at the same time. Data is stored on the magnetized sur- face of the platter in concentric circles called tracks (colored pink). Each track is divided into a number of pie-shaped wedges called sectors (colored red). Each sector contains a fixed number of bytes, usually 256 or 512.

The read-write head is a tiny electro- magnet that flies above the surface of the disk. When current is applied to the electric coil, the head becomes magnetic and orients the magnetic particles in the track, which is "write" mode. If no current is applied, the head picks up the magnetism of the track and induces a current in the coil. These elec- trical impulses are converted into digital sig- nals that the central processing unit can understand. This is "read" mode.

Binary bits (representing the numbers 1 or 0) are stored on the platter in microscopic magnets called domains. Before new data is written, the domains are oriented by the read-write head so that the magnetic poles all point in the same direction. The head then changes the polarity of some domains according to whether the data needs to be stored as a 1 or a 0. Each 8-bit grouping of domains is termed a byte.

into the platter and render the hard disk inoperable, so drives are sealed against contamination and built to withstand shocks up to 100 times the force of gravity.

The arms are moved to the right place on the hard drive by closed-loop positioning technology, in which the read-write heads are adjusted by electronic control devices until they are in the right place to retrieve data. Because the signals the head picks up from the platter are weak, they have to be amplified by a flex circuit inside the drive mechanism so that the chips on the drive's circuit board can convert these electrical signals into digital signals. The drive operation controls are also situated on the circuit board. Hard drives in most personal computers and work stations operate continuously while the power is on, whereas laptops and notebooks have "sleep" modes to save battery power.

Storing information on hard disks

Hard disks store information in concentric circles on the surface called tracks. These tracks are further subdivided into sectors, which can themselves be grouped into clusters. Current hard disk drives contain 2,000 tracks per in. of disk radius compared with the 135 per in. of a typical floppy disk. Improvements in the way disks are made has also enabled twice as many sectors (120) to be allocated in the outermost track than in the inner tracks (60), making them more efficient. Earlier hard disk drives contained the same number of sectors in all tracks.

Tracks and sectors are established on the hard disk by low level formatting, which marks the start and end points of each sector and prepares the drive to hold blocks of bytes. It is followed by high-level formatting, which writes the file storage instructions onto the sectors. Because the read-write heads all move together, data is written up and down from platter to platter in a concept known as a cylinder. If, for example, writing begins on track 55 of the first platter, when that track is full, the file continues to be written on track 55 from head number two. Depending on how long the file is and how many platters are contained in the hard drive, the information will continue to be written on the same track for each head until they are all full, when it will then move to track 56 on the first platter. Tracks are numbered inward from the outer edge. When the drive receives an address for the data to be retrieved, the heads move directly to the location in the order requested. The ability to store and retrieve data instantaneously was the chief reason for the demise of the tape system, which has a

▲ Hard disk drives being tested in a computer assembly plant. The decrease in size of hard disks from the early 24 inch platters to 3.5 inch drives together with the corresponding fall in price has done much to make personal computers affordable and within the reach of ordinary users.

clumsier search and retrieval mechanism because of the way it has to wind and rewind the tape.

A file is a named string of bytes that code for a discrete piece of information, such as a record in a database, an instruction in a software application, a screen color, and so on. When a file is requested by a program, the bytes are retrieved from the hard disk and sent one at a time to the central processing unit. How quickly the drive can respond is called its data rate—between 5 and 40 MB per second are common for personal computers. The time taken to access the data is called the seek rate. About 15 milliseconds is all it takes for the central processing unit to request a file and start receiving the first byte of data.

Removable storage

While hard disk drives can store most of the data a computer needs, portability and security considerations often make other forms of storage media necessary. Floppy disks are commonly used to transfer data between different computers but have a limited storage capacity that makes backing up large data files a lengthy process. The flexible disk surface is clamped to the surface of the recording head during operation to provide the necessary alignment of head with disk surface. Zip disks are a development of the floppy and have about ten times the storage capacity of an ordinary floppy disk.

To cope with the increasing amount of data used by and stored on computers, a number of high-capacity removable storage devices have been developed for archiving data or storing programs. Their use is largely dictated by performance, cost, capacity, and suitability to the task.

Tape drives

Magnetic tape was first used to store data on mainframe computers. The main drawback to using tape systems is that the information is stored sequentially on the tape and has to be wound or rewound to the location of the data. Nevertheless, improvements in the speed of tape drives and the introduction of digital audio tape (DAT) make it useful for backing up network servers and storage of critical data.

The magnetic tape used on large mainframe computers resembles that used on sound recorders but is usually 2,400 ft. (732 m) long and 0.5 in. (13 mm) wide, wound on 10 in. (25.4 cm) diameter spools. Magnetic tape units use 7, 9, or 24 tracks running along the length of the tape, and some can handle both 7 and 9 track requirements. The head assembly contains a read-write head for each track so that the machine can read or write all tracks simultaneously. All tracks are

▲ The data storage tape library of the CIA is so vast that it uses robotic arms to locate and retrieve the items needed.

usable for data recording except one, which is the one in which the parity bits are written. To give a built-in accuracy check on each row of bits written across the tape, the controlling system counts the number of ones in a row before it is written, and writes either a one or a zero in the parity track so that the total number of ones in each row is always an odd number (odd-bit parity) or an even number (even-bit parity). The row of bits is read immediately after writing, and if the parity check is incorrect, that is, the data bits have been wrongly written, the tape is backspaced and the row of bits rewritten. If the error is still present when the parity is checked again, the presence of the error can be indicated to the machine operator.

Data is written in short blocks with a small space left after each one, and the precision of the read-write heads allows very dense packing of the data. The space between the blocks of data allows the unit to operate one block at a time if necessary, as it allows the machine time to stop the tape at the end of one block and restart it again and reach proper operating speed before the next block is read.

With recording densities as great as 9,600 bytes (rows of bits) per inch (about 3,800 bytes per cm) and tape speeds of 200 in. per sec. (508 cm/s), the tapes must be stopped and started with great precision. In the latest tape drives, this precision is achieved by the use of motors with very light moving parts, high acceleration and deceleration speeds, and very precise braking mechanisms. To reduce the amount of fast stopping and starting and changes of direction of the tape spools and to permit more precise handling of the tape, tape reservoirs are provided between each spool and the head area. The tape runs down from each spool into a column placed directly below it and is drawn back up out of it by the tape drive capstans when needed. Sensing devices in the reservoir columns ensure that the amount of tape in each column is maintained at an optimum level, the spool drive motors feeding more tape in or out of the columns as necessary.

The number of tape drives used depends on the size and requirements of the computer system. Control units link the drives to the central processor, each control unit serving several drives. One of the tape reels is fixed permanently into the drive unit, and the other is removable so that the recorded files of data can be removed from the machines when not needed, freeing them for further work. The tapes of data prepared on one computer can be processed on any other similar machine, giving a measure of flexibility to this method of data storage. To prevent irretrievable loss of important data, most users have more than one copy of important tapes, so if one is lost or damaged, there is always a spare.

Modern magnetic tape drives solve the problem of interblock gaps and consequent loss of space for data by directly writing to or reading from a magnetic disk under program control, but by bypassing the conventional data transfer methods of the processor. Artificial interblock gaps are used, but a far greater packing density of information is possible. This process is known as streaming. Many streaming systems use a superior type of cassette that is more suitable for computer work than the conventional type of audio cassette.

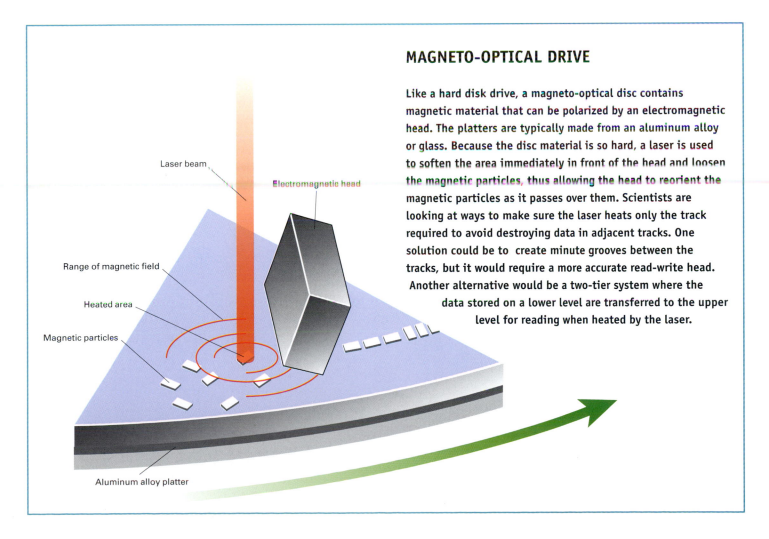

MAGNETO-OPTICAL DRIVE

Like a hard disk drive, a magneto-optical disc contains magnetic material that can be polarized by an electromagnetic head. The platters are typically made from an aluminum alloy or glass. Because the disc material is so hard, a laser is used to soften the area immediately in front of the head and loosen the magnetic particles, thus allowing the head to reorient the magnetic particles as it passes over them. Scientists are looking at ways to make sure the laser heats only the track required to avoid destroying data in adjacent tracks. One solution could be to create minute grooves between the tracks, but it would require a more accurate read-write head. Another alternative would be a two-tier system where the data stored on a lower level are transferred to the upper level for reading when heated by the laser.

Laser beam

Electromagnetic head

Range of magnetic field

Heated area

Magnetic particles

Aluminum alloy platter

Optical systems

Optical systems use lasers to read from and write to their media. Three types of optical disc are commonly used—the compact disc-read only memory (CD-ROM), the write once read many, or WORM, drives, and rewritable optical discs. CD-ROMs are popular for multimedia applications because they can store vast amounts of data. Software programs and encyclopedias are frequently distributed as CD-ROMs, as they are cheap and easy to mass produce. As with audio compact discs, lasers create a master disc and a mold is made from the master. Copies are made by pressing plastic into the mold and then lacquering the surface to protect the pattern of pits and lands (areas burned out of the disc surface by the laser to give a profile of high and low surface areas corresponding to 1 and 0 in binary digits). When the laser reads the disc, it scans the pits and lands and converts them into binary signals that the central processing unit can understand. Although they can hold large quantities of data (between 128 and 2,000 MB), optical discs have slower access times than hard disks—30 to 50 milliseconds is typical.

Rewritable disc drives are becoming more common as the cost of the technology becomes more affordable to the ordinary user. Usually these discs are used for holding massive files like pictures or graphics. Where it is important that the data cannot be changed after writing, such as on public records, WORM drives are used instead.

Although CD-ROM drives are common in most personal computers, they are slowly being supplanted by another optical system, the digital versatile disc, or DVD. These have storage capacities of up to 4.4 GB compared with an average 650 MB compact disc and are ideal for storing movies and for other image-intensive applications. Some models of Apple's iMac come with a DVD drive as standard, showing the probable direction of future home computing.

Magneto-optical discs

The magneto-optical disc is a hybrid technology that combines magnetic and laser media. Using the laser allows very high densities of magnetic media to be packed onto the discs, which come in 3.5 and 5.25 in. sizes. Like magnetic disks, the magneto-optical disc has a read-write head, but because they are made from materials that are resistant to magnetic fields at room temperature, a laser is needed to heat the magnetic particles enough for the read-write head to realign them as it passes. One advantage of using a laser is that the read-write head doesn't need to be as close to the surface of the disc, avoiding the possibility of a head crash and loss of data.

The laser is also used to read data from the disc. It does this by picking up reflections from the

▼ A compact disc being lacquered after pressing. Compact discs are frequently used to hold large databases or for multimedia applications. The development of the CD writer has made them useful to companies that need to keep large amounts of information, as they are cheap to produce and easy to store.

magnetic particles—depending on their polarity, the particles will either reflect or not reflect—and this response is converted into a digital 1 or 0 signal. Writing to the disc is more difficult, as the drive mechanism needs to pass over the disc twice—once to orientate all the domains in the same direction and then to change the polarity of some according to the data being written. Although magneto-optical drives revolve at the same speed as hard drives, this double pass makes them slower to write to.

Memory cards

Increasing miniaturization of computing devices such as palmtop computers, battery-powered notebooks, personal organizers, and even mobile telephones and digital cameras has created a need for lightweight and portable memory devices. This niche has been filled by the development of the memory card, also known as a PC card. Cards vary in thickness according to use but are about the same size as a credit card. Type III cards are actually tiny 1.8 in. hard disk drives, while Type I and Type II cards use solid-state memory chips and are expensive, as doubling the memory size effectively means using twice as many chips. However, they have low power consumption and are resistant to shock and vibration.

The uses of PC cards depend on the type of chip installed and how the data is programmed into it. Read-only memory (ROM) cards come with the data or program already built into the chip and will usually work only in equipment for which they have been designed. One-time-programmable (OTP) cards are built as blanks and need special writing devices to install the requisite information. As the name suggests, once the card has been programmed, it cannot be changed or rewritten. Although both can store data without a power source, the speed at which software programs become obsolete makes them an expensive and inflexible method of storage.

Another type of memory cache is the SRAM (static random access memory) card, which has the advantage of being rewritable. The main drawback to their widespread adoption is that they need a constant trickle of power to retain the data stored on them. The power is provided by the host device and backed up by a small watch battery on the card itself. While a battery can run for about a year before it has to be replaced, there is always the risk that the battery may discharge suddenly, thus wiping the data stored on the card. Typical cards can store up to 4MB of data, but capacities greater than this are very expensive.

Flash cards are another development that combines the nonvolatile nature of ROM and OTP cards with the ability to rewrite data of the SRAM card. Although flash cards are ideal for use in lightweight, portable computer equipment, their maximum capacity of 40 MB is significantly lower than a comparably priced hard drive.

SEE ALSO: ANALOG AND DIGITAL SYSTEMS • AUDIO AND VIDEO RECORDING • BINARY SYSTEM • COMPACT DISC, AUDIO • COMPUTER • DIGITAL VERSATILE DISC (DVD) • ELECTROMAGNETISM • INTEGRATED CIRCUIT • LASER AND MASER • LINEAR MOTOR • MAGNETIC TAPE AND FILM • MAGNETISM • MICROPROCESSOR • MULTIMEDIA

Density

alternative way of measuring density is to compare the mass of a certain volume of a substance with the same volume of water. This type of density measurement is known as the specific gravity (SG) or relative density of the object—and it is a dimensionless number because it is the ratio of two masses. The specific gravity of iron, for example, is 7.9. It is worth noting that specific gravity is always numerically the same as the density in grams per cubic centimeter because the density of water is very close to 1 g/cm^3.

The practical uses of measuring specific gravity were first demonstrated by Archimedes of Syracuse (in Sicily) in the third century B.C.E., when, according to legend, he was consulted by Hiero, the ruler of Syracuse, as to how it would be possible to detect whether the gold in a crown had been alloyed with silver by the goldsmith. The story goes that Archimedes hit on the answer when taking a bath, and he ran home through the streets of Syracuse shouting, "Eureka, I have found it." He had realized that, when he immersed himself in the bath, the volume of water that overflowed was equal to the volume of his immersed body—and hence, that if equal weights of silver and gold were immersed, the denser gold would displace less water. He then showed that the crown displaced more water than an equal weight of gold, so proving that forgery had taken place.

Measuring the SG of liquids

Archimedes also realized that when an object is immersed in liquid, the liquid surrounding it must be exerting an upward force (the buoyancy force) that would just support the same volume of liquid if the body were not there. The object must experience an upthrust equal to the weight of liquid displaced by it—this is the usual statement of Archimedes' principle. For a body that is denser than the liquid, the buoyancy force must be equal to its weight, and it will then float with part of its volume out of the liquid. This is the principle of the hydrometer, an instrument for measuring the specific gravities of liquids.

In its simplest form, a hydrometer is just a float made of a glass bulb weighted with lead shot, with a long narrow neck that rises above the surface of the liquid. When the hydrometer is floated in different liquids, it must always displace the same weight of liquid (equal to its own weight), so the volume displaced depends on the specific gravity of the liquid. The level of the liquid surface at the neck of the hydrometer indicates the

In everyday life, the word *heaviness* is often not used in its strict sense of referring to the weights of objects—for example, gold is thought of as being a heavier metal than aluminum even though an aluminum saucepan weighs more than a gold ring. The important idea here is that equal volumes of the two materials should be weighed. The mass of a standard volume of a substance is called its density, and the actual value of the density depends on the units in which the mass and volume are measured, though these are usually grams and cubic centimeters. The density of iron, for example, is 494 lbs. per cu. ft. (7.9 g/cm³). An

▲ A Galileo thermometer works on the principle that temperature affects buoyancy—the colder a liquid gets, the denser it becomes, and the more weight it can support. The tube contains differently weighted floats that sink as the liquid gets warmer. The lowest float still supported by the water indicates the temperature.

A HYInfused

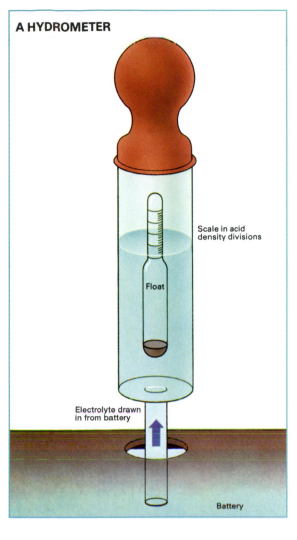

Scale in acid density divisions

Float

Electrolyte drawn in from battery

Battery

◄ The hydrometer works on the principle that when a body floats on a liquid, the weight of the liquid displaced by the submerged part will equal the weight of the body. Thus the volume visible above the liquid surface can then be used to measure the density of the liquid.

▼ The performance of racing cars is improved by the use of a heavy gasoline containing toluene, which increases the specific gravity of ordinary gasoline from 0.75 to 0.94. Adding toluene also improves fuel economy, a major consideration in racing cars, as it reduces the need for pit stops to take on extra fuel.

Vapor density

The density of gases and vapors is about a thousand times less than that of solids and liquids, so correspondingly accurate techniques are required to measure it. The measurement of the vapor densities of substances that are normally liquid (at room temperature and pressure) has been particularly important in chemistry because it is related to the molecular weight of the substance. One accurate method is to balance two evacuated containers in an atmosphere of the vapor and to puncture one so that buoyancy forces no longer act on it. The upthrust on the other is equal to the weight of vapor now in the punctured container, and so, from this force and the volume of the first container, the vapor's density can be calculated.

The density of the atmosphere changes all the time because it is affected by temperature, pressure, and water vapor. Air density is lowest on a hot day at a high elevation when the atmospheric pressure is low and highest at low elevations when the pressure is high and the temperature is low. Humid air is less dense than dry air because water vapor molecules replace some of the heavier nitrogen and oxygen molecules. The density of the air is an important factor for pilots—less dense air decreases engine power and thrust because more lifting force is needed to get the airplane off the ground. The planes also need longer runways to take off and land and cannot climb as quickly.

depth at which it floats, and because this depends on the volume of the liquid displaced, it is possible to graduate the neck in terms of the specific gravity of the liquid.

In a practical hydrometer, the float is usually in a glass container that is filled with liquid by suction using a rubber bulb. This way it is easier to see the liquid level, and less liquid is needed. Probably the best known use of a hydrometer is for measuring the state of lead–acid batteries, in which the liquid (electrolyte) has a specific gravity of 1.28 when fully charged; this number decreases as the battery is discharged. Hydrometers are also used for measuring the proof of spirits and for following the fermentation of liquors, whose specific gravity falls as the sugar in solution is converted to alcohol.

Another device used to determine the densities of liquids is the pycnometer. It consists of a calibrated glass vessel with a fixed volume. The vessel is weighed using an analytical balance and then filled to the calibration mark with the liquid and weighed again. Subtracting the mass of the empty vessel gives the mass of the liquid, which is then divided by the volume of the pycnometer to give the density of the liquid.

SEE ALSO: AIR • ENERGY, MASS, AND WEIGHT • GAS LAWS • PRESSURE • VAPOR PRESSURE

Dentistry

Dentistry is the part of medicine and surgery that is concerned with the mouth cavity, the teeth, the bones of the jaws, and the overlying soft tissues together with the prevention, diagnosis, and treatment of diseases of these parts.

To deal with dental decay, toothache, and loss of teeth, the Egyptians in 4000 B.C.E. used an assortment of medicaments, and the Chinese in 2000 B.C.E. treated dental complaints with herbs and acupuncture. The ancient Greeks in the fifth century B.C.E. described the operation of dental extraction, and the Romans in the first century C.E. carried out extractions and fillings and constructed false teeth. It was not until the 18th century that medicine and surgery were again influenced by a revival of scientific spirit. The first clinical demonstration of local anesthesia was given by Halsted in 1884, using an intradermal (within the skin) injection of cocaine to render an area of the body insensitive to pain during surgery while the patient remained fully conscious.

The treatment of dental disease and the development of techniques to restore the teeth then advanced rapidly. Electricity was used to speed up the dental drill and to provide better illumination in dental surgery. The discovery of antiseptics, X rays, antibiotics, and plastics and progress in metallurgy, materials, and drugs have all played a part in the advancement of modern dentistry.

Structure of teeth

Healthy teeth are hard, mineralized structures that are held by strong fibers in sockets in the bone of the upper and lower jaws. The root is the part of the tooth attached to the jaw, and the crown is the visible portion.

Teeth are composed of four different tissues: enamel, dentine, pulp, and cementum. Enamel is the highly mineralized, insensitive outer covering of the crown and the hardest tissue in the body.

Dentine, which forms the bulk of the tooth, is a sensitive tissue receiving its nourishment from a fluid that permeates the dentine structure through tubules. This fluid is derived from the tooth's pulp cavity.

Pulp is the nerve of the tooth and is situated in a chamber in the dentine extending down into the root end. Through the roots, blood and nerve fibers are supplied to the pulp.

Cementum, which covers the outside of the roots, is a bonelike substance that provides attachment for the fibers of the supporting periodontal membrane. It is this membrane that holds the tooth in the bone socket. The gingiva, or

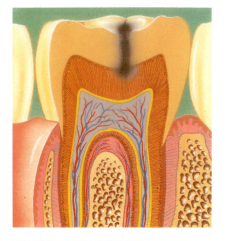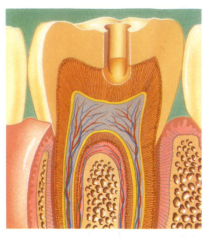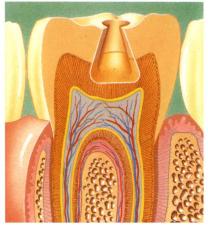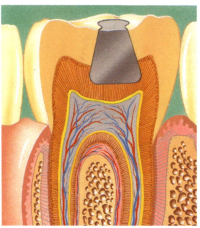

gum, surrounds the neck of the tooth and prevents infection from penetrating between the tooth and the bony socket.

Orthodontics

The bone of the jaw supporting the teeth is a living substance that reacts to and is molded by the forces acting upon it from using the teeth and from general muscular stresses. Any abnormal forces lead to gradual changes in teeth positions, and irregularities can occur. The prevention and correction of such irregularities is the study of orthodontics.

In orthodontic treatment, the plastic quality of the surrounding bone structure is exploited to reshape the jaw and reposition the teeth through the application of a continuous gentle pressure. Stainless steel springs, elastic bands, and screw fixtures are used. Where there is overcrowding of the teeth, some may have to be extracted to make space for the correct repositioning of the remaining teeth.

Tooth decay

Dental caries, or tooth decay, is one of the most universally prevalent diseases affecting teeth. It is found particularly in children and young people who eat a diet rich in sugars and other highly refined carbohydrates.

▲ Decay has penetrated the outer layer of enamel into a tooth core (top left). A hole has been drilled (top right), removing the decay. The cavity is then shaped, making it wider at the bottom than at the top to anchor the filling (bottom left). If too much of the tooth is drilled away, as is likely if the area of decay is large or if the tooth is filled on three or more occasions, the cavity can lose its wedge shape so that the filling (bottom right) is easily dislodged.

When debris is allowed to collect undisturbed on the tooth surfaces, it quickly forms an adherent film (dental plaque) filled with multiplying bacteria, which break down sugars and produce a strong acid that attacks the enamel. After a period of time, the enamel disintegrates and bacteria invade the unprotected dentine. If left undisturbed, the infection will finally approach the pulp as the dentine is softened and destroyed—leading to toothache.

Without treatment, the pulp and nerve endings are killed leading to a temporary relief from pain—but the infection continues down the root, causing pain and swelling of the jaw. This is the dental abscess, or gumboil.

Treatment

When teeth are damaged by dental caries, the infected area can be removed and the cavity filled with an amalgam (a mercury-based alloy). The extent of damage is not always visible, however, and X rays are taken of the teeth to show the internal damage. This technique, known as dental radiography, is frequently used in the examination of teeth and jaws for the presence of disease.

A piece of photographic film, protected from light and moisture by a suitable packet, is held in the mouth behind the teeth, and a beam of X rays is aimed at it from outside the mouth. The rays pass through the teeth, supporting bone, and soft tissues and throw a varying shadow upon the film. When the film is developed, it will show details in and around the teeth that cannot be seen by the naked eye.

Once the extent of the damage has been determined, the correct treatment can be applied. First, the tooth can be rendered insensitive with a local anesthetic injection. Then the infected and softened parts of the tooth are removed by using either a dental drill or handheld instruments. The cavity is extended to the desired outline so that the filling can be fixed firmly. The walls are smoothed, cleaned with warm water, and dried with air, and a protective cement lining is inserted. Often zinc phosphate cement is used for the lining; it is made by mixing a liquid and powder together in the required proportions and then molded into the cavity to provide the final shape for the amalgam. This cement acts as an insulating lining to protect the tooth interior, for example, from heat, which can easily pass through the amalgam and be extremely painful.

Dental amalgams

An amalgam is composed of a mixture of one or more metals with mercury. The alloy is made by combining finely ground particles of the constituent metals—usually at least 65 percent silver and 25 percent tin together with copper and zinc and a measured amount of mercury. The resulting amalgam is at first soft and plastic enough to be packed into the prepared cavity and contoured to shape before it sets. When hard, it has an impervious crystalline structure, resistant to wear and the chemical effects of mouth fluids. Dental amalgam alloys of this type have been developed so that they do not alter in size as they harden. Contraction could lead to a loose filling and expansion to an overstressed cavity. When the amalgam is hard—after a few minutes—it is carved to restore the lost tooth shape, and 24 hours later it can be polished with rotary brushes.

Disease of the gums

Gingivitis and periodontal disease are diseases of the gums and supporting structure of the teeth. Although less dramatic than dental caries, they are responsible for the loss of many teeth in people over 35. The first stages are, however, detectable in adolescence.

Inflammation of the gums may be due to general ill health (requiring medical attention), but the most common factor is poor oral hygiene. Again, sugars and bacteria build up between the teeth, forming a plaque, which causes irritation of the gums and leads to swelling and bleeding when the teeth are brushed.

If this first stage is neglected, a breach is made between the tooth and the socket, and hard tartar or calculus builds up in the pockets so formed.

▼ Stages in the fitting of crowns to replace an upper jaw of badly filled, discolored teeth. First the teeth are cut down to stumps (top left) on which the crowns will be firmly based. A cast of the upper teeth (top right) is prepared, and the crowns are set in place to check they will fit properly and look right.

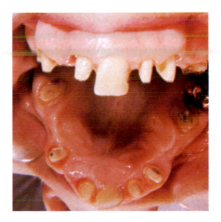

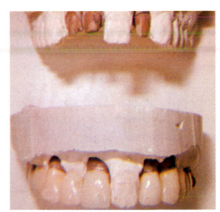

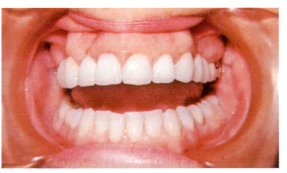

◄ The final result of the crowning process is a set of partly artificial teeth that are strong, clean, and filling free, and that match their owner's remaining healthy natural teeth perfectly.

A slow and insidious but often painless breakdown of the supporting structures commences, and the teeth inevitably loosen unless treatment is sought in time. Originally, an operation called gingivectomy was commonly performed to remove this unattached gum, but it is being superseded by plastic surgery, in which tissue is transplanted from the roof of the mouth to a place where the gums have receded.

Newer techniques try to regenerate the periodontum, the delicate layer of cells that glue the tooth to the gum and also to the bone itself. One involves transplanting fresh bone and marrow tissues, taken from the patient, around the teeth to form a new attachment apparatus. Another takes freeze-dried bone, which has fewer antigens than fresh bone, from genetically similar donors. Barrier membranes are placed over the wounds around the teeth because they selectively allow certain types of cells to enter the wound area.

Preventive dentistry

The traditional preoccupation of dentistry has been with the practical problems of repair and treatment of disease. Although these remain important, with preventive dentistry much can be done to eliminate the causes of dental disorder.

Today's children and young adults have far fewer filled or missing teeth than their parents. In the 1940s and 1950s it was discovered that people living in some areas developed far less tooth decay than those in other areas; the difference was due to traces of fluoride ion in the water. Since then, many states have added fluoride to the water supply with dramatic effects on the dental health of the population. Despite public concern about the possible dangers of fluoride, it is harmless in the doses used, though topical use in toothpaste is thought to be more effective. The dramatic decrease in tooth decay has changed dentistry from the old-fashioned drill-and-fill methods to some exceptionally high technology.

The holy grail for dental researchers is a vaccine that will prevent tooth decay and gum disease. Despite a serious research effort, nothing has been produced yet, but the next few years offer hope. Meanwhile, dentists have made huge progress in other forms of prevention and treatment.

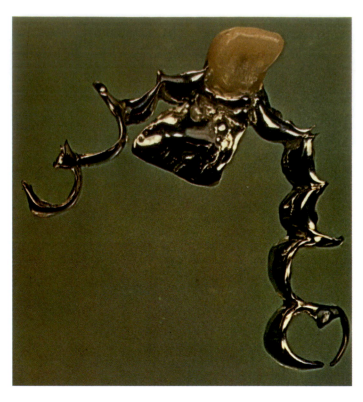

▲ The support for this one false tooth is ingeniously designed. The hook-shaped parts on each end clip onto other teeth.

Tooth replacement

Since 1980, it has become increasingly common for teeth that have been knocked out to be replaced. The tooth should be placed in milk, which will protect the delicate cells that stick it to the gum, and taken with the patient to the dentist. If no dentist is available, in an emergency, the individual can replace the tooth temporarily, using firm but not excessive pressure.

A new technique of tooth implantation, called osseointegration, was developed in Norway by Per-Ingvar Brane-mark in 1986. It has since become a commercial success. By 1990, there were 36 companies worldwide competing to produce the titanium parts for this procedure, in which a biologically compatible implant eventually becomes fused to the bone structure underlying the gum. Such implants need frequent follow-up treatment and scrupulous aftercare.

Dental decay is caused by bacteria that feed on sugar in the mouth, producing lactic acid and plaque; the presence of sugar also allows the bacteria to multiply rapidly. The plaque provides a housing for the bacteria, and calcium in the saliva allows it to "fossilize." The importance of cleaning teeth after eating sweets has been known for decades, but recent research has shown that brushing before eating sweets also protects the teeth, as there are fewer bacteria left in the mouth to multiply.

A new technique for preventing decay is the use of sealants. Even before a child has any signs of decay, a soft plastic is applied to the tooth surface to fill in the pits and cracks where food and bacteria can accumulate. The plastic is then hardened with ultraviolet light or a chemical.

A concern that the mercury used in amalgam fillings may cause chronic poisoning often results in replacing such fillings at huge expense to patients. However, research has shown that dental amalgam does not release mercury into the body and that dentists, who handle a great deal of amalgam and would be the first to be poisoned, suffer no harm. Mercury remains one of the best filling materials, as it is malleable when first mixed, lasts for many years, and does not crack under the forces of biting, chewing, and extremes of hot and cold temperatures in food.

Dental tools

The dental drill is an instrument used in dentistry for the deep penetration of tooth structure. It is used to remove infected and softened parts of decayed tooth substance (dental caries) and also to shape and prepare the remaining sound tooth to receive the filling or restoration. Rotary instruments similar to or attached to drills are also used to cut, grind, and polish the teeth in many other dental procedures.

Originally, cavities in the teeth were prepared with hand instruments such as tiny spoon-shaped excavators, chisels, and files. Over the centuries a variety of drilling tools evolved—first mechanically driven, from the 1870s, electricity was increasingly used to power drills. However, these instruments sent vibrations through the patient's jaw, and their use was often more painful than the original toothache.

Air turbine drill

In 1957, the first air-driven turbine handpieces became available, and they transformed modern operative dentistry by providing a free-running speed of 300,000 rpm. In 1962, this drill was even further improved by the use of air bearings to 800,000 rpm. It was found that operating speeds in excess of 250,000 rpm were above the level of vibratory perception of the patient, who was only aware of a whistling noise as his or her teeth were drilled.

The principle of the dental air turbine is that a foot-controlled flow of compressed air is carried via a flexible hose to a hand piece where it is

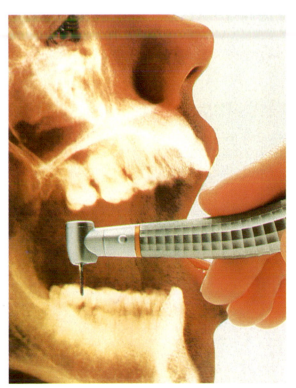

◀ The slim, flat-angled design of a typical high-performance turbine dental drill makes it easier to use and reduces muscular tension. A large number of drills, burrs, and polishing attachments can be rapidly fitted and disconnected from the permanently powered handle.

directed against the blade of a miniature air turbine, causing it to spin. The air is exhausted partially from the head of the hand piece, returning through a tube back to the control box. An oil mist was introduced into the compressed air to provide lubrication of the turbine motor, but it interfered with the adhesion of the filling material and has been replaced by special spray cans.

The burr, of diamond abrasive or tungsten carbide, is held in the central shaft of the turbine by a friction grip chuck and is easily interchangeable, although each shape of instrument is more versatile and long-lasting at these ultra-high speeds. An air and water burr coolant is conducted by a concentric tube to be blown accurately upon the burr from jets in the head of the headpiece.

The cutting efficiency of the air turbine is outstanding. A very light pressure is used and the hard tooth substance gently wiped away. If the pressure on the tooth is in excess of 5 to 6 oz. (140–170 g), the engine slows and stalls. The ultra-speed air turbine is used for rapid removal of bulky amounts of tooth substance, while the relatively slower high-speed drills are used for other purposes, such as finishing the cavity surfaces. Rotary instruments are still used at low speeds for slow removal of decayed tooth in circumstances where the operator's sense of touch is needed, and they are also employed for polishing.

Air-motor drill

Air motors have since been developed where the turbine is larger and has a greater torque, or turning power. Their normal speeds range from 5,000 to 25,000 rpm, but, fitted with specially geared heads, they can become as slow as 50 rpm. In all modes, the drill is powered by the same compressed-air sources as the air-turbine drill.

Early versions of the air motor were based on rotary piston systems, which had an extremely high torque but were somewhat bulky. The latest units, complete with a turbine blade motor in the handle section, are no larger than the dental hand piece of 20 years ago that required a bulky separate motor drive to make it functional.

Most of the recent air motors and turbines can be sterilized in autoclaves at temperatures up to 275°F (135°C), which provides a degree of patient protection not previously available.

As with air-turbine drills, special lubricants are applied from a pressurized container that simultaneously cleans and lubricates both the delicate motor and the turbine blades in the one operation. Both types of drill have air and water supplied directly to the hand piece for cooling and lubricating, and a fiber-optic system incorporated

FACT FILE

- Tooth transplantation was a speciality of some 18th-century dentists. Poor people were induced by advertisements to sell their healthy teeth, which were extracted at the same time as those of the paying customer. The healthy tooth was planted firmly in the empty socket. Most of these transplants failed to take root or had to be extracted owing to infection.

- Some modern resins used for false teeth can be shaped and fitted while in a malleable state and then hardened by means of intense light or ultraviolet radiation. The intermetallic compound titanium-nickel (TiNi), which has a shape memory, can also be bent to shape for orthodontic braces and becomes securely tensioned in the mouth when warmed.

- Queen Elizabeth I of England had badly decayed teeth but was so afraid of 16th-century dentistry that she would not have any pulled. To encourage her, the bishop of London, in 1578 during a very bad bout of royal toothache, allowed the surgeon to pull one of his few remaining teeth as an example, and the monarch then submitted. Eventually the queen lost so many teeth that she padded her cheeks with fine cloth when she was making public appearances.

- Modern dentistry is currently turning to high-tech tools such as computer-imaging systems, surgical lasers, fiber optics, and CAD-CAM systems. A company based in Sacramento, California, Professional Services Institute, offers an imaging system that dentists can use to preview the cosmetic result of dental work such as orthodontic treatment (straightening) or tooth capping.

- Another computer-imaging system—PreView Dental Imaging System from McGhan InstruMed Corp, Carpintaria, California— is modified from a French system used by plastic surgeons. These methods mean that the dentist does not have to make a physical model of the reconstructive work that he or she proposes and can communicate with the laboratory by electronic mail or by mailing a floppy disk.

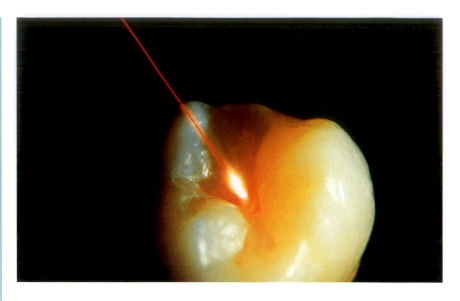

into the hand piece head conducts light to the working area of the mouth. Burrs are changed effortlessly by simply pressing a button.

Miniature lightweight electric motor drills are used in both the dentist's office and the laboratory, and the latest types now have a micromotor built into the hand piece. The electric motor typically operates on 12 V, and while micromotor drills do not have the high rpm of the air turbine, speeds of up to 50,000 rpm are available to the operator together with good speed control and excellent torque.

Developments

Future developments that can be anticipated include a revival of a system that was first investigated in the early 1950s and involves the use of ultrasonic vibration with an abrasive particle slurry that can be used for cavity preparation.

The use of laser beam cutting is also proving successful. By 1992, some 21,000 dentists worldwide had acquired lasers to vaporize tooth and gum disease. The pain of exposed teeth is caused by tiny tubules in the dentine, the outer layer of the root. Lasing the exposed surface closes these tubules; one course of laser treatment works for up to three years. Lasers can also be directed into the pockets between teeth and exposed gum, killing the bacteria and allowing the gum to cement itself to the tooth again. The CO_2 laser is effective at removing soft tissues and allows large areas to be treated at one sitting. The Nd:YAG laser, named for the rare earth element neodymium, which is its active medium, has proved effective in clinical trials for removing decay and for treating periodontal pockets.

▲ A laser being used experimentally to remove tooth decay. Lasers are concentrated beams of light that can be used as a surgical tool to cut through damaged tissue or specifically destroy diseased cells. Unlike conventional dental drills, they do not cause vibration in the patient's mouth and do not have the accompanying high-pitched sound that puts many people off a trip to the dentist.

SEE ALSO: ABRASIVE • ANESTHETIC • FORENSIC SCIENCE • LASER AND MASER • TOOTHPASTE • X-RAY IMAGING

Desalination

Desalination, or desalting, is the process of removing salt and other dissolved impurities from seawater or brackish water and turning it into water fit for drinking, washing, and a myriad of other uses in homes, farms, and industry.

We use vast amounts of water. In Europe and the United States, each person uses on average 55 to 80 gallons (200–300 l) of water every day; in developing countries, it can be as little as 2.5 gallons (10 l) a day. As the world's population increases and living standards rise, more and more water is needed. The natural supplies of fresh water are inadequate in some places—not just in the arid parts of the world, such as the Middle East. There are many desalination plants in the United States and some large ones in Europe—the Netherlands, for example. Saudi Arabia currently accounts for 30 percent of desalinated water output from 23 plants along its coast.

The sea, containing 97 percent of the world's water, is potentially a limitless source of water for our needs, but removing the dissolved salt (35,000 parts per million, or ppm) in seawater down to a level fit for drinking (500 ppm) takes considerable amounts of energy and is expensive. (Brackish water contains 5,000–10,000 ppm of salt.)

There are a number ways of desalinating water, and most commonly use boiling or evaporation processes. Distillation methods rely on the fact that when water vaporizes, the salt is left behind, and condensing the vapor provides pure water. Freezing methods use a similar natural phenomenon. Ice formed from seawater is salt-free. In addition, there are a number of direct methods, such as osmosis, electrodialysis, and ion exchange (this is the method used in domestic water softeners).

The method used depends on the circumstances. A very simple technique that can provide moderate amounts of water and salt as a byproduct is the solar still, but this is only suitable for small communities in very sunny countries.

Where larger amounts of water are needed, the choice will be governed principally by the available energy sources. If the energy is expensive, the best possible use must be made of it. In this case, the plants are complex—as well as expensive. Some methods, such as electrodialysis, are only practicable for brackish water, as the electricity needed increases rapidly with the amount of salt that has to be removed.

Because of the need for plentiful energy, desalination plants are often sited next to power plants and use the waste heat from the plant; the

▶ A flash chamber evaporator. The flashing can be seen as a foam of seawater and vapor. Water enters from a higher pressure chamber (left) and passes to lower pressure on the right, as can be seen from the scale.

combination of nuclear power plants with desalination plants has been studied widely. In many countries, the combined supplies of water and electricity form a center for industrial development. At the other end of the scale, Russia has developed small wind-powered units that can produce up to 16 gallons (60 l) of water an hour.

Distillation techniques

The simplest distillation technique, boiling water and collecting and condensing the steam, presents problems in practice. Above 160°F (71°C), below the normal boiling point, seawater deposits scale, similar to that found in kettles in hard-water areas. This scale insulates the pipes, making heating less efficient. Hot seawater is also very corrosive. If the pressure is reduced, the water will boil at lower temperatures, but this method is not so efficient. Modern processes try to overcome these problems by using modified low-temperature techniques.

Multistage flash distillation is the most important method of desalination, with many installations throughout the world using this method. Seawater is heated to about 250°F (121°C) and passed into a chamber at low pressure. Some of the water immediately boils and evaporates—known as flashing—and the vapor is passed over the condenser to give pure water. The remaining

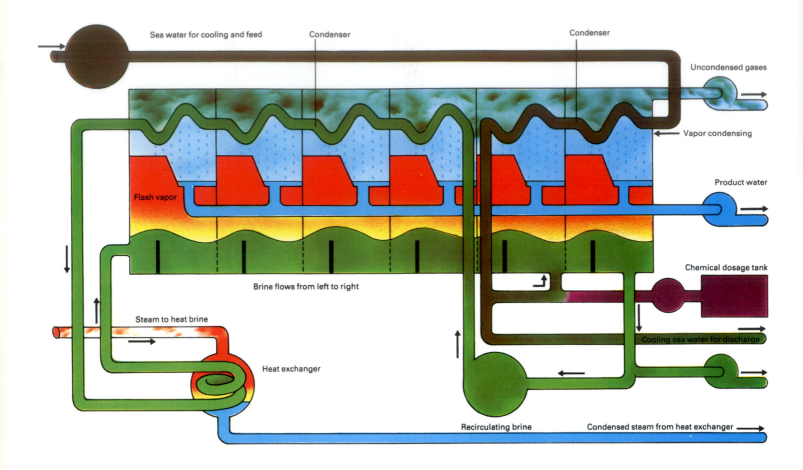

seawater is cooled slightly by the flashing and passes on to the second chamber at even lower pressure. Flashing occurs again, and the remaining water passes on to a third chamber, and so on, for many stages. The incoming seawater flows through the condensers. As the vapor condenses, it heats up the seawater. Large plants of this type are capable of producing millions of gallons of fresh water a day.

Vapor reheat flash distillation is similar to multistage flash distillation except that the fresh water, not the incoming seawater, is used to condense the vapor. The heat is transferred from the fresh water to the seawater in heat exchangers. The advantage is that there is less scaling; the disadvantage is that the system is more complex and more expensive to build.

Multiple effect evaporation (also called the vertical tube evaporation process) uses three or more evaporators to evaporate some of the seawater. The heat given out as the vapor condenses is used to evaporate more water, and so on.

Vapor compression distillation (also known as vapor compression evaporation) uses the fact that the temperature of steam, like any other gas, rises if the steam is compressed. The vapor from boiling seawater is compressed mechanically. Its temperature rises, and it is then used to heat further warm seawater, condensing as it does so to give

pure water. The pure water is quite warm and is used to heat the incoming seawater.

Solar distillation uses free energy, that from the sun. Seawater is placed in a large shallow basin with a black lining to absorb the sun's heat. Over the top of the basin is a transparent plastic or glass domed roof that acts as the condensing surface. Sunlight passing through the roof is absorbed by the black lining, which heats the water, producing vapor that condenses on the surface of the dome. The drops run down the roof into collecting trays. (A similar effect of heating and condensing can be seen in the small seed propagators with plastic lids that gardeners use.)

This is a small-scale technique and only suitable for very sunny climates. One square yard (1 m²) of water surface is needed to produce a gallon (3.8 l) of drinking water a day in areas such as Greece. It can be a useful survival technique.

Humidification is a simple process suitable for units of up to about half a million gallons (1.9 million l) a day output. Seawater is heated, either by the sun or by a fossil-fuel boiler, and sprayed down a tower. Dry air is passed up the tower and becomes saturated with vapor. The saturated air passes to a second tower, where the vapor is condensed and the fresh water collected.

Direct freezing involves spraying salt water into a vacuum, causing some of the water to evap-

▲ A multistage flash distillation (MSF) system. MSF is essentially a series of stills that operate at successively lower pressures as the salt is removed from the feed water as it passes from still to still. Distillate from this type of plant is very pure, with a total dissolved solids content of less than 50 ppm.

orate. The water left is cooled, and small crystals of pure water form. These crystals are separated out from the brine and melted. This method uses comparatively little energy and scaling is minimal, but the plants are expensive to build. Secondary refrigerant freezing makes use of the low boiling point of some organic liquids, such as butane. If methylated spirits is put on the skin, it evaporates quickly, cooling the skin. In the same way, if butane is mixed with seawater and then allowed to evaporate, ice crystals form in the water, as with direct freezing. Less energy is needed with this method, but traces of butane have to be removed from the thawed crystals. In practice, freezing is not an economically viable process for obtaining large quantities of water.

Membrane processes

The other main techniques of desalinating water use membranes and the phenomenon of osmosis to separate out dissolved salts. Electrodialysis takes advantage of the ability of salt water to conduct electricity. The salt, sodium chloride, splits into positively charged sodium ions and negatively charged chlorine ions. If electrodes are placed in seawater, the sodium will move toward the negative electrode and the chlorine will move toward the positive electrode. In desalination, the salt water flows through a large tank full of membranes arranged in series, with membranes that allow the sodium but not the chlorine ions to pass alternating with membranes that let the chlorine

► Desalination by reverse osmosis through a semipermeable membrane. The solvent of a solution passes through but not the dissolved substances—in this case, pure water and salt.

but not the sodium ions pass. At either end of the tank are a positive and negative electrode. When a current flows, the ions start to move but soon come up against a membrane they cannot pass through. In this way, the spaces between the membranes fill alternately with pure water and water even saltier than the original water, and the pure water can be led off. In practice, only brackish waters are treated this way. It is a common technique for dealing with such water and is used in the United States.

Reverse osmosis is the direct opposite of osmosis. When a pressure greater than the osmotic pressure is applied to a solution of salt in water, the water can be forced through a semipermeable membrane, giving pure water on one side and salty water on the other. The membrane is a film a few ten-thousandths of a millimeter thick on a porous support. The membrane can be tailored to the concentration of salt, but the pressure needed increases with the salinity.

Ion exchange uses special resins to remove the salt. The granular resins are packed into towers through which the salt water flows. The resins trap the sodium and chlorine ions in the water and pure water flows out. The resins must be recharged regularly by passing through other solutions—it could be acid, ammonia, or lime, depending on the process. This method is expensive for very salty water and is sometimes used as a second-stage treatment after a membrane process, particularly if ultrapure water is required for a manufacturing industry.

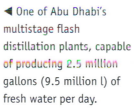

◄ One of Abu Dhabi's multistage flash distillation plants, capable of producing 2.5 million gallons (9.5 million l) of fresh water per day.

SEE ALSO: Distillation and sublimation • Osmosis • Salt production • Solar energy • Water • Water supply

Desktop Publishing

Desktop publishing is the use of powerful desktop and laptop computers to create and manipulate text and images to produce computer files from which documents can be printed. Such documents range from party invitations printed on household laser or bubble-jet printers to books and magazines printed on commercial presses. Desktop publishing, or DTP, started in the 1980s, when desktop computers became sufficiently powerful to fulfill the processing requirements of document-preparation programs.

Text preparation

Almost all printed documents contain some amount of text, or copy. The text might be simply the date, theme, and location of an event, or it might be the contents of an encyclopedia, with many thousands of words arranged into chapters, sections, subsections, and paragraphs.

In most cases, text is generated using the word-processing program of a computer, either by typing on a keyboard or by speaking into a microphone and letting voice-recognition software convert the sounds into text. If a typed manuscript is to be used, it can be converted to a form that can be edited in a word-processing program by optical character recognition (OCR). In the OCR process, an electronic image of the typed copy is first generated using an image scanner; software then identifies the individual characters of the text and converts them into passages of editable text. In the cases of voice recognition and OCR, the text requires corrections where the software has made errors: voice recognition can confuse homophones—like-sounding words, such as "their" and "there"—while OCR can easily misread "modern" as "modem," for example.

Once the text is in electronically editable form, an editor assesses it for content, clarity, and length, making adjustments where necessary. The editor must also ensure that the punctuation of the text enhances its clarity and that consistent rules of punctuation are used throughout. In many cases, an editor applies rules of punctuation and spelling according to a style sheet, which might be imposed by a publishing house or simply developed as the editing work progresses.

Word-processing programs help an editor in a number of ways. First, a spellchecker program identifies potentially misspelled words by looking for each word in a dictionary database. If the spellchecker cannot find a given word, the program draws the editor's attention to the suspect word and offers the options of replacing it with a

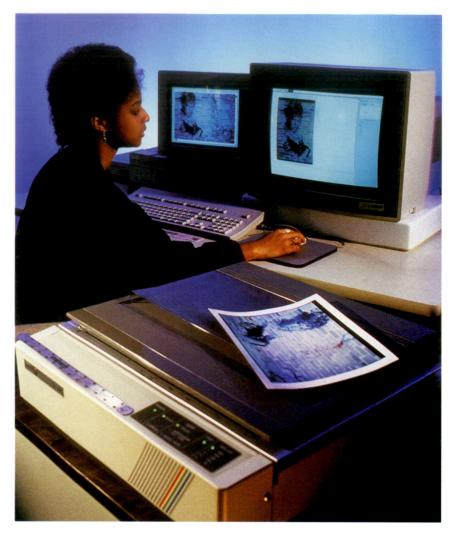

different spelling or adding the suspect word to a dictionary so that the word will be recognized as correct in subsequent checks. If the dictionary contains words that are similar to the suspect word, the spellchecker offers them as options for replacing the unidentified word.

Once the spellchecking operation is complete, the editing software checks the grammar of the text. Often, the editor can configure this program according to the requirements of the style sheet. If the program detects suspect grammar in a passage of text, it prompts the editor to confirm or correct the contents of the suspect passage. More sophisticated versions of this type of software detect phrases that are characteristic of imprecise or long-winded writing, so the editor has the opportunity to rewrite the afflicted passages more succinctly before the text goes to press.

Finally, the editing software can calculate the total number of words in a text, from which it is possible to estimate how well a text will fit its allotted space in a publication. Similar software calculates the average word count per sentence and the average number of sentences per paragraph. The greater these values, the more difficult the text will be to read and comprehend.

▲ An optical scanner produces an electronic image from a physical image, such as a photograph or a page of text. Beams of light scan from side to side and from top to bottom across the image, and sensors convert the intensity of reflected light into an electrical signal. Computer software creates an image file from the scanner's output.

TYPOGRAPHY

The use of different typefaces and styles can help make the text of a document more attractive to read and more effective in communicating its content than the same text would be if a single typeface were used throughout. Desktop publishing gives authors and designers access to numerous combinations of typefaces and styles by a few clicks of a mouse button.

A set of characters that is designed to have a consistent appearance is called a typeface, or font. Companies that create new typefaces are called foundries—a term that dates from an era when letters and numerals for use in printing presses were cast from hot metal—even though fonts are now created in electronic form.

While the scope for designing new fonts is unlimited, less than one hundred distinct fonts have established themselves in common use by virtue of the ease with which they can be read. Highly stylized fonts tend to become fashionable for a short while but then become dated and fall out of use within a few years.

Fonts are broadly classified according to whether or not they have serifs, which are small ticks at the ends of the main curves of characters. Sans-serif fonts have no serifs—sans is French for "without"—and their characters have a more clean-cut appearance than those of serif fonts; serif fonts lend a more classical appearance but can appear staid and fussy in the one-line copy of an advertisement, for example.

Sans-serif fonts are best used for headlines, poster captions, and other circumstances where a few words have to "shout for attention," because the simple lines of a sans-serif font make each character highly legible. Serif fonts are best used for longer paragraphs of text—so-called body text—because the serifs lead the reader's eyes from one letter to the next within each word, making it less tiring to read long stretches of continuous text.

The script fonts form a third class of typeface. They are simulations of hand-writing and are sometimes useful for informal documents, such as invitations. In order to give the appearance of joined-up writing, each character must connect to its neighbors at the same height on a line.

When composing a document, care must be taken to choose fonts that are appropriate for the specific functions of different types of text. Because of their clarity, sans-serif fonts are useful for the headings of chapters and paragraphs, since the function of such headings is to announce the content of the following text, which is usually in a serif font. A sans-serif font may also be used to draw a distinction between a self-contained block of text, such as a caption, and the main flow of the document's text.

The choice of fonts for a document is largely a matter of individual taste, but the number of fonts used should be less than four if a confusion of styles is to be avoided.

While pairings of sans-serif and serif fonts can help create refreshing contrasts within a document, pairings of different serif fonts are difficult to achieve with success. With pairings, the similarity between serif fonts can lead a reader's brain to perceive one font as a distorted version of the other—an effect called conflict. The same risk exists with similar sans-serif fonts; thus designers generally pair a single serif font with a single sans-serif font.

Headings can be emphasized by using a greater character height, for example, while remembering that the impression of size given by a font depends more on its x-height—the height of a lower-case x—than its point size, which is a measure of the overall character height of a font. Hence, a sans-serif font can appear larger than a serif font of the same point size but with a smaller x-height.

Emphasis can also be created by using bold or italicized characters. Characters in bold type have thicker lines but the same overall form as the standard version of the font, called the roman font. Bold type is most often used to emphasize whole lines of text, such as headings. Italicized characters are used to emphasize individual words or short phrases. Their lines are of the same thickness as those of roman characters, but they lean to the right. Italics are notably used to highlight words of foreign origin and to indicate that a group of words is the name of a ship or locomotive, for example.

Italicized text is sometimes used to distinguish captions from the body text of a document, but the slant of its characters can make for a tiring read if italics are used in longer blocks of text.

Avant Garde is an example of a sans-serif font.
Times New Roman is an example of a font with serifs.
Mistral is an example of a script font.

Sans serif makes headlines
Serif fonts, on the other hand, are more appropriate for longer stretches of text, which would be tiring to read if they were presented in a sans-serif font.

The juxtaposition of two serif fonts often creates a conflict, since a reader's brain perceives one font as a distortion of the other. The same effect can occur when two sans-serif fonts are paired in the same document.

A serif font usually seems to be smaller than a sans-serif font of the same overall height, or point size, because sans serif fonts typically have greater x-heights and their characters may be wider than those of a serif font.

Headings
A larger version of the basic body-text font can be sufficient to distinguish a heading from the main body of text.

Bold and *italic*
Bold text is useful for highlighting a line of text, such as a heading. Italicized characters can emphasize a *word* or *group of words* but are tiring to read in long blocks of text.

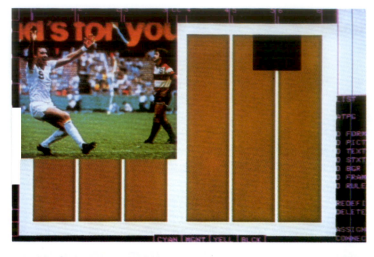

Image preparation

One of the original distinctions between desktop publishing and simple word processing was that DTP had the potential to combine images with text, whereas word processing did not. While that distinction is no longer strictly true, the use of images to reinforce the content of a text continues to be a major feature of DTP.

Photographs are an important source of visual information for a DTP document, since a single photograph can say much more than any amount of text about a new design of a sport shoe or a historic building, for example. If a photograph is available as a print or as a transparency, its image must be converted into an electronic format before it can be used in a DTP document. Devices that perform this task are called optical scanners.

One type of optical scanner, the flatbed scanner, has a transparent glass platform on which prints are laid face down for scanning. A scanning head moves under the glass from one side of the image to the other, illuminating strips of the image with beams of red, green, and blue light as it goes. Detectors in the head measure variations in the reflected intensities of the three colors along each strip, and software in the computer that controls the scanner converts these variations into an electronic map of the variations in color and brightness throughout the image. Such a map can then be used to recreate the image on a computer screen or to print the image on paper.

A principal parameter in scanning is image resolution, which is measured in dots per inch (d.p.i.). The resolution determines the quality of the electronic image and also the scanning speed and the size of the resulting electronic file. An image resolution as low as 72 d.p.i. might be suitable for rough work, and thus scanning time and memory demand are kept to a minimum. When a document goes to press, the image must be scanned at much higher resolution to avoid an effect called pixelation, whereby the individual dots of the image map are visible as blocks in the image or as a general graininess of image.

Digital cameras produce electronic images directly, so that there is no need for intermediate printing and scanning. While high-quality digital cameras are currently much more expensive than the equivalent film cameras, it is likely that the convenience of using a digital-camera image will lead to an increase in the number of photographic images produced in this way for DTP.

▲ Stages in the composition of text and pictures onto pages. Working to a three-column template, pictures that have been scanned and stored in the computer's memory are placed in the required positions on the page. The text is then flowed in and fitted onto the page, where it can be made to wrap around shapes such as the circular picture. Headlines and subheadings are added to provide visual breaks in the text. Once all the elements have been placed, the pages are proofed for editorial corrections.

Image enhancement

Once a photograph has been scanned, specialist image-manipulation software can be used to improve its appearance. Scratches and other marks can be removed by sampling the color around the mark and applying that color over the area of the mark. Other functions of this software can be used to improve the overall brightness, color balance, and contrast of an image, to enhance the sharpness of its edges, and to add blurring, false colors, or other effects. If this type of software is used, it must be applied to the high-resolution scan of a photograph that will be used in the final printing process. A low-resolution version of the manipulated image, for rough work, can be formed by sampling occasional dots in the original image to form an image with less detail and a correspondingly smaller memory demand.

Illustrations

Illustrations can provide images that are not possible by photography: a cutaway that shows the decks inside a supertanker, for example, or a computer-generated molecular model. A small proportion of illustrations are drawn by hand, in which case they are captured as digital images by optical scanning, just as an electronic copy of a photograph is made. Most illustrations are generated using illustrator programs, which are a type of computer-graphics software. Images produced in this manner are electronic files that can be used directly in desktop publishing.

Creating a layout

The key software in desktop publishing is a program that unites text and images in a single document. A DTP designer typically starts a project by creating a standard page layout with margins that will be maintained for any page within a document. A so-called baseline grid on this layout consists of evenly spaced horizontal lines onto which images and lines of text can be locked to ensure a consistent appearance. Vertical guides provide a reference for positioning the edges of text columns and images.

Once the standard layout has been established, individual pages are created by creating frames to hold the text and images of the document. These frames may be square, rectangular, or circular, for example. Other regular forms can be selected from software menus, and irregular forms can be created by defining points on the page and joining them by straight lines. Smooth-edged frames, such as kidney-shaped forms, can be created by setting the frame border to pass smoothly through the points that define the frame. The angle of inclination of the border can be modified at each defining point by moving an onscreen handle using the mouse pointer. The software then calculates the form of the frame outline that provides a smooth curve between all the points that define the frame.

Text is inserted into a page by copying it into a text frame from a word-processing program. By linking frames, the overflow text from the first frame appears in the frame designated for continuation. Many text frames can be linked together in this way, and if the size of the one frame changes, the text in the subsequent frames reflows to fill the frame that has changed.

The characteristics of paragraphs and other blocks of words are set using style sheets, which are established at the start of a project. Each style defines a typeface, style, and point size, as well as instructions for the automatic insertion of hyphens to break lines and for the alignment of the text against the frame border. Text can be fully justified, in which case the spacing of words adjusts automatically to fit the ends of each line to its left and right margins, or it can align to either the left or the right margin. Centered text does not fit flush to either margin but is equally distant from both margins. A block of text is styled by first selecting the text and then selecting the style from the onscreen style menu.

Images are inserted into a page by copying them into image frames. Only that part of the image that is within the frame appears in the printed document. The interaction of text and images is controlled by layering and runarounds: the top layer is the one that always appears in print, and the runaround is the function that makes the text in a lower layer flow around the outside of a frame in the upper layer.

▼ The interaction between text and an image in a DTP document. The image frame occupies a layer above the text frame, and the runaround of the image frame ensures that the text flows around the image.

Instead of making text flow around an image, the designer may wish to make text flow inside a part of an image, in which case a text frame must be created in the correct position in a layer "above" (in front of) the image. Alternatively, a text column may sit above any image frames so that the text flows over all image borders.

Preparing to print

Once the final design and layout of a document has been decided, the DTP file may be saved onto a disk for dispatch to a printer, or it may be sent by electronic mail. The DTP file contains the text of the document and instructions on type styles and how the text and images are positioned within the document. The DTP designer must also send computer files that define the text fonts as well as the high-resolution image files associated with images within the document. The printer's software then has all the information necessary to reconstruct the document in a form suitable for creating instructions for automatic typesetting.

Typesetting before DTP

Desktop publishing has only been used since the late-1980s. To appreciate the impact that desktop publishing had on the publishing process, it is necessary to consider the techniques that were used before the introduction of DTP.

From around 1450, documents were printed using a process invented by Johann Gutenberg, a German printer. Small blocks, individually engraved with raised letters or other characters on one face, would be held together in a frame. The frame would be smeared with ink and pressed onto paper, when the ink on the raised parts of the blocks would transfer to the paper. Once the required number of copies of a particular frame had been printed, the frame would be taken apart and the blocks filed for subsequent use.

Invented in the 1880s, the Linotype machine was the first major development in mechanized printing. The Linotype used brass blocks, called matrices, that had a character engraved in one face. The matrices were stored by character in racks, and a matrix was released from a given rack by pressing the appropriate key on a keyboard. Reading from an edited manuscript, the Linotype operator pressed keys to release matrices in the correct sequence to complete a line of text. An assembler would then insert the appropriate spaces between characters and fix them into a frame. Hot metal poured into the frame would solidify to form a cast with raised characters. The lines of a page would then be mounted in a frame, spaced using plain metal bars, called leading, and mounted in the press. Once a print run was com-

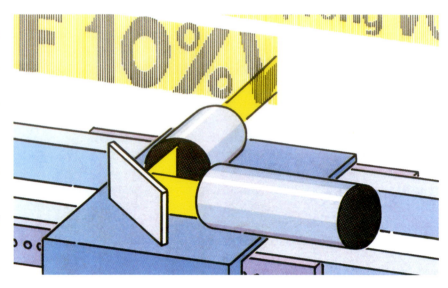

plete, the strips of type would be melted down and the metal reused in a subsequent print run.

From the 1940s to the 1970s, a series of typesetting devices were invented for used with lithographic printing presses. In the preparation of plates for a lithographic press, a light-sensitive coating on the plate cures to form a varnish where it is exposed to light but remains liquid where it is not. After exposure, the plate is washed to remove the uncured coating, and the varnish that remains is the part of the plate that accepts ink and transfers it to paper in the printing process.

The use of light to prepare lithography plates for printing is called phototypesetting. The operators of the earliest phototypesetting machines would select characters in order by pressing keys on a keyboard. The machine's exposure unit would then place a negative film image of the character to be typeset between a light source and the photosensitive coating of the plate. In this way, the coating would cure in the form of the character, and the exposure unit would then move to the position of the next character.

In a development of the early phototypesetters, negatives of all the available characters would be mounted around the edge of a rotating wheel. The coating would then be exposed to a given character by a burst of light timed to coincide with the negative of that character being in line with a window between the rotating wheel and the position for the character on the plate. With DTP, the publisher's electronic files of a document provide all the information required for a laser to produce cured varnish in the forms of text and images as it scans across the photosensitive coating on a lithographic plate.

▲ A crude representation of the scanning head that reflects a laser beam onto a lithographic plate under instructions generated from the DTP file of a document. In fact, the laser scans around 100 lines per inch to form a high-definition image.

 SEE ALSO: COMPUTER • COMPUTER GRAPHICS • COMPUTER PRINTER • OPTICAL SCANNER • PRINTING • WORD PROCESSOR

Detergent Manufacture

The word *detergent* has become a loose description for both the traditional soap and the newer nonsoapy synthetic materials. There are different kinds of detergent products ranging from simple tablets and flakes to complex powders, liquids, and tablets formulated to cope with various washing systems.

When washing skin, for example, a dense lather is needed to trap and remove any dirt, so the product must produce a good lather without becoming mushy with use. In addition, it should not interact adversely with the skin. A more complex product, however, is that needed for washing fabrics. It must eliminate calcium and other substances present in natural water that would otherwise hinder the removal of dirt. Furthermore, the dirt must be removed efficiently with a minimum of mechanical force and be kept in suspension so that it cannot become redeposited on the fabric. Stains must be removed and off-color caused by aging counteracted, but in carrying out all these functions, the product must not harm the fabric or the machine. It is also important that detergents are biodegradable—capable of being broken down naturally by bacteria after use.

Detergent constituents and action

The key to all detergent action is the surfactant, so-called because it modifies the surface quality of the water by weakening the forces between water molecules. In simple terms, it helps the water to more readily wet the object being washed.

There are two kinds of surfactant: soap, made from fats, and nonsoapy detergents (NSD), made mostly today from petroleum byproducts, such as alkylbenzine sulfonate. NSD itself is not as good a detergent as soap. For one thing, it does not lather so well. Finding out why has led not only to a better understanding of the mechanisms of dirt removal but also to all-round improvement in detergent products. For example, to meet the need of minimal lather in front-loading washing machines, a nonlathering NSD had to be developed—alkyl phenol polyethylene oxide is the one most widely used. Conversely, to improve the lathering power of a general-purpose NSD product, a lather booster must be incorporated.

Most products contain anything up to a dozen or so constituents, each with a specific purpose, though not every one is involved in detergent action. Washing powders, for example, will contain an anticorrosion agent to protect the drums

▲ Soap has been used for centuries as a means of personal cleanliness, but is not very good for washing clothes because of its poor rinsing properties. Modern detergents are better at removing dirt from fabrics and can incorporate bleaches, enzymes, and stain removers that improve the performance of the washing process.

of washing machines. Tablets and flakes are the only products that depend substantially on surfactant alone. Both are based on soap and rely for their product properties on the selection and treatment of the fats used for conversion to soap, and on the subsequent processing of the soap. In all other products, detergent action is shared for the most part by the surfactant and a builder, so named because it builds up the surfactant into a more complete detergent. The usual builder is sodium tripolyphosphate. Broadly speaking, the surfactant, which may be either soap or NSD, takes care of fatty dirt, and the builder takes care of solid particulate dirt, but there is some mutual support. The balance of the two ingredients varies, but in most fabric-washing products the percentage of soap to NSD is very small or nonexistent. For dish-washing, there is little mineral dirt and the surfactant predominates.

Fatty dirt is removed and dispersed in the wash liquor as minute negatively charged globules, and solid dirt as entrapped particles in nega-

THE MOLECULAR STRUCTURE OF A TYPICAL DETERGENT ION

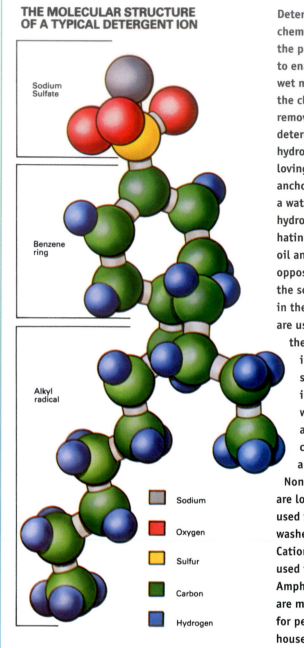

Sodium Sulfate

Benzene ring

Alkyl radical

■ Sodium
■ Oxygen
■ Sulfur
■ Carbon
■ Hydrogen

Detergents are organic chemicals that change the properties of water to enable the surface to wet more quickly so that the cleaning agent can remove soiling. Typical detergents have a hydrophilic (or water-loving) head, which anchors to the surface of a water molecule, and a hydrophobic (or water-hating) tail that attracts oil and grease. These opposing forces loosen the soil and suspend it in the water. Surfactants are usually classified by their ionic properties in water. Anionic surfactants are used in laundry soaps, washing-up liquids, and household cleaners and produce a lot of suds. Nonionic surfactants are low-suds producers used for laundry, dishwashers, and rinse aids. Cationic surfactants are used in fabric softeners. Amphoteric surfactants are milder and are better for personal hygiene and household products.

detergent action. The most suitable for soap powders is a mixture of sodium silicate and sodium sulfate. Liquid products contain highly concentrated constituents that are mostly immiscible (unwilling to mix) with each other. A solubilizing agent, such as sodium xylene sulfonate, is added to induce them to do so.

Manufacturing methods

The manufacture of traditional soap is based on a mixture of fats that is fed proportionately with an alkali solution into a reaction vessel where it is saponified. After saponification the soap is purified for further processing.

To make cakes of soap, the molten soap is cooled and flaked, dried to 96 percent soap mixture with trace constituents, such as perfume, triple milled between steel rollers, "plodded" (compressed and extruded in bar form), cut, and stamped. When soap flakes are required, the molten soap is cooled and flaked, mixed with trace constituents, and milled to the required thickness between steel rollers, which also cut it to shape.

For soap-based powders the molten soap is mixed with a builder and conditioners. The mixture is then heated and spray cooled by extruding it at high pressure through nozzles at the head of a cooling chamber. It falls as granules through an uprising current of cool air onto a conveyor belt.

In the manufacture of NSD-based powders, a paste is formed of the NSD, lather booster (if required), builder, and conditioners. The mixture is spray dried by pumping it through nozzles into the headspace of a drying tower. The spray falls through an uprising current of hot air that dries the drops to hollow granules. The powder is collected in the same way as soap powder, and heat-labile (unstable when heated) constituents, such as bleach, enzymes, and fragrance, are metered in as the powder travels along a conveyor. The latest high-density powders can be packed in much smaller containers or compressed as tablets.

The manufacture of liquid NSD products is essentially simple. The process is one of obtaining a stable solution or suspension by mixing, and no complex technical procedures are involved. Products are based on NSD, which must be either near liquid or extremely soluble. Lather boosters of more than average solubility must also be used. Small quantities of many exotic detergent constituents find their way into these products, the formulation of which provides far greater complexity than does manufacture.

tively charged molecular cages, which are formed by compounds in the cleaning product. To prevent their redeposition on fabric, it is given a repulsive charge by antiredeposition agents, each preferentially attracted to a particular type of fabric. Stain removal is commonly dealt with by a chemical bleach, sodium perborate, which performs well at the elevated temperatures and in the alkaline environment of the wash liquor. Off-color is corrected by an optical brightener, a fluorescent material designed to adhere well to fabric and emit a bluish-white light. Enzymes, which act as catalysts in breaking down protein stains, such as blood, may also be included in a detergent.

Washing powders need to contain substances that help to produce a readily pourable and easily dissolved product without detracting from the

SEE ALSO: Chemistry, organic • Enzyme • Soap manufacture

Dialysis Machine

Before the development of hemodialysis, diseases that caused failure of the kidneys (renal failure) resulted invariably in death within days or weeks. Now, using dialysis techniques, it is possible to replace most functions of the normal kidney artificially, and patients can live their normal span.

Once irreversible renal failure has occurred, dialysis is usually continued until a suitable kidney becomes available for transplantation. Dialysis is also used on a temporary basis to treat patients with sudden loss of kidney function (acute renal failure) whose kidneys often return to normal after the initial damage is treated. Modern dialysis techniques are so successful that many patients are able to perform their own dialysis at home without close supervision, thus enabling them to lead more normal and independent lives.

Renal failure

The normal kidney is a complex organ with many functions. Principal among these is the excretion in urine of the potentially harmful nitrogenous waste products of protein metabolism. It also plays a key role in the body's water balance, excreting excess and retaining water during episodes of dehydration. Other functions include the regulation of important electrolytes, such as sodium and potassium, and the maintenance of a steady neutral pH value (acid-base balance) within the body. In cases of renal failure, blood concentrations of products of protein metabolism build up to lethal levels. These can be measured as concentrations of urea, creatinine, and

▲ A patient undergoes dialysis. This man has a fistula (an artery joined to a vein) and has been shown how to insert his own needle. Recent trends toward patient and family education have alleviated the need for constant medical supervision, making home dialysis in many parts of the world commonplace. A worldwide network of dialysis units, as well as the use of portable kidney machines, makes travel a possibility.

uric acid in the blood, but there are many other related molecules, more complex and less understood, that contribute to uremia. In addition, excretion of potassium and excess acid (hydrogen ions) is impaired, contributing to the disease process and eventual death. Water excretion is also affected in renal failure, and patients may become waterlogged because they are unable to excrete all the water they drink. Dialysis artificially removes these substances from the blood stream.

Principles of dialysis

The cornerstone of dialysis is the semipermeable membrane. This is a synthetic sheet of material containing pores that allow the passage of small molecules. If solutions of a substance at differing concentrations are placed in containers on either side of this membrane, there is a tendency for molecules to pass to the side of lower concentration until the two concentrations become equal (assuming the membrane's pores are large enough to allow the molecules through). This process is diffusion. At the same time, solvent (fluid) molecules will pass through the membrane by the same principles by a process called osmosis. The rate of diffusion or osmosis depends on the size of the molecules, the larger ones traveling more slowly across the membrane than the smaller ones.

Osmosis can be increased by placing the fluid on one side of the membrane under pressure—known as ultrafiltration. In hemodialysis, the patient's blood, with its high concentrations of toxic waste products, is brought close to a specially prepared solution (the dialysate) across a semipermeable membrane in a dialyzer, or artificial kidney. The dialysate contains no uremia waste products, so they pass across from the blood by diffusion. Those substances, principally electrolytes, that should remain in the blood are present in the dialysate in normal blood concentrations, so diffusion of these occurs in both directions through the membane with no net change in concentration. Because of the size of the pores in the membrane, larger molecules such as proteins and blood cells are not lost.

Substances that are deficient in renal failure can be passed to the patient by adding them to the dialysate in suitable concentrations. Excess water can also be removed from the patient by ultrafiltration, if dialysate pressure is reduced or blood pressure increased. Thus, essential kidney functions can be mimicked by the dialysis machine. The dialyzer contains continuously circulating blood and dialysate, so maximum efficiency is obtained by

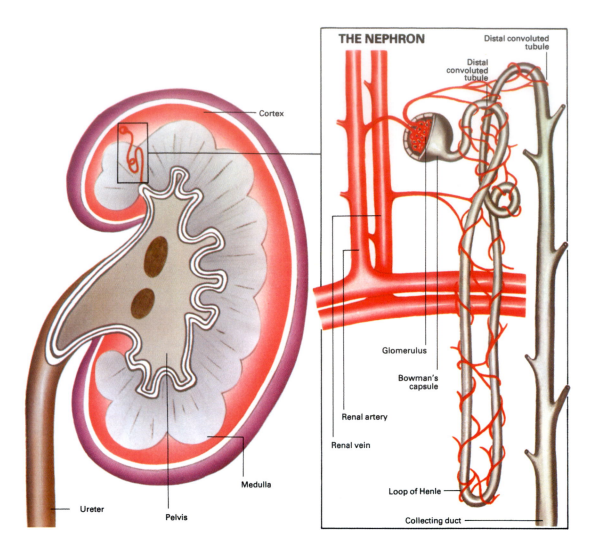

THE NEPHRON

Distal convoluted tubule

Distal convoluted tubule

Cortex

Glomerulus

Bowman's capsule

Renal artery

Renal vein

Loop of Henle

Collecting duct

Medulla

Ureter

Pelvis

◄ Diagram showing the arrangement of the kidney filtration unit and supplying vessels. The renal artery divides into arterioles that subdivide into capillaries at the end of each nephron. Large molecules are filtered out by the pressure of blood in the arteriole. Salts in solution are passed along the tubule for reabsorption by the cells lining the walls. Unwanted products (urine) are passed to the bladder.

ensuring constant concentration gradients across the semipermeable membrane. This efficiency is enhanced by running the two circulations in opposite directions on either side of the membrane.

History of dialysis

Dialysis was first performed in experimental animals in 1913. Technical advances that made the system more practical for use in humans did not occur until World War II. They included the development of cellulose acetate (cellophane) for use as the semipermeable membrane and a suitable anticoagulant—a drug that prevents blood in the dialysis machine from clotting. The first artificial kidney was used by Wilhelm Kolff in Holland in 1943. It consisted of a cellulose tube containing the patient's circulating blood wound around a drum rotating in a bath of dialysate. This machine was unwieldy and required close supervision. Improvements meant that by the 1960s patients could perform their own dialysis alone at home.

The artificial kidney, or dialyzer

There are many modern types of dialyzer, although they mostly fall into two categories. The coil dialyzer consists of cellophane tubing, contain-

ing the patient's blood, wrapped around a mesh drum through which dialysate is circulated at right angles to the blood flow. The plate, or parallel-flow, dialyzer consists of a film of circulating blood sandwiched between two layers of membrane, with dialysate circulated through grooves in the polypropylene boards that hold the two membranes together. The main advantage of the plate type is that resistance to blood flow is lower, so an electric pump is not required. Artificially pumped blood circuits can cause undesirable membrane rupture owing to the high pressures involved.

Most modern dialyzers consist of one square yard of membrane made of either cellophane or extra-thin cuprophan. The pores in the membrane are approximately 50 Ångstrom units in diameter (1 mm x 10^{-7}). They allow the passage of molecules with a molecular weight of less than 40,000. The larger the molecules, the more slowly they pass; those with a molecular weight of less than 5,000 pass with ease, so urea (mol wt. 60), creatinine (113), and urate (168) are quickly dialyzed. The efficiency of dialysis may be increased by using a thinner membrane, although if a membrane is too thin, it could rupture, mixing blood and dialysate.

Because of the risk of transferring infection from one patient to another, disposable dialyzers are now often used, usually of the multiple-layer plate type. These are, however, expensive and many hospitals reuse them several times, sterilizing thoroughly between dialyses.

Blood circulation

In hemodialysis, the patient's blood has to pass through the dialyzer in an extracorporeal blood circulation (see diagram below). To achieve sufficient blood for this purpose, some form of access is required to the high-pressure, arterial side of the patient's circulation (that closest to the heart's main pumping chamber). A further portal of entry is required into the low-pressure, venous side so that blood can be returned to the body after dialysis. The access portals are usually situated at the wrist or ankle, where they can be easily reached and where main arteries and veins are in close proximity. One form is the arterio-venous shunt (A-V shunt), which consists of two silastic tubes, one sewn to the end of a vein, the other to an artery. Between dialyses, they are joined with a Teflon connector, so the blood flows straight from artery to vein. During dialysis, the tubes are clamped, disconnected from each other, and attached to the blood lines of this machine before unclamping in readiness for dialysis. The second form of access is an A-V fistula. Here, the walls of an artery and a vein are directly sewn together by the surgeon so that after a few weeks a thick-walled, high-pressure blood vessel has formed. Into this, needles are inserted by nurse or patient under sterile conditions at the commencement of dialysis. This is the preferred form of access, as the patient does not need to take anticoagulant drugs permanently to prevent clotting and there is less risk of serious bleeding if the silastic tubes are displaced. The shunt, however, is very useful for patients who are averse to using needles.

Blood then flows along clear plastic tubing to the dialyzer and back to the patient. Average flow rate is around 0.4 pints (200 ml) per minute. Depending on the type of dialyzer, a variable-rate blood pump is used to maintain blood flow. Soon after leaving the body, the anticoagulant (heparin) is added, usually by slow infusion directly into the blood line. After passing through the dialyzer, blood flows through a bubble trap before returning to the patient. This trap serves to collect any bubbles that may have formed in the dialyzer, as

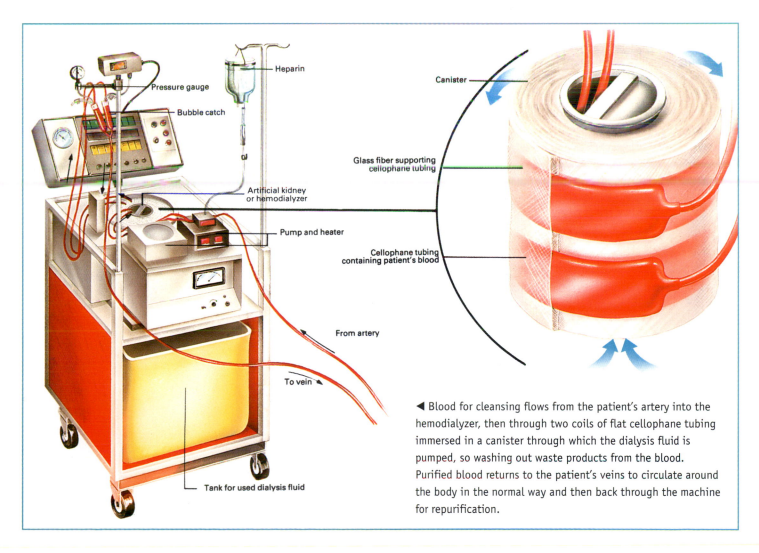

Heparin
Pressure gauge
Bubble catch
Artificial kidney or hemodialyzer
Pump and heater
From artery
To vein
Tank for used dialysis fluid

Canister
Glass fiber supporting cellophane tubing
Cellophane tubing containing patient's blood

◄ Blood for cleansing flows from the patient's artery into the hemodialyzer, then through two coils of flat cellophane tubing immersed in a canister through which the dialysis fluid is pumped, so washing out waste products from the blood. Purified blood returns to the patient's veins to circulate around the body in the normal way and then back through the machine for repurification.

air reaching the patient's circulation is potentially dangerous. This is also a convenient site to measure pressure in the blood circuit. Any sudden changes in pressure may signify blockages or leakage in the system.

The dialysate circuit

Safe hemodialysis depends on careful preparation of dialysate fluid and close monitoring of its concentrations and pressures in the dialysis machine. Like the monitors in the extracorporeal blood circulation, these machines are fitted with alarms to alert the patient or nurse in the event of malfunction. The fluid may flow straight through the dialyzer to the drain in a single pass or be recirculated. The former system is used with parallel-flow dialyzers, but a combined system in which recirculating fluid in the dialyzer is continually being replaced is used with coil dialyzers. The single-pass system uses up much more dialysate—up to 100 gallons (400 l) may be required for one dialysis. Normal flow rates are approximately 1 pint (500 ml) per minute.

The dialysate consists of specially treated water in which the appropriate substances are dissolved to make up the concentrations required. Tap water has to be pretreated because it contains some ions or trace elements that may be passed to the patient and cause toxicity, such as aluminum, which can cause bone disease and brain damage in dialysis patients.

Before use, the fresh dialysate must be heated to 104°F (40°C) to prevent the patient's blood from cooling. The fluid is then continuously monitored for temperature and conductivity. The conductivity meter measures the passage of an electrical current through the dialysate. Changes in conductivity warn of changes in dialysate concentrations, and if these are excessive, the fluid supply is diverted from the dialysis machine and an alarm sounds. Because temperature variations also affect conductivity, the two meters are connected so that these variations can be compensated for. Possible dangers if these systems fail include mass destruction of the patient's blood cells, if dialysate is too hot or too dilute, or gross ion overload, if the solution is too concentrated.

Before passing through the dialyzer, the fluid's pressure is measured, and often a flow meter is sited after the dialyzer. A pressure monitor is used when water is being removed—the more negative the pressure, the more water is removed. The flow meter also ensures dialysate is not passing through at a rate that may exhaust the supply tank.

Last in the dialysate circuit before the pump drawing fluid through to the drain is the blood leak detector, consisting of a light beam shining through the dialysate stream onto a photoelectric cell. Presence of blood in the fluid absorbs light, triggering the blood-leak alarm, and the blood pump usually stops automatically. The detector has to be highly sensitive and may also be triggered by bubbles in the dialysate—hence the importance of deaerating the water and efficient flow metering.

Dialysis fluid consists of a solution of sodium, 130 mmol/l (millimols per liter; potassium, 1.0 mmol/l; magnesium, 1.0 mmol/l; calcium, 3.05 mmol/l; chloride, 100 mmol/l; acetate, 35 mmol/l; and dextrose, 75 mmol/l. Sodium, magnesium, calcium, and chloride do not need to be removed, so they are at similar concentrations to those in normal blood. Potassium is at a low concentration, as blood concentration tends to be high in renal failure, and so potassium must be removed. Acetate is an anion at similar concentrations to an equivalent substance, bicarbonate, in the blood. Finally, the dextrose renders the dialysate isotonic with blood.

Dialysis procedure

The average kidney patient has to undergo hemodialysis for 10 to 15 hours per week divided into two or three sessions. Before starting, the nurse or patient thoroughly checks the dialysis fluid supply, alarms, and other components of the machine. The sterile dialyzer is then attached to the dialysate circuit, and flow is started so that the membrane is soaked and warmed to optimize its function and temperature and conductivity can be checked. Next, the blood lines are primed with saline. A-V fistula needles are then inserted, the A-V shunt is connected and blood flow is commenced. The first dose of heparin is given. During dialysis, the patient lies in bed and may even sleep. The dialysate fluid pressure is altered to remove excess water from the body. The amount is determined from the weight gain between dialyses, which is mostly retained water. Blood specimens may also be taken before or after dialysis to measure urea or creatinine levels so the efficiency of dialysis can be monitored. Between dialyses, the patient lives a normal, everyday life, although travel must obviously be limited.

▼ This portable dialysis machine revolutionizes life for victims of kidney disease. It allows the patient to use ordinary tap water to produce the sterile solution needed for peritoneal dialysis, allowing greater freedom of movement than was possible using older methods of treating water.

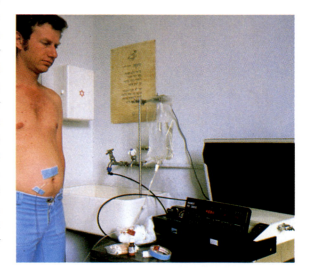

SEE ALSO: BLOOD • FLOWMETER • MEDICINE • pH MEASUREMENT • UROLOGY

Diamond

Diamonds were first discovered more than 2,000 years ago in India. In 1726, the Brazilian diamond fields were discovered, followed in 1866 by the South African diamond strike. Currently, South Africa produces more mined diamonds than any other country. As well as being among the rarest and most beautiful of gemstones, diamond is the hardest substance known, and thus, it is widely used in industry for cutting, etching, and drilling. Since 1953, synthetic diamonds have been manufactured for industrial use.

Geological source

Natural diamonds occur in certain deposits of an igneous rock called kimberlite, which is found in the pipes of extinct volcanoes. Such pipes typically have circular or oval cross sections, and cross-sectional areas that range from a few square yards (m^2) to several hundreds of acres (hectares).

Kimberlite is a blue-gray rock that weathers to form a yellow clay near Earth's surface. The two forms of kimberlite are known as blue ground and yellow ground, respectively, and the mineral is named for Kimberley, a location in South Africa where it occurs in vast quantities. Kimberlite often occurs together with other minerals—ilmenite, diopside, garnet, and zircon, among them—that serve as indicators for prospecting geologists. It is a silicate mineral formed by the solidification of molten rock from Earth's mantle. A diamond-bearing kimberlite deposit may yield one to two carats (0.007–0.014 oz., 0.2–0.4 g) of diamond for every 10 tons (9 tonnes) of ore.

Although almost all the diamonds on Earth are believed to have formed in volcanoes (the exceptions formed through meteorite impacts), not all diamonds are found in volcanic locations. Many occur in alluvial deposits—silty materials deposited by flowing water. These deposits originate from kimberlite that has been eroded by weathering, carried away by river systems, and deposited far from the original source. The most important alluvial deposit in Africa was built up along the Atlantic coast of southwestern Africa in this manner. The diamonds were probably carried by the Orange River from a distant inland source.

It is estimated that during the two millennia that have passed since the discovery of the first diamond, no more than 300 tons (270 tonnes) of diamonds have been mined; to obtain them, more than 5 billion tons (4.5 billion tonnes) of rock, sand, and gravel had to be moved. In alluvial deposits there are usually between 15 and 30 million parts of waste to one part of diamond.

Strip mining

Originally, all kimberlite deposits were strip mined, and the deepest such mine—at Kimberley, South Africa—was approximately 800 ft. (240 m) deep. A typical example of a modern strip mine is the Finsch Mine, also near Kimberley. The Finsch pipe has a diameter of 1,750 ft. (535 m) at its widest point, was covered by a 40 ft. (12 m) layer of topsoil and rubble, and extends to a depth of at least 1,000 ft. (300 m) below the original surface level. The kimberlite at Finsch is stripped out in layers 40 ft. (12 m) thick by blasting with high-explosive charges from the rim of the pipe and carrying the shattered ore in dump trucks to treatment plants.

Deep mining

Some tubes are mined through shafts sunk as deep as 3,000 ft. (900 m). The oldest method for deep mining diamonds, called chambering, was first used at Kimberley in the 1890s. In the chambering process, vertical shafts are sunk at some point away from the pipe. Horizontal tunnels called drifts are then driven into the pipe, and from them a complex of short tunnels is driven into the blue ground, forming chambers as the blue ground is mechanically removed.

While a typical chambering mine can yield around 5,000 tons (4,500 tonnes) of kimberlite per day, most modern deep mines use a more productive technique called block caving. In this technique, vertical columns of kimberlite are made to collapse under their own weight. A vertical haulage shaft is first sunk, and a drift is then cut into the pipe. A number of inclined shafts around 4 ft. (1.2 m) square are cut into the sides of the drift approximately every 11 ft. (3.5 m) on alternating sides of the drift through the pipe. These are the draw points for the ore. A cone is

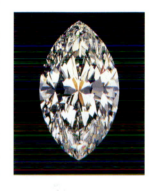

▲ A number of traditional cuts have been developed to exploit the brilliance and fire of diamonds for use as gemstones. One of the most popular cuts is the brilliant (top left); others (from top right to bottom) are the oval, pear, marquise, and emerald cuts.

cut out of the rock above each draw point so as to funnel the ore through the inclined shaft when it collapses. When the draw points and cones have been prepared, a horizontal slice 6 ft. (1.8 m) high is then mined some distance above the cones over the entire area of the pipe. The unsupported mass of kimberlite then starts to crumble and fall through the cone-shaped openings to the draw points in the drift below. Mechanical scrapers collect the broken kimberlite and load it into trucks for transportation to underground crushers. The crushed ore is then hoisted to the surface. When waste rock appears at draw points in the scraper drifts, mining of that level is complete, and production commences from a new set of drifts and draw points hundreds of yards deeper.

Alluvial mining

The alluvial mine on the coast of southwestern Africa is typical of alluvial mining in general. There, diesel-powered scrapers strip away 3.3 million cu. yds. (2.5 million m³) of sand each day to reveal the diamond-bearing gravel bed, which is then bulldozed into stockpiles to await delivery to a screening plant. Since diamonds accumulate in the lower reaches of the gravel bed, the surface of the underlying bedrock must be thoroughly cleaned. If conditions permit, a giant vacuum cleaner called a Vacuveyer is used. As the mining face advances, screened gravel and sand are used to cover the cleaned bedrock behind it.

For some time, gravel deposits on the sea bed off the coast of southwestern Africa were mined by suction from large floating platforms. This operation has now been discontinued.

◀ Diamond-edged abrasive wheels are used to cut intricate designs in glass without causing it to shatter. The fluid assists the cutting process by flushing away debris.

▶ Diamond polishing using a dop, tang, and scaife. The scaife is a cast-iron wheel impregnated with diamond powder, while the dop is the holder on which the diamond is mounted and the tang is the arm that holds the dop in the correct position.

Screening

Screening employs mechanical methods to recover diamonds from the ore or gravel where they occur. The first step is to carefully crush or mill. Then, some form of gravity-concentration device separates the diamond-rich fraction, or concentrate, from the barren portion, or tailings.

The oldest type of gravity-concentration device is the rotary washing pan developed in Kimberley around 1874. The pan is filled with puddle—a viscous slurry of decomposed kimberlite and water—which keeps the lighter particles in suspension while heavier particles, including any diamonds in the ore, sink to the bottom of the pan. The tailings flow over the edge of the pan.

Other types of gravity-concentration devices use a heavy medium—a slurry of ferrosilicon powder with a density 2.7 to 3.1 times that of water. Light particles float on the surface of the slurry, while heavy particles sink and are collected. One such heavy-medium device is a cone-shaped tank with a shaped agitator inside that clears the walls of the tank just enough to allow heavy particles to sink past it, while keeping the slurry agitated so that the lighter particles flow off at the top. Another type of separator is the lifting wheel, a rotating drum half filled with slurry that has paddles on its inner surface. They pick up heavy particles that have sunk through the slurry and dump them in a pan at the top. Finally, the hydrocyclone sets up a vortex swirl out of which the heavy particles are pulled by centrifugal force.

Once the gravity concentrate has been separated from the tailings, it is mixed with water and passed over a grease table. The greased-surface separation technique, which was invented in Kimberley in 1896, takes advantage of differences in the relative affinities of diamonds and other minerals for water and grease. Most of the heavy minerals in kimberlite have a relatively high affinity for water, so they are carried over the greased surface with the water. Diamonds have a much weaker affinity for water, so they adhere tenaciously to the greased surface of the belt or table.

Synthetic diamonds

Diamond is one of the physical forms, or allotropes, of the element carbon; the other is graphite. The carbon atoms in diamond occupy a structure that is much more dense and regular than the structure of graphite; thus, diamond has a relative density of 3.52, compared with a value around 2.3 for graphite. As early as the 19th century, researchers theorized that graphite could be converted into diamond by the simultaneous application of great heat and pressure to loosen the bonds in graphite and force the atoms into the more closely packed structure of diamond.

Early attempts to synthesize diamonds failed to generate the extreme conditions required—a temperature around 3600°F (2000°C) and a pressure of 90,000 atmospheres. On February 15, 1953, ASEA—a Swedish company—produced the first synthetic diamonds after 23 years of design and development work. The ASEA process used a remarkable hydraulic press with six pyramid-shaped pistons, one of which also had heating cables at its peak. The pressure generated at the center of the sphere formed by the pistons was equal to the pressure applied at the outer faces of the pistons multiplied by the ratio of the outer to the inner face areas. Thus, an applied pressure of 5,800 atmospheres was magnified to 97,000 atmospheres at the center of the press.

Synthetic diamonds have similar physical, chemical, and optical properties to natural diamonds, but they appear pale gold or gray-black in color. To date, the largest synthetic diamonds that can be produced economically are around 120 stones to the carat (0.07 oz., 0.2 g), and these are used for industrial purposes, such as drilling.

Objects made of metals or other heat-resistant materials can be coated with a diamond film using a process called chemical vapor deposition (CVD). In this process, the object to be coated is heated to 1350 to 2000°F (730–1100°C) and exposed to a gaseous mixture of 2 percent methane (CH_4) in hydrogen. Microwave radiation activates the gaseous mixture, causing it to deposit a thin film of diamond on the hot object.

Diamonds in industry

Diamond has many superlative properties that make it useful for industrial applications. Apart from being the hardest of all materials, diamond is also extremely resistant to high temperatures and chemical attack, so diamond is unaffected by extremely harsh environments. Diamond has the lowest compressibility of all materials and an extremely low coefficient of thermal expansion, so the dimensions of a diamond hardly change, even when it is subjected to extreme changes in pressure and temperature. It is a good conductor of heat and a good electrical insulator, although it can be made semiconducting by the addition of appropriate dopants. Colorless diamonds are also completely transparent to all frequencies of visible light as well as to infrared and ultraviolet light. Finally, diamond is compatible in biological systems, which makes it suitable for implants.

Most of the early industrial uses of diamond exploited its hardness above all other properties: diamonds are believed to have been used for engraving in India as long ago as 350 B.C.E., and a diamond drill was first used in 1751. In 1819, a patent was issued in England for drawing wire through a diamond die, and in 1870, diamond lathe tools were manufactured in New York. By 1900, 700,000 carats of industrial-quality diamonds were used each year. (The current annual consumption of natural and synthetic diamonds is more than 100 million carats per annum.)

Some 75 percent of all industrial diamond is used as abrasive powder, formed by crushing small diamonds. Mixed with resins, metals, or ceramics, diamond powder forms the cutting surfaces of grinding wheels, bandsaws, files, drills, and many other tools. These tools are used to cut or shape a wide variety of substances from glass and ultrahard alloys to stone and concrete. Whole diamonds are used in the drill bits of oil wells and in the cutting tools for turning nonferrous metals.

Diamond tools are remarkably durable when compared with tools made from other materials. Wire can be drawn through a diamond die at speeds of up to 100 mph (160 km/h), for example, which would destroy a metal die in seconds. A good high-speed steel tool can cut a path through phosphor bronze up to 5 miles (8 km) long, while a diamond tool will last 1,250 miles (2,000 km) under the same conditions.

The exceptional durability of diamond means that tolerances of 0.0001 in. (0.0025 mm) can be maintained for long periods; no other tool material can maintain such precision for so long.

The properties of diamond make it useful in diverse applications, from the nose cones and heat shields of space rockets to machines for cutting and planing concrete for construction work.

▼ The lumps in this drill bit are embedded chunks of bort—a form of rough diamond—that enhances its cutting performance. Drill bits of this type are used to bore oil wells.

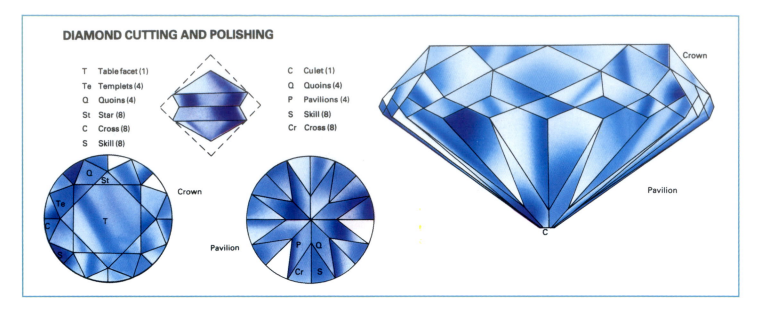

DIAMOND CUTTING AND POLISHING

T Table facet (1)
Te Templets (4)
Q Quoins (4)
St Star (8)
C Cross (8)
S Skill (8)

C Culet (1)
Q Quoins (4)
P Pavilions (4)
S Skill (8)
Cr Cross (8)

Crown

Pavilion

Crown

Pavilion

Diamonds as jewels

Diamond has an extremely high refractive index; thus, a well cut diamond sparkles because the high refractive index causes light to reflect off the rear surfaces of the crystal. The refractive index depends strongly on the wavelength of light, so white light is split into its colored components as it reflects. This separation of wavelengths, called dispersion, causes the "fire" of a diamond.

Few diamonds are flawless: most contain spots and other types of inclusions, usually amorphous carbon, and these can detract from the appearance of the gem. The position of flaws and their size is important in the cutting of a clean gemstone. The principal diamond-cutting centers—Antwerp, Bombay, New York, and Tel Aviv—specialize in the types of diamonds that they cut. Antwerp cuts diamonds classed as cleavages, maccles, and chips, while New York cuts larger stones, Tel Aviv cuts medium-sized diamonds, and Bombay cuts mostly small brilliants.

The task of a diamond cutter is to produce a gemstone that is free of defects and whose faces are cut to angles that take full advantage of the optical properties of diamond. The four processes used in converting a rough diamond into a gemstone are cleaving, sawing, bruting, and polishing.

Cleaving

Any crystal has planes along which it is relatively easy to cut. These are called planes of cleavage, and they are used by diamond cutters to perform the preliminary shaping of a rough diamond. A skilled and experienced cutter can determine the directions of the planes of cleavage of a rough diamond from features of its surface, such as chips that have revealed a flat surface. The cutter then makes a scratch mark, known as a kerf, using the hard edge of another diamond. A metal blade is inserted in the kerf with its blade in the plane of cleavage. A sharp blow to the blade with a wooden mallet causes the diamond to split along its cleavage plane, exposing a flat surface.

Sawing and bruting

Preliminary shaping can be done using a high-speed splitting saw—a thin phosphor–bronze disk that turns at around 5,000 rpm. The edge of the disk is coated with a paste of fine diamond dust and olive oil to make it more abrasive.

Bruting is a process that produces round crystals. The diamond to be shaped is mounted on a lathe chuck and spun as another diamond presses against it, roughly rounding it.

Polishing

Diamond powder is rubbed on or impregnated in a cast iron wheel known as a scaife. The diamond to be polished is mounted in a dop and tang. The dop is a holder into which the diamond is fixed with cement or mechanically held. The tang is an arm that presents the diamond in the dop to the revolving scaife. The skill of the diamond polisher lies in the correct presentation of the diamond to the wheel along its planes of cleavage.

The most widely used cut is the brilliant cut, which requires 58 separate faceting operations. Other popular cuts include the emerald, marquise, oval, and pear cuts. A large diamond can take months to polish into such a cut. While a machine called the Piermatic can cut diamonds up to half a carat (0.004 oz., 0.1g), diamond cutting and polishing is still largely the reserve of highly skilled and trained individuals.

▲ Cutting a single rough diamond can often yield two brilliant-cut diamonds (top left). The upper part of a brilliant-cut diamond is called the crown, and it consists of six distinct types of facets (bottom left). The lower part, or pavilion, consists of four types of facets (bottom center). In all, there are 58 facets in a brilliant-cut diamond. The facets are angled to reflect incoming white light off the inner surface of the pavilion, splitting it so that reds and oranges emerge at right angles to the table facet, while colder colors of light are scattered to the sides, so enhancing the "fire" of the diamond.

SEE ALSO: ABRASIVE • CARBON • CRYSTALS AND CRYSTALLOGRAPHY • DRILL • DRILLING RIG, OIL • MACHINE TOOL • STONE CUTTING

Diffraction

Diffraction is the spread of wave motion that occurs when a stream of wave energy emerges from a hole or slit or passes a solid object. It is how waves spread through a harbor from an opening in a harbor wall and how sound can be heard from around a corner even when there are no surfaces to reflect echoes. The diffraction of X rays is put to scientific use to determine the structures of crystals and molecules.

Diffraction of light

The diffraction of light was first observed by Francesco Grimaldi, a 17th-century Italian Jesuit. Grimaldi found that thin rods illuminated by narrow shafts of light did not cast sharp shadows, as would be expected if light traveled only in straight lines. Instead, Grimaldi noted bright lines just inside the edges of the shadows. Diffraction was one of the optical effects that led Grimaldi to propose the wavelike nature of light.

Optical diffraction effects are not noticeable unless small, intense light sources or fine-mesh filters are used. If a clear light bulb is viewed through a fine mesh, for example, the image of its filament appears fragmented into a series of images that become fainter as their distance from the main image increases. In this case, each hole in the mesh acts as a tiny light source, and the perceived image is formed by interference between light from the holes. The fragmentation of an image gives the effect its name—*diffraction* is from the same Latin root as *fracture*.

The diffraction of light is responsible for a number of striking optical effects. Video-camera operators can produce starlike halos around bright lights by placing a mesh over the camera lens, for example, and the spiked halos on some photographs of stars are caused by the diffraction of light around support vanes inside the telescope used to take the photographs.

Aperture and wavelength

When a wave passes through a harbor wall from open sea, curved wavefronts spread over the protected waters in the harbor. If the opening in the wall is narrow relative to the interval between wave crests, the wavefronts will be almost semicircular and centered on the opening. If the gap is larger, the wave fronts are less curved; where there is no wall, they are straight. This is an example of how the aperture—size of opening—influences the degree of diffraction for a given wavelength. Light, whose wavelengths are more than a million times shorter than waves on water,

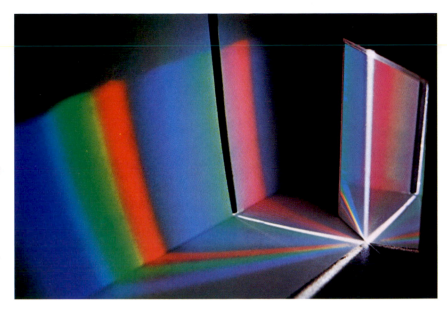

requires an aperture that is correspondingly narrower in order to diffract significantly. This is why high-quality diffraction gratings for light have up to 30,000 lines per inch (12,000 lines/cm). The gaps between the lines act as slits that are narrow enough to diffract light effectively.

X-ray diffraction takes advantage of the fact that the particles in crystal lattices are separated by distances similar to the wavelengths of X-ray photons. This makes crystals able to function as effective diffraction gratings for X rays, and the patterns formed by interference between diffracted X rays can be used to calculate the relative positions and precise spacings of particles in highly regular crystal structures.

Dispersion

Just as the aperture size must decrease with wavelength in order to achieve effective diffraction, so the extent of diffraction increases with wavelength for a given aperture. This leads to an effect called dispersion. When white light diffracts through a mesh or grating, for example, the images formed by diffraction have a blue fringe at one side and a red fringe at the other. This is because red light diffracts through a greater angle than blue light, which has a shorter wavelength.

Dispersion also happens with sound. When a marching band approaches an avenue from a side street, for example, a listener some distance along the avenue will hear the bass drum first, while the piccolos are not clear until they are directly in view. This is because the bass notes of the drums have longer wavelengths and diffract better than the shrill, high-frequency notes of the piccolos.

▲ A mirror (right) reflects the components of white light diffracted through a slit (center). Most of the light is not diffracted and reflects off the mirror as a white beam. The first-order diffracted image of the slit splits into components of different wavelengths. Short-wavelength blue light diffracts least and forms an image close to the white beam; long-wavelength red light diffracts through a greater angle. The whole pattern is repeated more faintly at yet greater angles.

SEE ALSO: Crystals and crystallography • Light and optics • Spectroscopy • Wave motion

Digestive System

Digestion is the means by which animals—and some carnivorous plants—extract nutrients from foods. The digestive system is a group of organs that break foodstuffs into molecules that can pass through the intestinal wall and into the bloodstream for distribution around the body. The digestive process in humans could be said to start when we cut up food with implements such as knives and forks, something for which nontool-using animals use their sharp cutting teeth at the front of the mouth—the incisors—and also their pointed holding teeth just behind the canines.

The mouth

The mouth is the first part of the digestive tract. In it, food is ground up by the premolar and molar teeth (the big flat teeth toward the back of the mouth). During this process, the food is either warmed or cooled, to bring it closer to body temperature, and lubricated by saliva.

Saliva is produced by three sets of glands—the submandibular and sublingual, which lie in the lower jaw, and the parotid glands, which lie farther up near the ear and secrete the enzyme ptyalin. Ptyalin is an amylase—an enzyme that acts on starch, starting its breakdown into maltose, a simple sugar. Enzymes are essentially catalysts without which digestion cannot take place, as digestion is basically a chemical process whereby complex molecules of protein, fat, and starch are broken down into simpler molecules that are easily absorbed. This process is one of hydrolysis, which is chemical decomposition by water. During the process, long molecular chains are broken and water is introduced where the chemical bond is broken. To aid the digestive process, an adult produces about three pints (1.5 l) of saliva per day.

Once a mouthful of food has been treated by the teeth and saliva, it is pushed to the back of the mouth by the tongue and into the esophagus, which lies behind the trachea (windpipe). The trachea is covered by a flap of cartilage while the food, which at this stage in the digestive system is called a bolus, passes over it. The esophagus is a muscular tube, and the bolus passes down it by means of waves of muscular contractions that push the bolus along. This muscular process is called peristalsis.

The stomach

The esophagus leads into the stomach, a muscular sac with a mucous lining that is situated in the upper left hand side of the abdomen, just below

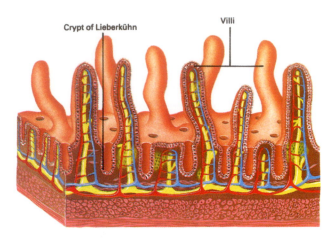

Crypt of Lieberkühn Villi

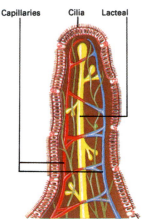

Capillaries Cilia Lacteal

▲ Thousands of minute fingerlike projections, called villi, line the ileum, increasing its surface area to speed up the absorption process.

▲ The villi contain capillaries that absorb the food and form a network of veins that carry usable products of digestion into the bloodstream for immediate use.

the diaphragm (the muscular sheet that separates the thorax or chest from the abdomen). The stomach is capable of holding and storing a large amount of food—without it, a human being would have to eat every 15 or 20 minutes to stay alive. While in the stomach, the food is constantly churned by the stomach's muscles. There are three sets of these muscles—the outer, which runs from bottom to top; the middle, which runs around the stomach; and the inner oblique muscle, which runs diagonally down.

In the mucous lining there are secreting glands that open into small holes called gastric pits. From these pits is produced the gastric juice, which contains pepsinogen; mucin, which lubricates the food; and hydrochloric acid. The acid acts on the pepsinogen, an inactive enzyme, turning it into pepsin, which breaks down the big protein molecules into simpler compounds called peptones. The production of gastric juice is stimulated by the sight or taste of the food and the action of the hormone gastrin.

Those enzymes that are concerned with digesting protein are produced initially as inactive substances so that they do not digest the walls of the stomach or the intestine itself. However, once they are released into the digestive tract and activated, the linings of the tract are protected by secreted mucus. Also present in the gastric juices is rennin, which curdles milk. This enzyme is important in young children, but in an adult, it may not be active or may be missing.

The food, when it has been acted on by the gastric juices and churned by the muscle contractions, becomes a thin gruel-like fluid called chyme. Some water, glucose and alcohol is absorbed by the stomach wall, but most of the chyme is passed, a small amount at a time, through the pyloric sphincter at the bottom of the stomach, and from there, it travels into the duodenum.

The small intestine

Here, in the first part of the small intestine, the acidity of the chyme is neutralized by an alkaline secretion from the pancreas and bile from the liver. The pancreas lies below the stomach and produces insulin, which passes straight into the bloodstream, as well as three enzymes that are secreted into the pancreatic duct. This duct joins with the bile duct and then enters the duodenum at the ampulla of Vater. The three enzymes are amylase, which turns starch into maltose; lipase, which acts on fats to split them into fatty acids and glycerol; and trypsinogen, an inactive protein-splitting enzyme.

The duodenum itself produces enterokinase, which activates trypsin from trypsinogen to break down proteins into peptones; erepsin, which reduces peptones to amino acids; invertase and maltase, which turn sugar into glucose; and sodium carbonate, which neutralizes the acid. Bile, which is made by the liver and stored in the gall bladder, emulsifies fat, that is, it breaks it down into small globules with a large surface area for the liver to work on.

The duodenum also produces hormones similar in action to gastrin. They are secretin, which makes the pancreas produce pancreatic juice; enterogastrone, which slows the emptying of the stomach and controls its churning action; and cholecystokinin, which is produced when fats are present and causes the gall bladder to empty bile into the bile duct. The sphincter of Oddi controls the opening and closing of the joint bile and pancreatic duct and lies just below the ampulla of Vater.

Little absorption of food takes place in the duodenum—absorption mainly takes place lower down in the small intestine. The food passes down the intestine by means of peristalsis. After the duodenum, it enters the jejunum—the second part of the small intestine. Here erepsin, amylase, and lipase continue their activity, and maltose, sucrose, and fructose disaccharides are broken down into glucose monosaccharide by maltose and invertase. From there, the food passes to the third part of the small intestine, the ileum.

The small intestine runs from the pyloric sphincter to the ileocecal valve where it joins the large intestine. There are two sets of muscles—an outer longitudinal set running from top to bottom and an inner circular set running all around. Between these muscles lie nerves that control peristalsis. These nerves, which operate automatically and over which we have no direct control, are part of the autonomic nervous system.

▼ Food molecules broken down by enzyme action diffuse through the cell walls of the villi and into the blood and lymphatic systems, where they are carried all over the body.

◄ The ridged surface of the mucosa (at x2 magnification) is covered in millions of villi, which contain specialized food-absorbing cells.

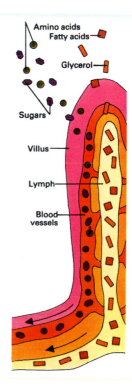

Amino acids
Fatty acids
Glycerol
Sugars
Villus
Lymph
Blood vessels

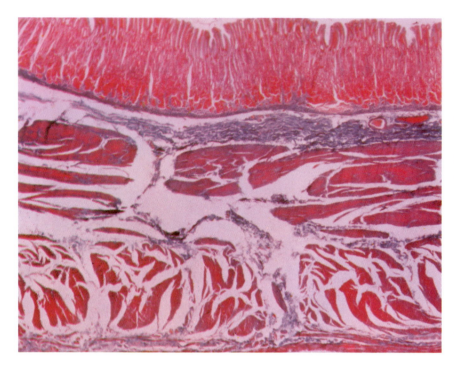

The mucous membrane lining of the small intestine, called the mucosa, is ridged and covered in thousands of small fingerlike projections called villi. They increase the surface area of the intestine and facilitate absorption. The epithelium (cell tissue lining) of the small intestine is very thin, which also helps absorption. Each villus has a network of fine blood capillaries and a lymphatic vessel. The amino acids, glucose, water-soluble vitamins, and salts are absorbed into the blood through the capillary walls. The capillaries join together to form veins that enter the main hepatic portal vein (literally, the vein that carries to the liver), which runs all around both the large and small intestines collecting the products of digestion and taking them to the liver. There they are processed into substances the body needs and either stored for future use or sent out into the bloodstream for immediate use.

The fatty acids are absorbed by the lacteals. The mechanism by which substances move through the intestinal wall is not fully understood, but it is doubtful whether diffusion alone is responsible. The lacteals empty into the lymphatic system, which itself empties into the bloodstream. Again, the fats find their way around to the liver, where they are used at once or deposited in fat cells for future use. Also present in the mucosa are sections of lymphoid tissue, called Peyer's patches, that help to combat infection.

Where the large and small intestines join, there is a blind alley, the caecum, attached to which is the vermiform (wormlike) appendix, which in humans is vestigial and appears to do nothing. In herbivores, however, it is much larger and is concerned with digesting cellulose.

▲ A magnified cross section of the stomach wall is stained to show layers of muscle (center) and the pits of the gastric glands (top).

The ileocecal valve and sphincter are in the right iliac fossa (the lower right-hand side of the abdomen), and from it, the ascending colon runs up toward the liver. It then crosses over the abdomen toward the spleen, and it is known here as the transverse colon. From the spleen, it becomes the descending colon as it runs down into the pelvis where it becomes the slightly narrower sigmoid colon, which terminates in the rectum and anus; there the anal sphincter controls the final elimination of solid waste from the body.

The large intestine

The large intestine is mainly concerned with the absorption of water and soluble salts. By the time the food enters the colon, most of the digestible goodness has been removed, and the residue of indigestible matter such as cellulose is termed fecal material. There are bacteria that live in the colon and aid the decomposition of the fecal material into some of the vitamin B12 complex gases and feces. The rectum is usually empty but when feces move into it by peristalsis, it distends and this distension causes defecation.

The digestive tract in humans is on average about 36 ft. (11 m) long from mouth to anus. The small intestine, where most of the absorption of usable food takes place, accounts for about 23 ft. (7 m) of this. The need for this great length lies mainly in the size of the animal—the bigger the animal, the more food it needs to supply its cells and the more it needs to extract from its food. It needs, therefore, a large absorbent surface area—hence the ridges and villi of the small intestine—and must also delay the passage of food through the body to allow the villi to do their work of absorption.

Another factor is the digestibility of the food itself. Animals that are herbivorous have the problem of digesting cellulose, and several of them, notably the ruminants, have solved it by having more than one stomach. In addition, after initial processing by the first stomach, the rumen, the food (called cud) is regurgitated and chewed again before being once more swallowed and passed to the second stomach.

The main division is between herbivores and carnivores. The carnivore's diet is high in protein and low in cellulose and, therefore, very nutritious. A lion, for example, may eat once a day and could go longer without eating again if need be. A herbivorous giraffe, though, must eat through most of its waking hours to survive, as its food is mainly cellulose. Humans, the omnivores, are a compromise. We eat on average three times a day, and our mixed diet, though more difficult to

THE HUMAN DIGESTIVE SYSTEM

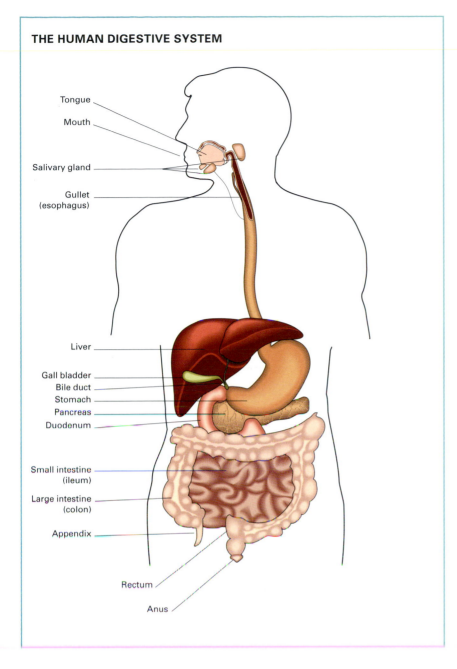

Tongue
Mouth
Salivary gland
Gullet (esophagus)
Liver
Gall bladder
Bile duct
Stomach
Pancreas
Duodenum
Small intestine (ileum)
Large intestine (colon)
Appendix
Rectum
Anus

digest than the nearly 100 percent protein of the carnivore, is much more quickly and easily digested than the herbivore's.

Indigestion is an uncomfortable feeling in the chest or abdomen that can result from eating or drinking too much or as a symptom of certain disorders of the digestive system, such as an ulcer.

Digestion in other organisms

Some of the lower orders of animals have much simpler systems. Unicellular creatures such as amoebas simply surround their food particle and enclose it inside themselves in a food vacuole—a small hole in the cell protoplasm. Any indigestible matter is simply left behind when the organism moves on. Primitive multicellular organisms such as corals have a somewhat more complicated procedure. Here, the different cells perform different tasks, and there are specialized cells concerned

▲ Components of the human digestive system. As food passes through, it is broken down, stage by stage, from complex chemicals to simpler ones that are more readily absorbed and used by the body.

solely with digestion. These cells line the inside of the creature, which is cup shaped, with only one opening through which food is taken in and waste matter excreted. The more complex the organism, the more cells it has, the bigger it is, and the more complex is its digestive process.

The type of dentition (teeth) an organism has may also affect how its digestive processes work. Some animals with no teeth concentrate solely on food that needs no chewing. For instance, the blue whale, the world's biggest mammal, has no teeth as such and lives off microscopic plankton that live in water. Other creatures, such as birds and some reptiles, have evolved a gizzard. This is a muscular stomach containing stones or gravel that pound the food into smaller particles. There is also another stomach for the more usual digestive processes.

Some animals with primitive dentition rely on extremely powerful digestive juices and retain the food for longer in the stomach to cope with the large lumps of food they swallow. Sharks are among this group. As well as having no grinding teeth, they are unable to move their jaws from side to side, an action vital for chewing. They merely seize their prey, bite a chunk off, and swallow it immediately.

Snakes are unable to chew their food. Their lower mandible is very loosely attached and can be dislocated at will to enable the prey to be swallowed whole. This process may take some days to complete.

Some creatures, such as leeches and vampire bats, suck the blood of their prey. Blood needs no chewing and is relatively easy to digest. Other creatures, including butterflies, also take their nourishment in liquid form in the shape of nectar extracted from plants.

A number of other insects such as flies digest food outside their bodies. They secrete digestive juices onto their food, and when these have acted, they suck the resultant liquid into their mouths.

Most plants make their food by photosynthesis (the making of food compounds by using chlorophyll and light) and by absorption through their roots, but some supplement this by being carnivorous. The Venus's flytrap uses sugary substances to lure insects. When insects alight on a carnivorous plant, they are trapped either mechanically, as in the Venus's flytrap, where the leaves fold over, or by the gluing action of an attractive substance, as in the sundew plant, or they are drowned, as in the pitcher plant.

SEE ALSO: ACID AND ALKALI • CARBOHYDRATE • ENZYME • FAT • MEDICINE • METABOLISM • MUSCLE • PROTEIN • STONE CUTTING

Digital Display

A digital display shows information in the form of characters, symbols, or points of light, rather than as the position of an indicator on an analog scale. The display of a digital watch, for example, shows the time in numerals, while an analog watch uses hands to indicate time by their positions on a dial.

The mechanism of a digital display may be electromechanical, electrical, or electronic; the information for display is usually provided in the form of an electrical signal. The processes that convert such signals into commands that operate displays are collectively called *interfacing*.

The choice of display mechanism depends on the requirements of the display and the type of information that is to be displayed. A wristwatch requires a display that is compact and light, and the information displayed consists of a few numerals and possibly an A.M.-P.M. indicator, so a liquid-crystal display is appropriate. An airport arrivals indicator must display several destinations at the same time in a form that is easily read from a distance, so an electromagnetic display with printed boards is suitable for this use.

Electromechanical displays

Electromechanical displays consist of banks of letters, numbers, words, or phrases printed on drums, disks, or plates. The display elements turn until the required message is in view. The advantage of such a display is that each element of the display can be printed clearly and precisely.

The drawbacks of electromechanical displays stem mainly from their drive systems—assemblies of electric motors, electromagnets, gears, and relays—and from the size and mass of the display elements. Such mechanisms are unreliable and difficult to service; they are bulky, expensive, slow, and noisy. Moreover, the slow response times of electromechanical displays make them useless where the information to be displayed can change rapidly, as in the case of a vehicle's speedometer. For these reasons, electromechanical displays tend to be used only where their clarity is a benefit that outweighs their weaknesses and where the display changes slowly. Such applications include scoreboards in sports arenas, large digital clocks and thermometers for public spaces, and indicator boards for airport, bus, and rail terminals.

The signals for electromechanical displays are generated by switches, keyboard inputs, or electronic devices such as clocks or thermocouple thermometers. Their interfaces simply convert command signals into position settings for the display, which are effected by the drive system.

▲ When the Dalai Lama made an address near the Washington Monument on July 2, 2000, a crowd of some 40,000 gathered. Few in the crowd would have been able to see him in detail had the address not been displayed on this huge LED video screen.

Matrix displays

A matrix display consists of a grid array of lamps set against a dark background. Such displays show characters and symbols by lighting appropriate patterns of lamps. They can show static images—roadside information signs often do this—or they can show moving strips of text and images for advertising and newscasting purposes.

The earliest matrix displays used incandescent filament lamps. The combination of the physical size and the heat output of such lamps meant they had to be well spaced to prevent overheating. Consequently, the displayed images could be perceived clearly only from considerable distances. Clusters of four lamps each—one clear lamp and others with red, green, and blue filter domes—could produce 15-color displays by illuminating combinations of lamps; the sizes of these clusters reduced the clarity and resolution of the display, however. A major failing of the earliest matrix displays was the tendency of incandescent lamps to fail—especially when subjected to severe vibration, as is the case in roadside locations.

The control interface for moving matrix displays was a machine that read rolls of punched paper tape. The paper would pass between an array of electrical contacts—one for each bulb—and a metal tablet. When a contact lined up with a hole, a current would flow to illuminate the bulb connected to that contact. For color displays, separate parallel tracks drove the clear bulbs and the three sets of colored bulbs. Each track would be prepared manually using a punch and templates.

LED matrix displays

While some incandescent filament-lamp displays still exist, most modern matrix displays use light-emitting diodes (LEDs), which are luminescent semiconducting devices. The advantages of LEDs over filament lamps include longer lifespans, lower power consumption for a given output, and lower operating temperatures.

An important characteristic of LEDs is their size: LEDs are more compact than filament lamps, so they can be used in small displays that are capable of moderately high-resolution images. Small displays—typically 3 to 6 ft. (1–2 m) long—are used to display next-arrival data on rail and subway platforms as well as at some bus stops. Other users include stores and entertainments venues, where typical messages include details of special offers and forthcoming events.

Older and more basic LED matrix displays use one color of LED—usually red—and are programmed by entering the message to be displayed on a keypad that plugs into the display. More sophisticated displays use two or three colors of LED and are sometimes driven by signals from a central processor that may control several displays on a local or wide-area network. In any case, a microprocessor translates the message and any effects—moving or flashing text and images, for example—into signals that switch the individual LEDs on and off with the appropriate timing to generate the desired images. Several messages can be displayed in programmed or random sequences, and the messages may be accompanied by—or interspersed with—local time, temperature, or air-pollution data.

Full-color video displays

Full-color video displays are sophisticated LED matrix displays. The elements of the matrix are clusters of three LEDs each—red, green, and blue—that are the equivalents of the pixels of a computer monitor. The initials of the three colors of LEDs in a full-color video display give rise to its alternative name: RGB display.

Each of the LEDs in a cluster can be switched off or illuminated to a number of intensities, so each cluster can produce a vast range of colors—more than 16 million colors if sufficient image information is available. The interface of a full-color video display behaves in the same way as a computer's graphics card, taking color information for each pixel of an image—in the case of an RGB display, for each cluster of three LEDs—and converting it into signals that illuminate each LED appropriately. Given sufficient processing capacity at the interface, RGB displays are capable of producing full-color moving video images.

Large-scale RGB displays are frequently used in arenas and at outdoor venues for concerts, sports events, and other gatherings. In such cases, they screen live video images of the proceedings on stage—affording a clear view to the whole audience—as well as prerecorded promotional videos and computer graphics that support the live event. Advertising agencies use outdoor RGB displays to show versions of television advertisements. Often, these displays are mounted in prominent roadside positions where traffic holdups are frequent and the occupants of cars may have an hour or so to view a series of video commercials. Such displays have attracted criticism from road-safety campaigners and from environmental campaigners, who consider them a source of so-called visual pollution.

Nixie tubes

Some of the first examples of electrical and electronic displays were used to show numerical data on electronic calculators. In many cases, these technologies later found uses in a diverse range of displays, including those of electronic watches, household electrical goods, such as video-cassette recorders and compact-disc players, and industrial instruments and digital gauges.

One of the earliest numerical displays was the Nixie tube—originally NIX I, for numerical indicator experiment number I. Launched in the 1950s, the Nixie tube was a glass cell that had a transparent metal-mesh anode on the front wall and contained a stack of cathodes, shaped like the numerals zero to nine, with low-pressure neon and a small amount of mercury vapor. Connecting a 180 to 200 V direct-current supply to the anode and one of the cathodes produced an orange-red discharge glow in the shape of that cathode. Nixie tubes had disadvantages; their display cells were bulky and the characters had an uneven appearance. Also, they often required their own power supplies, thus adding to the weight of equipment and making it less portable.

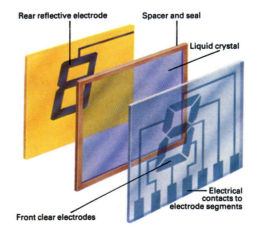

Rear reflective electrode   Spacer and seal

Liquid crystal

Front clear electrodes

Electrical contacts to electrode segments

◀ A seven-segment liquid-crystal display is capable of depicting all numerals—from zero to nine—and crude forms of some letters. This type of display is used for calculators and watches.

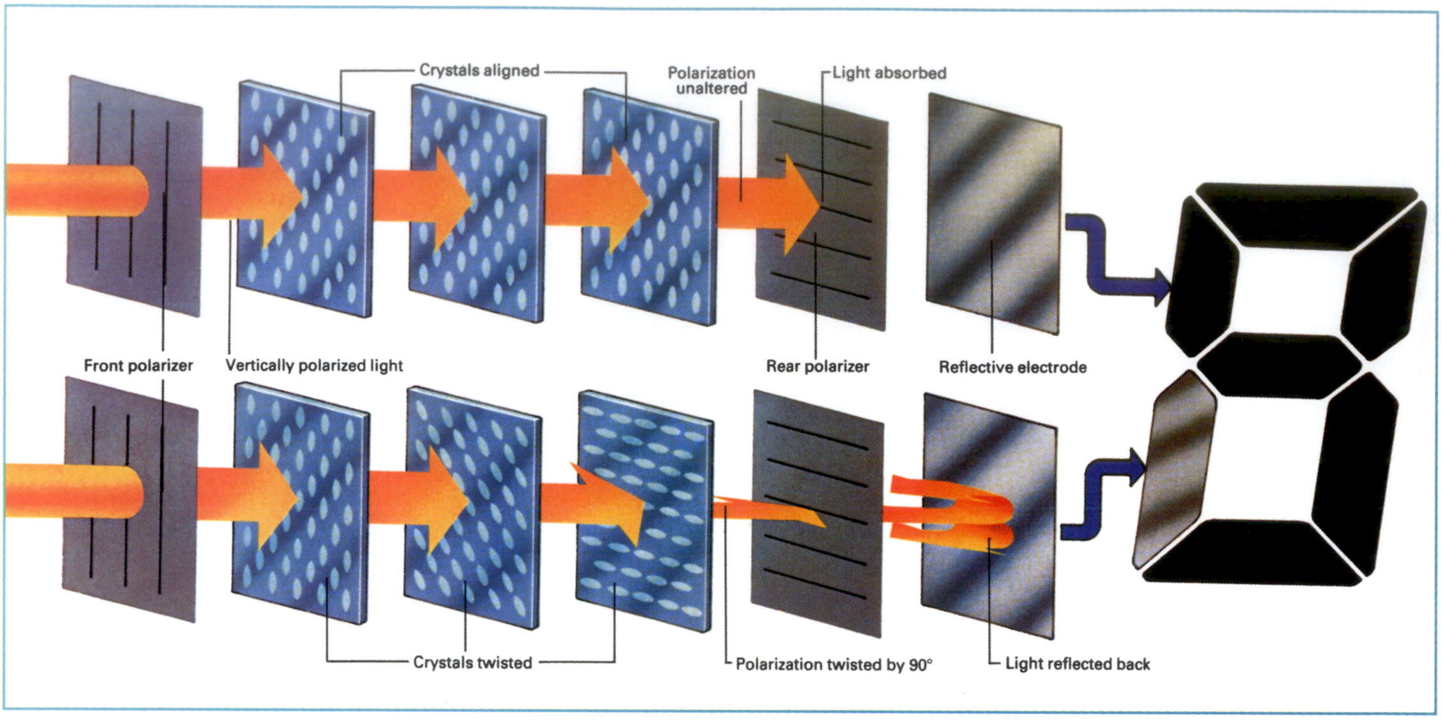
Crystals aligned
Polarization unaltered
Light absorbed
Front polarizer
Vertically polarized light
Rear polarizer
Reflective electrode
Crystals twisted
Polarization twisted by 90°
Light reflected back

▲ When a segment of an LCD is energized (top), the molecules in the liquid crystal line up between two cross-polarized filters. The filters then prevent light from passing through the segment. Switched off (bottom), the molecules form skewed layers that rotate the polarization of light so that it can pass through both filters. The segment then has a much lighter appearance.

Planar displays

A number of display technologies have been developed that show several characters in a single plane and are therefore less bulky than Nixie-type tubes. These technologies typically use seven rectangular segments, arranged in a form similar to a figure eight, to portray numerals zero to nine. The interface of such a display is more complex than that of a Nixie tube, since it must provide signals that illuminate the appropriate segments to represent each numeral rather than simply connecting the appropriate cathode to the supply.

One form of planar display uses the discharge glow between a transparent tin-oxide anode on a front glass panel and segments of conductive paint on a rear ceramic panel. As in Nixie tubes, the space between the anode and cathode is occupied by low-pressure neon gas and mercury vapor, so the glow is orange-red. In other systems, phosphor-coated anodes are used. These fluoresce red, yellow, or blue-green when current flows.

LEDs use the light produced by gallium-based semiconductors when a current is passed through them. Red, orange, yellow, blue, and green units are available. As with other planar displays, LEDs are arranged in groups of seven, and characters are produced by activating the appropriate pattern of diodes. The decode-and-drive logic circuits may be mounted within the same package as the display, thus saving space and reducing complexity. Standard integrated-circuit technology can condense a display onto a single chip for applications such as pocket calculators. Owing to their reliability and low power requirements, LEDs became widely used in the 1970s.

Liquid-crystal displays (LCDs)

LCDs are planar displays that draw much less power than equivalent displays that use other technologies. For this reason, LCDs are used almost universally for battery-powered equipment.

An LCD has two light-polarizing filters that are crossed, or set such that the polarized light that passes through one filter would be blocked by the other. A liquid-crystalline material fills the space between the filters, and its rod-shaped molecules align with minute grooves etched into the surfaces of the filters. However, since the grooves in the two filters are at right angles to one another, successive layers of molecules form a spiral between the two filters. As polarized light passes from one filter to the other, the spiraling layers twist the plane of polarization of the light so that it can pass through the second filter and reflect off a mirrored surface behind it. On the return journey, the plane of polarization of the light is again twisted so that it can pass through both filters, thus producing a milky-white appearance in the unenergized display.

The segments of an LCD are marked out by transparent electrodes on the two filters. When a potential difference is applied to these electrodes, the electric field between them causes the molecules to align with incoming light. They no longer twist its plane of polarization, so the filters block the light and the segment appears black.

SEE ALSO: Cathode-ray tube • Computer • Computer graphics • Discharge tube • Liquid crystal • Microprocessor • Polarization • Semiconductor

Digital Versatile Disc (DVD)

The digital versatile disc, or DVD, is a form of data-storage medium that has the potential to replace a whole range of storage media, including audio compact discs and CD-ROMs (compact-disc read-only memories), recordable CDs, rewriteable CDs, video tapes, and videodiscs. As such, DVDs have started to unite the home-computing and home-entertainment markets, since the same disc can be used to view a film using the DVD player of a home-entertainments system or the DVD drive of a computer, for example.

History of DVD

Since a major application of DVDs is as video-storage devices, the history of the DVD is largely that of video recording as a whole. In fact, when it was launched, the DVD was widely known as the digital video disc, rather than digital versatile disc.

In the early days of cinema and television, people had to adhere to the schedules of movie-theater owners and television broadcasters if they wished to view a film or television program. The launch of video-cassette systems in the 1970s removed that limitation: for the first time, affordable electronic equipment and magnetic tapes similar to audio cassettes made it possible for people to buy or hire their favorite movies to watch at home and to record television broadcasts for viewing at a time that suited them.

Around the same time that video-cassette systems became available, Philips launched the Laserdisc video disc—arguably the first direct ancestor of the DVD. Video discs held encoded information in a spiral pitted track on a disc of metal film some 12 inches (33 cm) in diameter; the film was sandwiched in transparent plastic for protection. Players used a low-power laser to illuminate tracks on the revolving disc, and variations in reflected light caused by pits in the track were converted into pulsed electrical signals. The great advantages of video discs over video cassettes were their fidelity—the exactness with which they reproduced the original image—their resistance to degradation of image by surface marks, and the speed with which the player could move from one part of the recorded program to another. These advantages won a niche for the video-disc system in the field of corporate training, since trainers could move with ease between sections of a training program to suit individual training needs.

▲ DVD players are the latest in audio and video entertainment systems. This model can be plugged into a number of output devices, but the latest DVDs are completely self-contained, with features such as a liquid crystal display screen and headphones making them completely portable.

► The Philips Laserdisc was the forerunner of both CDs and DVDs. The reading beam of laser light enters a multidirectional prism from top right. The prism reflects this beam onto the surface of the disc. The reflected beam follows the path of the reading beam at first but then passes straight through the multidirectional prism to fall on a detector that converts its varying intensity into a signal.

The great disadvantage of the video disc was the fact that it was impossible to record a disc using a simple player, whereas a household video-cassette machine could record programs onto blank tapes as well as play prerecorded tapes. This disadvantage prevented video disc systems from gaining widespread acceptance in the household entertainments system market. In June 1999, the last remaining manufacturer of video discs for entertainment announced that it would no longer release films on Laserdisc format. At that time, there were approximately seven million video-disc players in use worldwide.

To a large extent, the DVD's route to commercial success has been paved by another form of optical data-storage medium: the compact disc. CDs use similar technology to video discs but on small-format 4.75 in. (12 cm) discs. The first application of CDs was as a medium for pre-recorded audio data. During the 1980s, the CD rapidly replaced the long-playing vinyl record, and then the 45 rpm single record, as the most popular format for prerecorded music. This popularity was fueled by the superior sound quality of CDs and their resistance to wear and tear when compared with recordings in vinyl, which were easily ruined by accumulated dust and scratches. In contrast, error-correction software helps a CD player to read through all but the most severe marks and scratches by reconstructing the obscured data from the visible data around scratches.

Soon after the audio CD had made the general public aware of the quality of digital recordings on optical discs, the CD-ROM highlighted the versatility of optical discs as media for computer data. CD-ROMs rapidly became popular as high-density media for installing software programs on personal computers and for acting as read-only data sources for multimedia computer encyclopedias, for example. Such programs use data from a CD-ROM to construct text, photos, animated images, and video clips with soundtracks. The user can select links within text that direct the CD-ROM drive to read the part of the disc that contains the data pertaining to the link, so the user can progress rapidly through the content of the disc to information that is of interest. A CD-ROM has a capacity for 650 megabytes (MB) of data, which is equivalent to all the information required for a 74 minute full-color video with full stereo sound. CD-ROMs whose capacity is mostly or completely dedicated to video are called video CDs; they were introduced in 1994.

DVDs as advanced CD-ROMs

When DVDs were introduced in 1996, they fitted naturally into the roles established by CDs: as read-only data-storage media for audio recordings, computer programs and information, and videos. Standard DVDs are the same size as standard CDs—4.75 in. (12 cm)—and simple DVDs appear identical to CDs. For this reason, many manufacturers have resolved to use a different case size from that used for CDs in order to reduce the risk of customers confusing the two formats.

The crucial differences between the two types of discs are the total amounts of information that they can store and the rate at which that information can be read and transferred to a computer processor or devices for converting the raw data into video and sound signals. The capacity of a basic DVD—a so-called single-sided, single-layer 4.75 in. (12 cm) DVD-5—is 4.38 gigabytes (GB), compared with 0.64 GB (650 MB) for a CD-ROM. The standard rate of data retrieval is 1.32 MB per second, compared with 0.146 MB/s for a CD-ROM. In fact, both DVD and CD-ROM drives operate many times faster than this rate, so a "16x" DVD drive can read data at a rate of 21.1 MB/s (16 x 1.32 MB/s), for example.

The greater capacity of a DVD compared with a CD makes it able to store more text, greater numbers of more detailed images, longer films, or more hours of music, for example. DVDs have a greater capacity of information because the information is more densely packed than on a CD of the same size. High-frequency lasers in DVD readers are able to read the surface markings of DVDs in more detail than the lower-frequency lasers used to read CDs can. Consequently, the minimum pit size on a DVD is 0.4 micrometers compared with 0.83 micrometers for a CD, and the tracks of a DVD are 0.74 micrometers apart compared with 1.6 micrometers for a CD.

Other formats of DVDs

The basic DVD-5 is but one of a range of DVDs that each have different capacities. The lowest-capacity DVD is the DVD-1, which is a 3.1 in. (8 cm) version of the 4.75 in. (12 cm) DVD-5. The DVD-1 holds up to 1.36 GB—just under one-third the capacity of a DVD-5.

The capacity of a DVD can be almost doubled by imposing a semitransparent track over the base track. The separation between the two layers is 20 to 70 microns. A minimum pit size of 0.44 micrometers—10 percent greater than that of a single-layer DVD—helps reduce crosstalk, which is a type of interference between the tracks of the two layers. The disc runs 10 percent faster to compensate for the longer pits, and the disc holds just under twice the capacity of a similar single-track disc. The 4.75 in. (12 cm) single-sided double-layer DVD is coded DVD-9.

The capacity of the DVD-5 can be truly doubled by placing two single-layer discs back to back. The resulting DVD-10 has a capacity of 8.75 GB, but it has the disadvantage of having to be removed from the drive to read information from the different sides. The DVD with the greatest capacity is the double-sided, double-layer DVD-18, which can hold 15.9 GB—more than 100 times the capacity of a CD-ROM.

DVD video

Because of its demands for large quantities of information to be transferred at high rates, the reproduction of videos and films is a worthy application for DVD technology. The amount of picture and sound information for storage on DVDs is reduced from the raw signals by so-called compression techniques.

The video signal is compressed using a system called MPEG-2. The raw video signal is a stream of values that describe the color and brightness of every pixel of a frame, line by line and from top to bottom. One stage of MPEG-2 compression removes redundant information from the raw signal by identifying groups of pixels of similar color and brightness; instead of stating similar values for each pixel in a group, the compressed signal states a representative value once and gives the starting pixel for that value and the number of pixels for which it applies. The amount by which the final signal is compressed depends on the range of color and brightness values used: a more faithful representation of the original image is achieved with a broad palette of values, but the amount of compression is less. Another stage of the MPEG-2 process reduces the signal by describing only those parts of an image that change significantly from one frame to the next.

OPTICAL DISC MANUFACTURE

DVDs and similar optical discs, such as CDs and Laserdisc video discs, are copies of a glass master disc. One master may be used to produce several stampers, from which replicas of the master can be pressed.

First, a circular glass plate is polished until it is optically flat. It is then coated with a photoresist—a light-sensitive resin similar to that used in the manufacture of integrated circuits. The plate then rotates under a laser, whose pulses form a pattern of solid blocks in the photoresist.

The photoresist that has not hardened through exposure to laser radiation is washed away in a process called development. The result is a negative of the final disc, since ridges of hardened photoresist occupy the positions that will be occupied by pits in the metal of the finished discs.

The developed master is silvered and electroplated with nickel to form a "father" disc—a metal plate that has the same pattern of pits that will be present in the final disc. The father disc, once

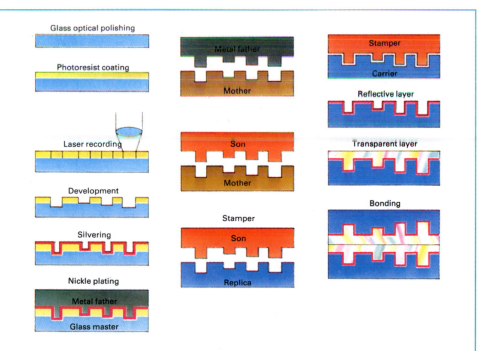

Glass optical polishing
Photoresist coating
Laser recording
Development
Silvering
Nickle plating
Metal father
Glass master

Metal father
Mother
Son
Mother
Stamper
Son
Replica

Stamper
Carrier
Reflective layer
Transparent layer
Bonding

peeled away from the master, is used to stamp "mother" discs, from which many "sons"—copies of the original father—are pressed. These sons are the stampers that are used to press thermoplastic carriers that will support the metal film in discs.

One side of the disc is then completed by coating the patterned surface of the carrier with a reflective metal layer and filling with more metal. The two sides of the disc are then united and bonded together using an adhesive cement.

CD/DVD PLAYER DVP-S735D

The most common system for encoding movie soundtracks is Dolby Digital, which usually encodes five full channels—left front, left rear, center, right front, and right rear—with an additional "subwoofer" channel that emphasizes low-frequency sounds. Because the information for the subwoofer channel is less detailed, this combination is described as 5.1 channel sound. Older movies might have a single sound channel, or two channels—left and right—that are processed to give the impression of a three-dimensional soundscape, or "surround sound."

DVD video compared with VHS

At present, DVD videos are read only: there are no systems for recording video on DVDs in the home. Although this is the only weak point of DVDs compared with VHS video cassettes, it is a major failing for many video enthusiasts.

The advantages of DVDs over VHS are many. DVD video images are much sharper than those from a VHS cassette, since a DVD portrays 500 lines of pixels for every frame, compared with 240 for video. Furthermore, the digital recording on a DVD does not deteriorate with age; a VHS tape stretches and loses magnetic particles with time, on the other hand, so its image quality declines. The quality of freeze frame and slow motion images is also far superior for DVD.

As well as the basic video and audio streams, a DVD can carry alternative soundtracks for other languages, optional subtitles to accompany the original-language soundtrack, and optional captions for the hard of hearing. Several different cuts of the same film can be included on a single DVD, and each cut may have several alternative camera angles that can be selected at will as the film plays. A film may be recorded in standard format with a 4:3 aspect ratio, meaning that the image is 1⅓ times wider than it is tall, or it may be recorded in widescreen 16:9 format. Playback of a widescreen recording on a 4:3 screen can be done by inserting black bars above and below the widescreen image or by filling the 4:3 screen with a selected part of the widescreen image—a technique known as pan and scan.

Recording on DVDs

Apart from the read-only DVDs so far described, there are also recordable DVDs (DVD-R)—"blank" DVDs on which data can be recorded permanently—and rerecordable DVDs (DVD-RAM), on which data can be recorded and erased countless times. The two types of recordable DVDs use different recording technologies.

DVD-Rs contain a clear layer of an organic material that is transformed into a colored dye when activated by the writing laser in an appropriate DVD drive. The points of dye left by pulses of the writing laser are then read by a low-power laser in the way that the pits of a standard DVD (DVD-ROM) are read. Since the activated dye cannot be returned to its original clear state, a given DVD-R can be written only once.

In a DVD-RAM, the recording material is a thin layer of a substance that exists either in a crystalline phase or an amorphous phase. The two phases have different reflectance values, and the writing process records data as changes between amorphous and crystalline phases.

More sophisticated DVD drives have optical systems that can read and record on the different types of DVD media as well as read CDs. DVD-video players are in development, but they will require immense processing power to compress raw video data for recording on DVD-RAMs as the video signal is received.

The future of DVD

Current development projects include DVDs that operate with blue or violet lasers, whose high frequencies will be able to resolve smaller pits and more closely spaced tracks, thus increasing the amount of information that can be packed on a single disc. A fluorescent multilayer disc (FMD) has also been made in prototype form. FMDs can have up to 50 layers per side and use recording material that emits light when irradiated by a laser. Such a disc will hold 25 GB of data.

▲ The DVD player is becoming a common feature of home entertainment systems, but unlike conventional video players it can only play prerecorded discs.

SEE ALSO: Compact disc, audio • Computer graphics • Data storage • Laser and maser • Sound reproduction • Video recorder

Diode

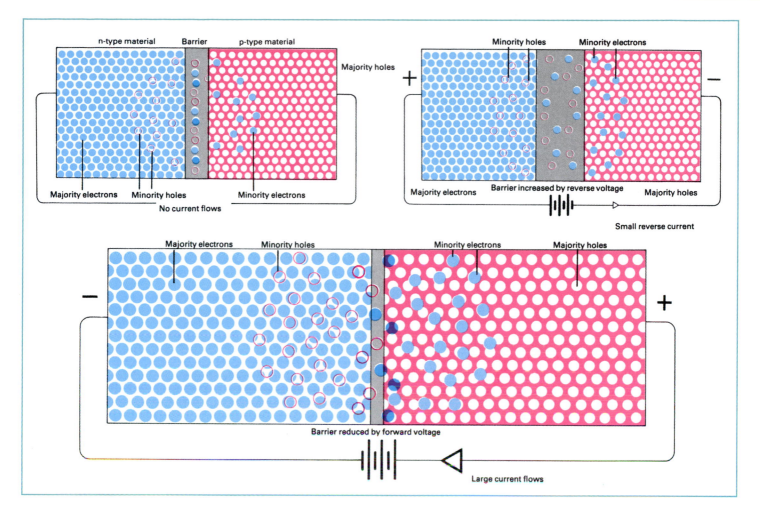

n-type material — **Barrier** — **p-type material**

Majority holes

Majority electrons — Minority holes — Minority electrons

No current flows

Minority holes — Minority electrons

Majority electrons — Barrier increased by reverse voltage — Majority holes

Small reverse current

Majority electrons — Minority holes — Minority electrons — Majority holes

Barrier reduced by forward voltage

Large current flows

A diode is an electronic device that permits an electrical current to flow in only one direction between its two terminals. Some diodes use semiconducting materials to control the direction of current flow, while others use vacuum tubes. One of the most important applications of diodes is in rectifiers, which are electrical circuits that convert alternating current into direct current electricity.

Vacuum-tube diodes

A vacuum-tube diode—a tube—consists of two electrodes and a heating element sealed in an evacuated glass tube. One electrode, the cathode, is made from or coated with a metal that readily gives off electrons when heated—an effect known as thermionic emission. The other electrode, the anode, is neither heated nor treated to give off electrons under normal operating conditions.

In use, a filament heats the cathode to its operating temperature and thermionic emission forms a "cloud" of free electrons around the cathode. If the anode is at a positive voltage relative to the cathode, the electric field between the two electrodes draws free electrons through the vacuum from the cathode to the anode and a current flows

easily through the device. This flow direction is called the forward current direction, and the device is said to be forward biased—rather like a switch in the on position. If the voltage across the device reverses, however, there are no electrons available to draw from the anode to the cathode. Consequently, no current flows and the diode is reverse biased. In this condition, diodes exhibit extremely high resistances and behave like a switch in the off position.

Vacuum-tube diodes have some disadvantages relative to semiconductors: they are bulky and prone to breakage; also, it takes time for the filament to heat the cathode when first switched on, so the diode does not function immediately. For these reasons, vacuum-tube diodes have been largely replaced by semiconductors, except in heavy-duty industrial applications.

Semiconductor diodes

A semiconductor diode is made from a sliver of a semiconducting material—silicon or germanium, for example. The sliver is cut from a single crystal of pure semiconductor, and its two faces are then treated with impurities to create layers that

▲ A semiconductor diode consists of n-type and p-type materials that meet at a junction. When there is no external voltage (top left), no current flows. When the n-type material is connected to a positive voltage relative to the p-type material (top right), the diode is reverse biased, and only a minute leakage current flows. When the diode is forward biased (bottom), a much greater current can flow.

have different electrical properties. The region between the two layers is called a junction, and it is this region that controls current.

In pure silicon, for example, each silicon atom has four electrons that it contributes to the bonding of the crystal. Those electrons are firmly held in bonds, so pure silicon is a poor conductor. If one face of a sliver of silicon is infused with atoms of an element that has only three valence electrons—aluminum or boron, for example—the inclusion of such atoms leaves electron vacancies in the bonding system of the crystal. These vacancies, called "holes," are centers of positive charge that can move with relative ease compared with the electrons in pure silicon. Hence, aluminum- or boron-doped silicon is described as a positive-majority, or p-type, semiconductor.

Doping the other face with atoms of an element that has five valence electrons—antimony, arsenic, or phosphorus—introduces electrons that are surplus to the requirements of the bonding system in silicon. Like the holes in p-type silicon, these electrons are relatively free to move. Hence, silicon doped in this way is called a negative-majority, or n-type, semiconductor.

Between the p-type and n-type materials is the p-n junction, where there is neither a surplus of electrons nor of holes. This region is also called the depletion layer, which refers to the depletion of its electrons and holes. The depletion layer acts as a barrier to the movement of both holes and electrons. By analogy, it presents a slope or gradient that only a few energetic holes and electrons can climb, the rest falling back to their respective sides. Because there are more holes in the p-type region than in the n-type region, it is far easier for positively charged holes to move from the p-type region to the n-type region than vice versa.

Similarly, it is easier for electrons to move from the n-type region to the p-type region. Hence, a significant current flows when the p-type region is at positive voltage and the n-type region at negative voltage—the forward-biased condition. If the voltage is reversed, few holes and electrons can jump the barrier of the depletion zone, so the reverse, or leakage, current that flows through a reverse-biased semiconductor diode is minute.

Semiconductor diodes are tiny yet robust relative to vacuum-tube diodes. For this reason, they have made a major contribution to the miniaturization of electronic devices as diverse as aircraft control systems and home stereo systems.

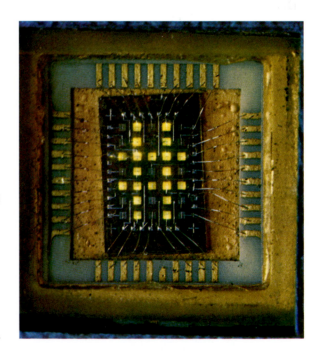

▶ The reverse of an electronic calculator's light-emitting-diode (LED) display. The fine wires connect in pairs to gallium-arsenide diodes that have been treated with phosphorus. When one of these diodes is forward biased, a current flows and the diode glows.

SEE ALSO: CHEMICAL BONDING AND VALENCY • CONDENSED-MATTER PHYSICS • SEMICONDUCTOR • SILICON

Discharge Tube

◄ A high-pressure sodium lamp consists of a translucent aluminum oxide tube that contains mercury, sodium, and xenon between two electrodes. A bulbous glass envelope shields the tube from air currents that could cool it from its optimum operating temperature. When first connected to a power supply (top center), the gas in the tube is pure xenon. After a while, heat from the pale xenon discharge vaporizes the sodium and mercury, and the intensity of the emitted light increases. A lamp of this type takes around three minutes to reach full power (bottom right) from a cold start.

Discharge tubes are devices that produce light as a result of an electrical current passing through a gas, usually at less than normal atmospheric pressure. They are used as energy-efficient lamps for indoor and outdoor lighting.

Naturally occurring luminous discharges include phenomena such as lightning and Saint Elmo's fire—the glow that extends from steeples and ships' masts during heavy storms. The first person to harness electrical discharges in evacuated glass tubes was Heinrich Geissler, a German glassblower and inventor. In 1858, Geissler invented a hand pump, which he used to remove air from glass tubes in whose walls electrodes were embedded. Other scientists who studied electrical discharges through low-pressure gases included Faraday, Crookes, and Thomson. The devices built by these workers were the forerunners of cathode-ray tubes, electronic vacuum tubes, and gas-discharge lamps. These early tubes differed in the shape of the tube, the distance between the electrodes, the operating voltage, the nature of the filling gas or vapor, and the pressure in the tube.

Basic principles

For a substance to conduct electricity, it must possess charged particles that are free to move. Under most circumstances, gases are excellent insulators: they consist entirely of electrically neutral particles. Under exceptional conditions, electrons break away from neutral atoms or molecules to leave positively charged ions. This process, called ionization, makes a gas able to conduct an electrical current.

The process of ionization requires an input of energy. Atoms and molecules can acquire the energy for ionization from collisions with cosmic rays or other fast-moving particles or by absorbing high-energy photons, such as gamma rays.

In a discharge tube, ionization is initiated by a strong electric field between the electrodes. Once a few electrons break free, they accelerate toward the positive electrode. The progress of the free electrons is interrupted by collisions with neutral atoms or molecules. If the free electrons have sufficient kinetic energy to cause ionization when they collide, an avalanche of ionizations results, and the gas becomes ionized and conducting.

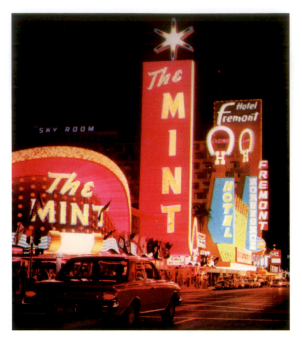

► Neon lights and other types of discharge tubes are a familiar sight in the entertainment centers of many large cities.

more stable pattern. The streamers fill most of the space between the electrodes, and their color is characteristic of the gas in the tube—pink for air and red for neon, for example.

By around 0.01 atmospheres, most of the tube is filled by two glowing regions: the negative glow—a small glowing patch near the cathode, or negative electrode—and the positive column, which extends from the anode, or positive electrode, through most of the discharge tube. Two dark regions are visible, named for the scientists who first recorded them: the Crookes dark space, which is at the surface of the negative electrode, and the Faraday dark space, which separates the negative glow from the positive column. Further reduction in pressure causes the positive column to become shortened and split into evenly spaced striations, which are luminous transverse bands. The striations become fewer as the pressure falls.

Whether or not an avalanche of ionizations occurs depends on the ionization energy of the gas, its pressure, and the strength of the electric field. The pressure of the gas determines how far free electrons travel between collisions: at high pressure, free electrons tend to collide before they have enough energy to cause ionization. Raising the strength of the electric field increases the acceleration of free electrons, so the avalanche effect can happen at higher pressures. Note that the strength of the electric field depends on the voltage and distance between electrodes—doubling the gap halves the field.

The passage of current through a gas causes it to become hot. Eventually, the thermal energy of the gas becomes sufficient to cause ionizations through high-energy collisions. In this state, described as plasma, the gas is highly conductive. In a plasma, electrons are continually knocked out of atoms and recaptured, emitting light as they fall into the empty orbitals of ions.

Visible phenomena

A simple discharge tube for laboratory demonstrations consists of a glass tube with a connection for a vacuum pump and two electrodes at the ends of the tube. An induction coil provides a potential difference of tens of thousands of volts between the electrodes. At normal atmospheric pressure—around 1 atmosphere—the current amounts to only microamperes and nothing is seen. As the pump is connected and the pressure falls to around 0.07 atmospheres, a larger current starts to flow and the electrodes are joined by glowing streamers of ionized gas that flit erratically around the tube. As the pressure continues to fall, the streamers strengthen, coalesce, and adopt a

▼ The Philips SL is a miniaturized fluorescent lamp that fits a conventional lamp socket. It consumes around 70 percent less power than a filament lamp of the same lighting power and lasts more than five times longer.

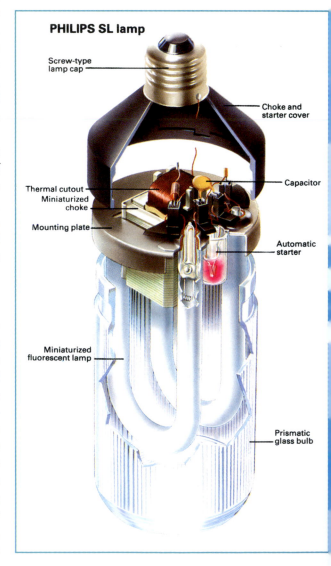

PHILIPS SL lamp

Screw-type lamp cap

Choke and starter cover

Thermal cutout
Miniaturized choke

Capacitor

Mounting plate

Automatic starter

Miniaturized fluorescent lamp

Prismatic glass bulb

Cathode rays and vacuum tubes

If a discharge tube is evacuated to less than 0.00001 atmospheres—$\frac{1}{100,000}$ times normal atmospheric pressure—the space inside the tube ceases to glow. This is because there are hardly any gas atoms to be ionized. Nevertheless, a small current still flows, and the glass wall of the tube fluoresces behind the anode. At first, these effects were believed to be caused by rays emanating from the cathode—hence the term *cathode ray*. In fact, the current is evidence of electrons being pulled out of the cathode by the electric field and flying directly to the anode; the fluorescence of the glass happens because some of the electrons fly across the tube but miss the anode. Instead, these electrons strike the glass and make it glow.

Vacuum tubes combine the ability of electrons to pass through a vacuum with a phenomenon called thermionic emission. In this effect, a metal emits more electrons as its temperature increases, since the thermal energy of the electrons helps them escape the body of the metal. In a vacuum-tube diode, one of the electrodes is heated by a filament. A much greater current flows if the heated electrode is the cathode than if the polarity is reversed. This is because a large number of electrons "boil" to the surface of the hot electrode to be pulled to the positive electrode. Until the invention of semiconductor diodes, vacuum tubes of this type were widely used to control the direction of current flow in electrical circuits.

Neon lamps

Lamps commonly called neon tubes are discharge tubes that contain a low pressure of neon or some other gas that emits visible light. The walls of such tubes are usually clear, so the color seen is the actual color of the gas discharge. This type of discharge tube can be softened by heating and formed into letters and other shapes that are ideal for use in decorative and promotional displays.

Neon tubes generally operate on alternating current (AC), so the two electrodes function as the cathode for different parts of the AC cycle. The electrodes are typically iron tubes with an internal coating of alkaline-earth oxides that promotes the emission of electrons. The discharge heats the electrodes to around 300°F (150°C).

The power supply to the tube is controlled by a ballast—an electromagnetic or semiconductor device that provides an initial-high voltage "kick" but restricts the current that flows once the gas has ionized and the resistance of the tube has fallen to nearly zero. Without a ballast, the current through the tube could increase uncontrollably, eventually vaporizing the electrodes.

Fluorescent lamps

Fluorescent lamps differ from neon lamps in a number of respects. First, the electrodes of the usual "hot cathode" fluorescent lamps are coiled tungsten filaments rather than iron tubes. A current passes through the filaments, heating them

▲ This photograph of a metal-halide discharge tube was underexposed to reveal the details of the discharge. A bright central core bridges the gap between the electrodes and is surrounded by a diffuse glow. The dark yellow droplets are condensed metal iodides.

to around 1650°F (around 900°C). The high temperature couples with the coating of alkaline-earth oxide to promote electron emission.

At startup, the tube contains argon, neon, or xenon at extremely low pressure together with a few drops of liquid mercury. The high-voltage "kick" from a ballast ionizes the noble gas first. The discharge then heats and vaporizes the mercury, which also becomes ionized.

The mercury discharge in a fluorescent lamp includes a large proportion of ultraviolet light, which can cause blindness by burning the retina of the human eye. For this reason and because ultraviolet radiation provides no illumination, the insides of fluorescent tubes are coated with materials called phosphors. The phosphors absorb invisible and harmful ultraviolet radiation and radiate it as visible light by a process called fluorescence. (Fluorescence is the conversion of a high-energy photon into a lower-energy photon as the electronic structure of an atom changes.)

The color of the light given off by a fluorescent tube depends on its mixture of phosphors, the most usual colors being shades of white. Sunlamps are fluorescent tubes whose coatings allow some of the less harmful frequencies of ultraviolet photons to pass through.

Fluorescent lamps produce much less heat than filament lamps do, so more of their power consumption is converted into light during continuous operation. This is why a 20 W fluorescent lamp produces almost as much light as a 100 W filament lamp does. The power demand of a fluorescent tube at startup is great, however, so switching fluorescent lights on and off on a frequent basis eliminates much of their economical advantage. Also, since each startup vaporizes a small amount of the filament coating, frequent startups reduce the lifespan of a fluorescent tube.

The two formats of fluorescent tube in common use are the large tube with separate ballast and power supply and the compact fluorescent lamp, whose tube and power-supply components form a single disposable unit that fits into a standard fitting of the type used for filament lamps.

Low-pressure sodium lamps

Low-pressure sodium lamps are the most energy-efficient of all light sources, producing more than seven times more light intensity than filament lamps of equivalent power consumptions.

The function of a low-pressure sodium lamp is similar to that of a fluorescent lamp, but the tube is uncoated glass and generally U-shaped. The starter gas is a mixture of argon and neon, and the tube contains a small amount of solid sodium that vaporizes when the lamp starts up. The discharge tube is enclosed in an evacuated glass bulb that traps heat and so helps maintain the operating temperature of the lamp.

The disadvantage of low-pressure sodium lamps is that their light is of two near-identical wavelengths in the orange-yellow part of the visible spectrum. Thus, it is impossible to determine the true colors of objects lit by low-pressure sodium lamps alone. Nevertheless, low-pressure sodium lamps have been in widespread use for street lighting in Europe since the end of World War II.

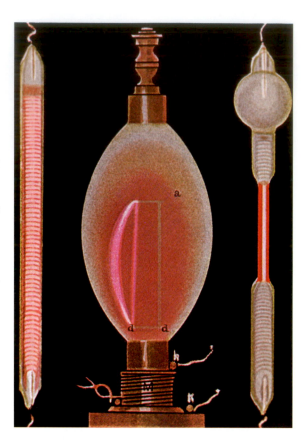

High-pressure discharge lamps

High-pressure discharge lamps operate near or above atmospheric pressure, although the discharge tube is well below this pressure when cold. High-pressure lamps combine energy efficiency with good color rendition, which makes them the favored light sources for roads and urban areas.

Mercury vapor lamps contain mercury and small traces of noble gases. They usually have an additional starting electrode near one of the main electrodes. On startup, the initial arc to the starting electrode vaporizes and ionizes the mercury. Once the resistance in the tube has dropped, the discharge passes to the main electrode. The discharge tube may be enclosed in a clear glass bulb that filters ultraviolet light from the blue-green light of the discharge, or it may be phosphor coated to give a warmer fluorescent light.

Metal-halide lamps contain mercury with some noble gases and iodides of mercury, sodium, and scandium. The iodides glow red, orange, or yellow, producing a more balanced white light than the mercury discharge alone.

High-pressure sodium lamps contain sodium, mercury, and some xenon in an aluminum oxide tube that resists attack by sodium vapor at high pressure. Their light is an intense warm white that is ideal for street lighting.

▲ Different forms of Geissler tubes, so named for their inventor. Air at low pressure was the most common filling for this type of tube during the 19th century. The tubes at left and right show the striations, or stripes of varying light intensity, which are typical features of discharges through gases at low pressure.

SEE ALSO: CATHODE-RAY TUBE • DIODE • MERCURY • VACUUM TUBE

Dishwasher

The first dishwashing machines, designed for restaurants and caterers, generally worked on the principle of passing the dirty dishes under jets of hot water by means of a conveyor belt or revolving basket. Modern dishwashers have reversed this procedure, the stationary dishware being washed by revolving jets above and below the basket.

A typical dishwasher is housed in an enameled cabinet designed to match and complement other large kitchen appliances. A drop-down door enables a plastic-coated basket to be pulled out on slides or rollers for loading. The door is fitted with a microswitch to shut off all operations if it is opened during a cycle—this is an important safety feature. The interior of the machine is finished in stainless steel, plastic-coated steel, or vitreous enamel.

Water supply

The water connections for the machine can consist of a hose connection from existing taps, or they can be plumbed in permanently. Most machines now take hot and cold water, but they also have their own heating elements. Waste water is removed by a pump via a drain hose. If the drain hose is plumbed in permanently, this must be done at the correct height in order to prevent accidental siphoning of the wash water out of the machine. As an additional precaution

▶ A late-19th-century dishwasher. The dishes were placed in the machine together with hot, soapy water, and when the handle was turned, the water was flung against the dishes by the motion of the paddles, effectively cleaning them.

against siphoning, the waste pipe can be vented to the atmosphere by means of an air hole.

The amount of water used varies from water-saving types using under 3 gallons (11 l) to those using 29 gallons (110 l), depending on the size of the machine, the wash cycle, and the brand. (Ordinary domestic machines are at the low end of this scale.) The temperature of the water, 122 to 158°F (50–70°C), is much hotter than hands can bear.

◀ In a modern dishwasher, very hot water containing detergent is sprayed onto the dishes by sets of rotating and fixed spray jets; the spray angles and pressures are designed so that all parts of the load are cleaned and food particles removed.

Heater, pumps, and motors

The heater rating can be from 1,800 to 2,750 W. Heaters are normally of the mineral insulated sheathed element type, consisting of a heating spiral contained in a metal tube but insulated from it. The insulation is typically made of compacted magnesium oxide powder. This type of element can be safely immersed in water; its operation is controlled by a thermostat.

Dishwashing machines have separate vane pumps to provide water pressure to the spray arms and to remove the dirty water. Some machines have one motor to operate both pumps, but most have separate motors. The motors are protected by overload cutouts embedded in the windings to shut them off if they exceed a safe operating temperature.

Operation

A dishwasher generally has several programs that can be selected by means of keys or push buttons, depending on the type of utensils to be washed and the type of food residues to be removed. A typical program begins with a cool or warm

◀ A cutaway view of a dishwasher with one loading tray removed for easy viewing. The revolving spray arms can be seen at top and bottom. Pumps and motors are installed in the bottom of the machine, and the controls and detergent dispenser are located in the door. Dishes are dried by the circulation of hot air.

rinse, continues with a hot wash with detergent, and concludes with several rinses. The rinse will probably include a rinse aid, which is essentially a wetting solution, and the final rinse will be hot, to aid final drying.

Many machines also dry the dishes, using the heating element as a heat source. Most also include a simple cold rinse to provide an initial cleansing for dishes if there is likely to be a delay before a proper wash can be undertaken, such as when a machine has space for many place settings.

The wash and rinse water is sprayed from above and below the dish basket by whirling arms through which the water is pumped, each of the arms having several spray holes in it. The detergent and the rinse aid are stored in dispensers that automatically release the right amount at the proper point in the cycle. The machine usually has a built-in water softener to which salt must be periodically added manually by the user.

A timing device, which automatically controls the selected cycle, is often operated by means of a simple round calibrated knob. Turning it in one direction starts the cycle, and it turns back slowly as the machine operates. Some machines have pilot lights that indicate which part of the cycle is currently in operation. Sometimes the knob has a push-pull off-on function so that the cycle can be stopped at any time to allow the user to put in or take out utensils.

Many domestic machines are about the size of a front-loading washing machine, but there are space- and energy-saving types available that are roughly half the width and will hold between four and six place settings. There are also tiny dishwashers that can stand on top of work surfaces.

SEE ALSO: DETERGENT MANUFACTURE • WASHING MACHINE

Distillation and Sublimation

Distillation separates the components of liquid mixtures according to their boiling points; sublimation separates the components of solids that become gases without passing through a liquid phase at temperatures called their sublimation points. In industry, distillation is used in the production of diverse substances, including gasoline, whiskey, fragrant oils, and oxygen. In some countries, distillation produces drinking water from saltwater. On a smaller scale, distillation and sublimation are important separation techniques for research and quality-control laboratories.

Aristotle reported distillation as early as the fourth century B.C.E., when he described the distillation of seawater to make drinking water. The Romans and Alexandrians (from Alexandria, Egypt) distilled pinewood resin to obtain oil of turpentine, a useful solvent and a medicinal oil. In this early equipment, vapors condensed in a downward-sloping air-cooled outlet from the top of the boiling vessel. While air cooling is sufficient to condense high-boiling substances, more volatile components escape to the atmosphere before condensing. It was probably the Arabians who first used a water-cooled outlet, which allowed them to isolate various essential oils—natural plant oils, used mostly as flavorings or perfumes—by distilling liquid plant extracts. Later in the Middle Ages, alchemists used a type of distillation apparatus, called an alembic, to prepare nitric acid and other mineral acids.

The preparation of fortified alcoholic beverages by distillation has taken place since antiquity. Distilled alcohol—probably first produced in Italy in the 12th century—was at first used as a medicine. The apothecaries and monasteries of the time possessed distillation rigs called stills, and their operators would sometimes flavor the distilled alcohol with herbs and spices. Liqueurs such as Benedictine and Chartreuse developed from these early medicinal experiments.

By the early 1800s, large-scale distilleries were producing spirits that are still popular today: brandy is obtained by distilling wine, while whiskey is made from fermented barley grain (malt) mashes, rum from fermented cane sugar, and vodka from fermented rye or potatoes.

Distillation is an early stage in petroleum refining. Crude petroleum that has been treated to remove traces of saltwater is heated and led into a fractional distillation column, where it separates into fractions with different boiling ranges.

Basic principles

Distillation is very similar to evaporation: in both processes, molecules escape from the surface of a liquid and form a vapor. In evaporation, the vapor is dispersed and the residue that remains is collected; in distillation, the vapor is subsequently cooled and condenses as a liquid that is collected.

The molecules in a liquid move around by virtue of the heat energy they possess. Far below the boiling point of a liquid, few molecules move fast enough to be able to escape the attractive forces of other molecules in the liquid, so the space above the liquid contains hardly any molecules that originate from the liquid. Closer to the boiling point of the liquid, more molecules have sufficient energy to leave the liquid. The evaporated molecules start to exert a significant pressure in the space above the near-boiling liquid, and this pressure is called the vapor pressure. A liquid reaches boiling point when its vapor pressure equals atmospheric pressure and bubbles of vapor form in the liquid.

When a mixture of two liquids with widely different boiling points boils, the vapor above it consists almost exclusively of the substance that boils at the lower temperature when pure. By condensing the vapor away from the boiling liquid, the lower-boiling component of the mixture can be obtained in high purity. When that component has been removed from the mixture, the temperature of the remaining liquid starts to rise until the higher-boiling liquid boils.

▲ A laboratory apparatus for vacuum distillation. The metal heating mantle at left provides energy to boil the liquid in the flask without presenting the hazard of a naked flame in case the flask breaks. Cold water flows through the condenser in the center of the picture to remove heat from the vapors as they condense, and the liquid that forms then runs into the receiver at right. The hose at top right leads to a vacuum pump, and the arrangement of taps allow for the main part of the apparatus to be kept at low pressure while the vacuum in the receiver flask is temporarily released and a new flask installed. After changing flasks, the new receiver must be evacuated before being opened to the rest of the distillation system.

◄ A 210 ft. (64 m) crude oil fractionating column dominates this scene of a typical oil refinery. The vertical pipes attached to this column and the smaller one at left tap off fractions that collect on plates within the column. The approximate heights of the plates are indicated by the positions of the service walkways on the towers.

Simple distillation

The simplest arrangement for a distillation apparatus is a still, or retort, in which the liquid is heated to boiling point. The vapors then condense in an arm of the vessel that may be cooled by the surrounding air or by a circulating cooling fluid such as water. The condensate then falls under gravity into a receiving vessel.

Simple distillation is only effective in separating a liquid from a solid or in separating liquids that have widely differing boiling points. Simple distillation is used in Kuwait to separate pure water for drinking from the salt in seawater; burning cheap natural gas from the local oil fields provides the necessary heat for the process.

Simple laboratory distillations usually employ a round-bottomed flask, a heat source such as an electric mantle, and a glass condenser. The most common type of condenser, the Liebig condenser, consists of a glass tube surrounded by a hollow jacket through which cold water circulates.

Fractional distillation

Simple distillation is ineffective in separating mixtures of liquids that have similar boiling points: the condensate obtained is only slightly richer in the lower-boiling component than the starting mixture. Far better results are achieved if the still head—the take-off point for the condenser—is separated by a fractionating column.

A typical fractionating column for laboratory use consists of a glass tube packed with ceramic or glass beads, rings, sticks, or tubes. As the distillation proceeds, hot vapors rise up the column and establish a temperature gradient within it, with the highest point of the column having the lowest temperature. As the vapor reaches the part of the column that is below its boiling point, it condenses and starts to run back down the column in a process called reflux. At each point in the column, descending liquid meets rising vapor on the large surface area provided by the packing material. The vapor that rises from each point is richer in the more volatile component than is the liquid that descends, therefore, the concentration of the more volatile component is greatest at the top of the fractionating column.

In effect, a fractionating column performs several distillations in a single operation, and the efficiency of a column is measured in terms of theoretical plates, with each theoretical plate achieving the equivalent separation of a simple distillation operation. The efficiency of fractionation depends on the vapor and liquid in the column always being in intimate contact with each other. The nature of the packing material determines the surface area available for this interaction, as does the overall size and shape of a column. Another factor is the reflux ratio, which is the volume of liquid that condenses at the still head and returns to the column for each volume of liquid collected as condensate.

Industrial fractionating columns

Industrial-scale columns are not packed, since it was found that refluxing liquid tends to form channels in the packing and flow down those channels, thereby avoiding the vapor. Various designs are in current use, but all feature horizontal plates that cross the column at several heights. The vapor bubbles through holes in these plates, and the liquid flows down from one to the other. Sieves with small disk valves over each hole or perforated bubble caps ensure thorough mixing as the vapor passes through the liquid.

Industrial columns are operated continuously, whereas laboratory fractionations are done in batches. In the laboratory, for example, each fractions is collected in turn from the head, with the temperature of the column gradually increasing. This type of operation is best suited to one-off fractionations of small volumes of mixtures. In continuous operation, fractions are tapped off at various levels in the column. The column is continuously replenished with mixture for separation, and the temperature gradient in the column remains constant once the column has reached a steady state of equilibrium.

In the petroleum-fractionating columns of the oil industry, preheated crude oil is fed into the column at around one-third the way up. At the bottom, vapor is produced by heating up the residue with steam, and at the top a reflux condenser returns liquid to the column. As soon as the whole column is in equilibrium, it is tapped at various heights, where condensates drain through valves at controlled rates. The top of the column yields the most volatile components: refinery gas, raw gasoline, and raw kerosene; higher-boiling gas oils collect around the middle of the column; and fuel oils collect near the bottom. The residue that collects at the base of the column is a mixture of heavy fuel oil, lubricants, and bitumen.

Another important fractional distillation process, but one that takes place at extremely low temperatures, is the separation of liquefied air into its component gases. The separation is so effective that not only oxygen and nitrogen but also the inert gases argon, krypton, and xenon may be recovered in commercial quantities.

Azeotropic distillation

Some mixtures behave as if they were single compounds: they have a fixed composition and characteristic boiling point. Such mixtures are called azeotropes, and their boiling points are either lower or higher than any of their components.

One example of an azeotrope is rectified spirit, which consists of 95 percent ethanol (ethyl alcohol) and 5 percent water. In order to obtain pure ethanol, a third component—benzene—must be added. Benzene, ethanol, and water form a second azeotrope, which boils out of the mixture at a lower temperature than the ethanol-water azeotrope. Once all the water has been removed from the mixture, a benzene-ethanol azeotrope boils off to leave pure ethanol in the pot.

Steam distillation

Steam distillation uses azeotrope formation to distil heat-sensitive organic compounds that are immiscible with water. Aniline is an example of such a compound, since it decomposes appreciably if heated to its own boiling point. If steam is passed into impure aniline, however, the temperature of the mixture rises until the aniline-water

azeotrope distils over. The condensed azeotrope separates into immiscible aniline and water layers. Steam distillation is also widely used to extract heat-sensitive essential oils from plants.

Distillation at reduced pressure

Distillation at reduced pressure—often called vacuum distillation—is an alternative to steam distillation for compounds that decompose below their normal boiling points. It has wider applications than steam distillation, since it does not require the distilled material to be immiscible with water. Vacuum distillation works by reducing the temperature at which a liquid boils, remembering that boiling starts when a liquid's vapor pressure matches the ambient pressure.

In a vacuum distillation, the whole system is sealed off from the atmosphere and the pressure is reduced by a vacuum pump. Pressures down to 10^{-9} times normal atmospheric pressure are used.

Vacuum distillation produces heavy fuel oils and high-viscosity lubricating oils from the residue of crude-oil fractionation, the residue of the vacuum distillation being bitumen for road surfacing. It also removes compounds with unpleasant odors from cottonseed and soybean oils to make them suitable for use in cooking.

▶ The spherical copper pot of a gin still sits in a heating jacket (the silvery cladding). Hot vapors from the top of the still pass through a copper pipe, just visible at top right, to a vertical condenser.

Molecular distillation

Molecular distillation is a variation of vacuum distillation that is used for materials that are either extremely sensitive to heat and cannot be heated to their normal boiling points or are readily oxidized if heated in contact with air. It is particularly useful for distilling compounds of high molecular weight, typically in the range of 500 to 1,000 mass units, including many complex organic molecules that occur naturally.

Under pressures of 10^{-6} times normal atmospheric pressure or less, the liquid mixture that is to be separated is sprayed onto a spinning, heated cone in a dome-shaped chamber—this apparatus is called a molecular still. The majority of the liquid spins directly off the cone into a collecting trough at its edge from which it returns to a reservoir for recirculation over the cone. Those molecules that receive enough heat to evaporate from the liquid on the cone condense on the cooled dome that encloses the cone. From there, the condensate drains into a receiver.

Molecular distillation protects sensitive compounds in a mixture from excessive exposure to heat by maximizing the surface area of the liquid on the cone, thus promoting evaporation, which occurs only at the surface of a liquid. Furthermore, the use of a molecular still minimizes the time the liquid spends in contact with the heat source. This process contrasts with a standard vacuum-distillation apparatus, in which the whole sample is constantly heated during distillation, yet the ratio of the surface area of the liquid to its volume is much smaller than in a molecular still and so much less favorable for evaporation.

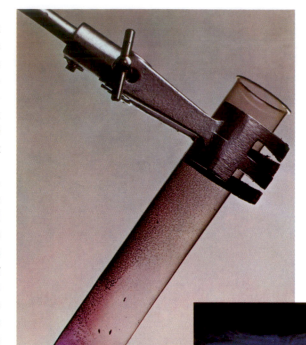

◄ Relatively few substances sublime—that is, pass directly from the solid to the gaseous phase without becoming liquid. Iodine (left) is one example of such a substance; carbon dioxide (below) is another. The clouds around the solid carbon dioxide are formed by airborne moisture that forms a fog in contact with cold carbon dioxide gas.

Sublimation

The vast majority of solid mixtures melt before evaporating, so that one or other form of distillation is usually the appropriate separation technique. A few solids pass directly into the vapor phase without becoming liquid. This process is called sublimation. The basic principle of distillation—separation according to differences in vapor pressure—also applies to separation by sublimation, but the equipment for sublimation must be designed in such a way as to not become blocked by accumulations of solid.

Destructive distillation

In destructive distillation, a high-boiling or high-melting substance is deliberately decomposed by high temperatures, and the products of that decomposition are collected. For example, coal—heated to around 1800 to 2200°F (1000–1200°C) in an airless sealed chamber, or retort—decomposes to yield coal gas, liquid hydrocarbons, and an ammonia-rich liquid. Coke remains as a solid residue in the retort, and the other components are further purified.

SEE ALSO: ALCOHOL • CENTRIFUGE • CHEMISTRY, ANALYTICAL • CHEMISTRY, ORGANIC • CHROMATOGRAPHY • DESALINATION • GAS LAWS • GASOLINE, SYNTHETIC • OIL REFINING • PRESSURE

FACT FILE

■ In the late-17th century, an Italian religious order called the Gesuati was suppressed by the Vatican for neglecting religious duties and employing the entire labor force on the large-scale distillation of scent and liqueurs.

■ In early-19th-century Ireland, the illegal distillation of poteen—a potato-based spirit—was so rife that members of the constabulary were awarded graded bonuses for discovering equipment. They received three pounds and three shillings for seizing an entire still, falling to five shillings for merely the "worm"—the spiral-shaped metal condenser in which the vapor was cooled to produce the extremely potent distillate.

Diving Suit

As the technology of diving has been developed over the years, rescue, salvage, and repair operations have required diving at great depths and in cold conditions; even in warm parts of the world, the water becomes cold as the diver goes deeper. The introduction of diving suits has been necessary for protection against hypothermia (lowering of the body temperature).

The effects of hypothermia are quite dangerous. An unclothed diver in water at freezing temperature would be unconscious in minutes. Even at 50°F (10°C), the diver's survival time would be little more than 3½ hours, but at this temperature, a good diving suit would increase the survival time to around 24 hours by preserving body heat.

There are two types of diving suits: the helmet suit, which includes the breathing apparatus and completely encloses the diver, keeping him or her warm and dry, and the free-diving, or scuba, suit, which is independent of the breathing apparatus. Scuba is an acronym that stands for Self-Contained Underwater Breathing Apparatus; the scuba is so called because it is used in conjunction with the aqualung. Scuba suits are subdivided into two further classifications: the dry suit, which keeps the diver completely dry, and the wet suit, which allows a thin film of water between the diver's body and the suit. The water inside the suit is soon warmed by the diver's body and acts as additional insulation against the cold water outside the suit.

The helmet suit

The helmet suit was suggested by the earlier diving bell; the helmet itself can be seen as a personal portable diving bell, with the air continually replenished by means of an air line to the surface.

The suit is made of rubberized fabric, and the diver enters it through the neck hole. The helmet is then attached to the suit with a waterproof seal. The helmet has glass ports that enable the diver to see and is connected to the surface by an air line through which compressors pump fresh air at ambient pressure, that is, at the pressure of the surrounding water. Expired air is released via an outlet valve into the water. There is also a secure line for hoisting the diver to the surface and usually a telephone line so that the diver has direct voice contact with team members above the water.

The helmet diver can work for long periods underwater because there is a constant supply of air, but because movement is limited by the lines and the cumbersome heavy suit, this type of div-ing suit is best used for stationary work such as may be involved in working on a wreck.

Free-diving dry suit

The free-diving dry suit is used in conjunction with foot fins, a mask, and an aqualung. A comparatively loose-fitting garment, it allows for undergarments. It is usually made of rubber or neoprene (an artificial rubber that is more resistant to corrosion) and is sometimes reinforced with fabric. Waterproof seals are provided at the neck and the wrist, and there is a waist seal where the top joins the trousers, which have boots attached. Some dry suits have a neck entry that eliminates the need for the waist seal.

When the diver is dressed, the undergarments retain some air, creating unnecessary buoyancy. The air must be vented by inserting a finger under a wrist seal and submerging until only the hands are above water; water pressure drives the air out. Some suits have a simple duckbill valve that does this automatically.

One of the disadvantages of a dry suit is that, as the diver descends, the residual air left in the undergarments is compressed by the water pressure. As the volume of this air decreases, the suit is pressed tighter to the diver, making it rigid and hampering movement. Sometimes the folds in the suit will trap and pinch the diver's skin, causing welts. For this reason the dry suit is less popular than the wet suit, except in extremely cold water, where warm dry undergarments are a distinct advantage, and in polluted water, where the dry suit is worn with a full face mask to protect the diver. Disinfectant can also be poured over the diver as a precaution.

Free-diving wet suits

The wet suit consists of a close-fitting material, usually foam neoprene, and is not watertight. Water seeps in and is trapped next to the diver's skin, which soon warms it, or warm water may be poured in at the start. The foam material, containing millions of tiny air bubbles, acts as an insulator.

The principal disadvantage of the wet suit is that the air bubbles make the diver buoyant, so the aqualung diver is provided with a weighted belt to

▲ A diver wearing a dry-helmet suit adjusts the flow of exhaust air from the suit.

help the descent. But as the diver descends, the ambient pressure reduces the volume of each air bubble, resulting in a loss of both buoyancy and insulation; the diver who is neutrally buoyant at the surface becomes overweighted and heavy at depth. (This is one reason why the weighted belt is equipped with a quick-release mechanism.) The experienced diver soon gets used to this change in buoyancy, and although it makes ascending more work than descending, the diver can generate quite a lot of power by kicking his flippers in a rhythmic manner.

Some methods of avoiding loss of buoyancy have been developed, particularly for commercial divers who spend long periods of time underwater and find the overweighting exhausting. The most simple is the adjustable buoyancy lifejacket. This is a bag to which is fixed a cylinder of compressed air. As the diver descends a little air is bled into the bag to increase buoyancy. On ascending the air is automatically vented or discharged manually. A more sophisticated method uses millions of tiny air-filled bubbles of glass instead of foam bubbles. The air in the glass bubbles cannot be compressed, so the diver's buoyancy and insulation remain more or less constant. This type of suit, however, is far more expensive than the standard version.

A recent advance in aqualung equipment, the rebreather, recycles air exhaled by the diver, increasing the air supply underwater an extra 45 minutes to 2 hours. The air is passed through a regeneration chamber in which carbon dioxide is removed; it is then mixed with oxygen and air from the cylinder and rebreathed. As the rebreather does not emit bubbles, the suits are also quieter.

Hot-water suit

The hot-water suit is a sealed suit supplied with hot water from the surface. The water flows through a series of passageways in the suit to cover the whole of the diver's body and then leaves the suit through valves, creating a constant flow of hot water to maintain the diver's temperature. This heat is especially important in saturation diving, where the diver breathes a helium–oxygen mixture. As helium conducts heat far more readily than air, hypothermia can occur much more rapidly.

▲ The combination of the free-diving wet suit and the self-contained aqualung opened up diving to the amateur sportsman and woman.

For deep diving operations—1,000 ft. (304 m) or deeper—the hot water may be supplied to the diver at temperatures up to 110°F (43°C) and up to 4.7 gallons per minute (18 l/min.).

Pressure suits

A diver in the Gulf of Mexico may descend to a depth of 1,770 ft. (540 m) 15 to 20 times a month to do maintenance work on an oil rig. Working with explosives and drilling tools, he can spend up to 12 hours under a pressure 70 times that of the atmosphere. When he comes back up, his ascent takes just a quarter of an hour. Before the early 1970s, this speed would have been impossible without the use of submersibles or a huge saturation diving complex.

Oil companies looking for ways to reduce the costs and risks of diving in deep waters found an answer in the form of a diving suit called JIM and its inventor, an engineer called Joseph Peress. JIM (named after Peress's mechanic and test diver, Jim Jaratt) was an atmospheric diving suit (ADS) so massive that a diver could safely take it into deep water and breathe air at ordinary atmospheric pressure. Peress designed JIM in the 1920s and used it in quests for sunken wrecks in the 1930s, but he had been disappointed in the 1940s when the British Royal Navy found no use for it.

A chance meeting in 1969 between Peress and engineers from Underwater and Marine Equipment Ltd (UMEL) of Farnborough, Britain, resulted in a highly successful demonstration of JIM. Peress was persuaded to restart development, leading to a modern version of the suit.

JIM is an elephantine device with a cast magnesium body and domelike head that flips down to allow the diver in and out. Four Plexiglas windows give all-around visibility, and the entire suit is coated with a film of waterproof sealant to prevent the magnesium from corroding.

What most intrigued the experts who rediscovered JIM was the skillful way Peress had solved the problem of its joints. Peress had no formal engineering training, but he created a ball and socket joint that included a fluid cushion—rather like a human joint. Without the cushion between ball and socket, water pressure would have forced the two together in paralytic immobility.

JIM and his more modern brothers have been a success. Operators discovered that, past a certain number of dives every month, ADSs are far more cost-effective than a saturation diving complex. JIM and his backup equipment may cost anything up to half a million dollars, but running costs are low and an entire four-ton diving unit can be flown anywhere by helicopter. By comparison, a saturation diving complex is hideously expensive to run: a day's work at 2,130 ft. (650 m) takes 35 days of compression and decompression for the divers concerned. If they are going to spend a month working under such conditions, it becomes worth it—they can live in a pressure chamber without having to decompress. However, few jobs are so lengthy as to justify this expense.

Hazards of the deep

Safety is an important consideration. Bone necrosis and the bends are well-known hazards of deep diving. Also, divers who breathe mixtures of oxygen and helium lose their body heat more quickly and need a hot water supply pumped down to them from the surface. Helium itself affects the nervous system—divers often get the shakes, or high pressure nervous syndrome—and also scrambles speech, meaning divers can barely be understood.

All these problems are avoided if an ADS is used. The suit can be lowered to the bottom on the end of a cable that also carries a telephone line for communication and a power supply cable. Otherwise JIM is totally self-contained, carries enough air to last 72 hours, has no need of a heating system, and the carbon dioxide that accumulates is scrubbed by a soda-lime filter that is replaced after every dive. Cylinders of pure oxygen on JIM's back replace the carbon dioxide without raising air pressure inside the suit.

It takes about an hour to get JIM from the seabed onto a tender, change the scrubber and diver, descend, and restart work. If anything goes wrong on the seabed, the diver can jettison the ballast weights and JIM floats to the surface. There is also an acoustic through-water link with the mother ship, or sonar pingers can be released. Pingers float about 16 ft. (5 m) below the surface and emit "pings" that are picked up by hydrophones on the ship's keel.

The suit weighs a hefty 1,100 lbs. (500 kg) on dry land but is surprisingly nimble under the water. Walking is quite simple, and JIM can even climb ladders. The arms float horizontally until moved, and JIM can be made to lie on its back or front simply by leaning forward or backward. JIM's hands are simple universal claw designs with a facility for holding portable tools like wrenches, grinders, and cable cutters.

JIM has grown up over the years into a family of ADSs. One of the great problems with JIM in his basic form was that the magnesium body was difficult and expensive to cast properly. UMEL coped with this problem for some years before opting for welded aluminum in their Mk 3 SAM suit. The suits used in the Gulf of Mexico and the North Sea, however, are made of glass fiber.

JAM

JAM is the name given to one of the new generation of atmospheric diving suits that enable divers to work at great depths without long periods of decompression. JAM has a glass-fiber body 1 in. (25 mm) thick and a double-layer acrylic dome head, and it can work at depths up to 2,300 ft. (700 m). It is, in effect, a person-shaped submersible in which the diver breathes air at normal atmospheric pressure.

▲ UMEL's Mark 4 suit—nicknamed JAM—with its glass fiber body and 2,300 ft. (700 m) depth rating is unbeatable in bottom-of-the-sea situations.

SEE ALSO: Air • Aqualung • Breathing apparatus • Gas laws • Lung • Pressure • Rubber, natural • Rubber, synthetic • Sea rescue • Submersible • Temperature • Undersea habitat

Dock

For many centuries, sea traders relied solely on the shelter afforded by natural harbors, inlets, and river estuaries in order to load or discharge, resupply, or repair their ships. While lying at anchor, their vessels were at the mercy not only of wind and tide but also of bands of marauders, to whom they were easy prey. The need for protection from such threats led to the establishment of basins, or wet docks, where sailing ships could be fitted out in safety and where their cargoes could be dealt with in relative security.

The word *dock*, which to this day is used fairly loosely to describe a variety of places where ships are berthed, was first used to describe "an artificial basin filled with water and enclosed by gates" during the 16th century—a period of considerable expansion in maritime trade. One of the first recorded enclosed dock basins was the Howland Great Wet Dock, which was built on the south bank of the Thames River, London, in the 17th century. Only in the late 18th and 19th centuries did the great dock-building period begin in earnest, often closely associated with canal- and railway-building ventures. This was also the period of the first iron steamships, but the tremendous growth in ship sizes since then has made many early docks obsolete.

The provision of gates at dock entrances is necessary because of the large tidal range that would otherwise cause the basins to have insuffi-

▲ Modern docks can handle a wide variety of cargo ships. Most are fitted with cranes and conveyor systems for loading and unloading containers and bulk goods, such as grain or crude oil.

cient depth of water at low tide. In many countries, the rise and fall of the tide is so insignificant that docks can be completely tidal. For example, in Melbourne, Australia, spring tides (those with the greatest range) rise less than 3 ft. (1 m), in Rotterdam about 6.5 ft. (2 m); and in Boston, about 10 ft. (3 m).

In Britain, however, with its large tidal ranges, more major dock systems are enclosed. The most notable exception to this is at Southampton, where all dock berths are tidal and where the effects of a 13 ft. (4 m) tidal range are minimized by a phenomenon known as the double tide, which gives six hours of high water a day. An extreme example of a tidal range that makes enclosed docks imperative occurs in the Severn Estuary, where Bristol, for instance, experiences a maximum variation of almost 49 ft. (15 m) between high and low water.

Enclosed docks may have a single pair of gates that are open only at high tide, when the water levels inside and outside are the same. In order to reduce tidal restrictions on shipping movement, it is more usual to have two or more pairs of gates forming a pen, or entrance lock, in which ships can be raised or lowered. Such docks are often impounded, that is, kept at a high level by powerful pumps drawing water from outside the dock to replace that lost during the locking of ships. Alternatively, water losses can be made good by opening up the lock at high water to refill the dock basin. If the dock walls have been built sufficiently high, there is no reason why the level of

◄ A floating dock in Hamburg, where ships of up to 70,000 tons (63,000 tonnes) can be lifted.

water in an impounded dock should not be maintained above the highest level achieved outside, a practice that has long existed in the Port of London to give greater depth.

Lock entrances

The dimensions of the lockpit inevitably govern the maximum size of vessel that can enter an enclosed dock. With the trend toward ever larger ships, the constraints of existing entrance locks have become a problem. The largest lock in Britain, at Tilbury, is 1,000 ft. (305 m) long and 110 ft. (33.5 m) wide, with a depth of 45½ ft. (14 m), whereas the largest container ships, now operating between Europe and the Far East, are 950 ft. (290 m) long overall and 106 ft. (32 m) in the beam and have a maximum draft of 42½ ft. (12 m). New entrance locks are being built to handle even larger vessels: at the West Dock at Bristol, Britain, a lock measuring 1,200 ft. (366 m) long and 140 ft. (43 m) wide has been constructed to take ships of 75,000 tons (68,000 tonnes) deadweight, and developments at Le Havre in France include a new lock 1,312 ft. (400 m) in length and 219 ft (67 m) wide, one of the world's largest and capable of accommodating a tanker of 500,000 tons (454,000 tonnes) deadweight.

The operation of an entrance lock is basically simple. By using a system of culverts and sluices, water is allowed to pass from the dock into the lock with both inner and outer gates shut. The water level, and with it any ship in the lock, rises until it reaches dock level, when the inner gates open and the ship moves into the dock. A departing vessel can then be penned in the lock and lowered by allowing water to escape through the outer sluices.

Lock-gate machinery is usually electrically or hydraulically operated. The gates themselves may each weigh 300 tons (270 tonnes) or more and are of hollow construction. Different types include gates that are withdrawn into recesses in the lock walls; flap gates, which are lowered like a drawbridge to lie flat on the lock bottom; and the more common hinged gates, which swing back to open. Large locks often have a third set of gates to form a short lock for handling small vessels more quickly and minimizing water

▼ A cargo ship at dock with a Stülcken derrick mounted centrally astride the hold. The derrick greatly simplifies and speeds cargo handling.

loss. Pairs of gates are invariably angled back slightly in a V against the head of water so that the water pressure keeps them tightly shut against a sill on the floor and water leakage is negligible.

Dock layouts

Although certain cargoes, such as coal or bulk grain, require specialized handling facilities, dock berths have traditionally been multipurpose and vary little in design, layout, and equipment. Usually the quay apron (the working area alongside ship) is equipped with rail tracks both for cranes and railroad boxcars and is flush-surfaced to give access to road vehicles. Quay cranes of three- to five-tons' capacity at an 80 ft. (24 m) radius are usually adequate for break-bulk general cargo operations (that is, where individual packages, drums, bales, and so on are handled piecemeal using cargo trays, nets, slings, or hooks), but cranes of greater capacity are installed where heavier cargo, for example, steel castings, is frequently dealt with. For even heavier items, many ports are equipped with floating cranes, often with lifting capacities exceeding 100 tons (90 tonnes).

Transit sheds adjacent to the quay apron give temporary covered accommodation to cargo prior to its loading aboard ship or collection by road or rail vehicles. Modern sheds have the maximum possible unobstructed floor area so that mobile equipment, such as forklift trucks, platform trucks, and mobile cranes, can be used to carry and stack cargo. To the rear of the sheds, loading bays with both road and rail access serve for the delivery of goods.

Container docks

The dramatic changes that have occurred in cargo transportation over the last 25 years have, however, completely transformed the layout of modern terminals. These new techniques include containerization—the carriage of general goods in large containers of internationally standardized dimensions—and roll-on roll-off vessels employing bow, stern, or side doors through which wheeled freight is loaded and discharged.

A typical container-handling dock has a large area of land serving each berth, ideally 20 to 25 acres (8–10 ha), for container marshaling. It does not usually have covered accommodation, except where container stuffing (packing) and unstuffing or customs examination are carried out, although warehouses with their own internal gantry cranes for stacking have been constructed in the vicinity of docks.

Two or three giant gantry cranes, with lifting capacities of up to 40 tons (36 tonnes) and capable of working a three-minute cycle (that is, loading and unloading 20 containers an hour), may be provided to a berth. For large ocean-going container ships, at least 1,000 ft. (305 m) of quay is allocated for each berth. Mobile handling equipment may include van carriers, which straddle, lift, carry, and stack containers three high; tractors and trailers; or side or front loaders, each with similar lifting capacities. Alternatively, the gantry cranes may span the entire stacking area, carrying out all movements between ship, container stack, and inland transport.

With large container ships carrying 2,000 or more containers and perhaps discharging half of these at one port and then loading a similar number, the operation of a container terminal is highly complex. For this reason, computer con-

trol of container movements is widely used, and studies are already in hand with a view to the automation of future container berths, perhaps with fleets of robot tugs responding to radio signals.

Ferry terminals

Although many roll-on roll-off ferry terminals accommodate passengers as well as freight, roll-on roll-off terminals consist mainly of a ramp, shore bridge, or linkspan onto which the ferry can open its doors and a large marshaling area for the vehicles it carries. In some cases, a simple concrete ramp built out from the quay wall is all that is necessary, but most shore bridges are tailor-made for the individual vessel using them, with electrically operated machinery able to compensate for the ferry's changing draft during loading operations. Like all very successful ideas, roll-on roll-off is a simple concept, and it has revolutionized the carriage of cargo on short sea routes.

Bulk terminals

The economics of transportation are resulting in the building of increasingly large vessels for bulk handling of raw materials, but arrangements must

▼ Roll-on roll-off ferries load cars and container trucks through a gate at the rear and front of the ship. Many ferries use a special bridge that can compensate for changes in the ferry's draft as vehicles enter or leave the vessel. Care is taken during loading to balance container trucks evenly. Foot passengers embark through a separate flexible structure, similar to those used for boarding aircraft.

◄ These modern crane vessels use flotation legs for stability. A computer-controlled ballast system compensates for uneven loads by pumping water ballast between compartments within the legs.

be made to accommodate them. *Globtik Tokyo* and *Globtik London*, two of the largest tankers afloat, are 477,000 tons (430,000 tonnes) deadweight and 1,253 ft. (382 m) long and have a draft of 92½ ft. (28 m). Oil tankers are usually brought to jetties sited in deep water, but a relatively new system of loading and unloading uses what is known as a single-point mooring buoy, or monobuoy mooring, linked by pipeline to the shore installations and placed as far out to sea as is necessary.

Special dock facilities exist for other bulk traffics, iron ore being a prime example. Vessels of 100,000 tons (90,000 tonnes) or more are regularly employed carrying ore. Modern terminals, such as the Associated British Ports' Port Talbot Harbour in South Wales, work around the clock 365 days of the year when necessary; their transporter cranes, which are fitted with 20 ton (18 tonne) capacity grabs, are capable of average discharge rates of around 1,800 tons (1,630 tonnes) an hour.

Dry docks and floating docks

At regular intervals, all ships need to be inspected in the dry and repaired. For this reason, most major ports are equipped with dry, or graving, docks, slipways being used for smaller ships.

Dry docks, which usually take one ship at a time, are simply basins that are capable of being pumped dry to leave a ship supported by an arrangement of keel blocks so that work can be carried out on the hull, propellers, or rudder. The procedure for dry-docking a ship is a precise affair and may take several hours; with the dock flooded, the gate is opened and the ship enters, then the gate is closed and pumping begins. Accurate positioning is vital as the ship settles onto the blocks, prearranged to fit her hull, and to facilitate this move, modern dry docks are usually fitted with guidance systems. In many international ports, dry docks are being constructed that are capable of handling the largest tankers afloat.

The purpose of a floating dock is the same as that of a conventional dry dock, only the method of getting the ship out of the water differs. Ballast tanks are used to raise the submerged dock toward the surface and with it the ship to be repaired. A large floating dock would have a lifting capacity of 20,000 tons (18,000 tonnes), which would enable it to deal with ships of up to 70,000 tons (63,000 tonnes) deadweight.

SEE ALSO: CRANE • FREIGHT HANDLING • HYDRAULICS • LOCK, CANAL • SHIP • TANKER

Doppler Effect

With any wave motion, the observed frequency—the pitch of a sound or the color of a light—depends on the rate at which wave crests reach an observer. If the source of the wave or the observer move relative to the medium in which the wave is traveling, the frequency observed differs from that emitted by the source. This is the Doppler effect, first investigated by the Austrian physicist C. J. Doppler in 1842.

The effect is often evident when a moving source of sound, such as an aircraft, racing car, or train (especially a train sounding a whistle or horn), passes close to the observer. The noise approaches as a high-pitched note and swiftly falls to a much lower pitch, passing through the true pitch for the source at the point where source and observer are closest together and have instantaneously no relative motion along the line joining them.

There are few applications of the Doppler effect with sound and similar vibrations involving matter, but in the case of electromagnetic radiation, it has already been put to many uses. When, in the 19th century, astronomers began to study the spectra of stars, they discovered that in many spectral light had been shifted in frequency. This shift was correctly attributed to the motion of stars relative to Earth. It is a simple step to convert the frequency shift into a velocity, either of approach or of recession, for a star.

In the 20th century astronomers came to realize that the light from the most distant astronomical objects is shifted to the red end of the spectrum—the so-called redshift, which all objects receding from Earth display in their spectra. In the 1920s, the American astronomer Edwin Hubble made the remarkable discovery that the farther away an object is, the larger its redshift. In other words, the farther an object is from Earth, the faster it is receding from us—evidence that the entire Universe is expanding in the aftermath of the Big Bang, in which the Universe was born about 12 billion years ago.

In the field of radar, Doppler effects have become enormously important. By 1950, military radars were beginning to incorporate MTI (moving target indication) by adding circuits that instantly detect reflected signals subject to a Doppler shift while ignoring reflections from fixed targets. Thus the radar could at once spot an aircraft approaching low down in front of a distant hillside. Today Doppler radars are so sensitive they can be used as burglar alarms. A miniature antenna can "illuminate" a courtyard or other space and signal the alarm if an intruder were to creep in at the slowest practical rate of human motion. Other Doppler radars are carried by aircraft as navigation aids to measure relative motion between aircraft and ground with special corrections being applied for wave motion when flying over the ocean. This principle is also used in radar speed checks on cars.

Earth | Light waves | Fixed star

Redshift

Earth | Receding star

◀ Astronomers use the redshift to calculate how fast stars are moving away from Earth. Light from a fixed source produces a consistent set of spectral lines. If this light source begins to move away from Earth, the spectral lines become shifted toward the red end of the spectrum. Conversely, if the light source was moving toward Earth, the spectral lines would be shifted toward the blue end of the spectrum.

DOPPLER EFFECT

As it travels, an airplane emits a sound wave in all directions. By the time the next wave is released, the airplane has moved forward toward the sound wave in front of it. The result is that the waves ahead of the airplane become compressed, giving a higher pitch. The sound waves to the rear are attenuated, giving a lower pitch.

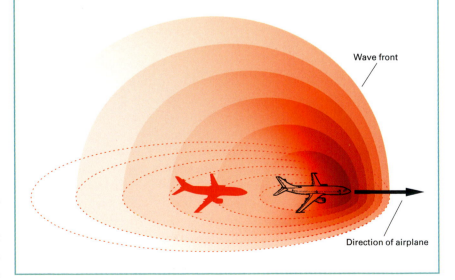

Wave front

Direction of airplane

SEE ALSO: Air traffic control • Astronomy • Astrophysics • Cosmology • Electromagnetic radiation • Light and optics • Navigation • Radar • Radio astronomy • Sound • Wave motion

Drainage

Drainage is the removal or control of surplus surface water, groundwater, and sewage. The main types of drainage are land drainage and urban drainage, which includes sewage disposal.

In its natural state, the earth can control its own drainage fairly well. Vegetation absorbs the initial rainfall and protects the topsoil, whose humus (decomposed organic matter) content can absorb water and whose structure assists the percolation of the remaining water. The surplus flows into streams or rivers or percolates still farther into the ground.

Soils, however, vary greatly in the main single factor that affects their natural drainage—permeability—for example, gravelly soils can be 50,000 times more permeable than clay (the permeability of soil is the rate at which water can seep through it). In addition, higher lands, with their steeper slopes, usually have good natural drainage. The ways that people use land, however, have tended to impair natural drainage. Soils are composed of roughly half solid particles and half pore space,

which is filled with air and water. Without drainage, the pore space can become waterlogged. The uppermost surface of the waterlogged zone is called the water table; in good land, the water table is deeper than 6 ft. (1.8 m) from the soil surface.

The main objectives of land drainage—land reclamation, erosion control, and flood control—are achieved by lowering the water table—that is, taking water from the soil faster than it can accumulate.

There are signs that the Chinese used drainage systems for land restoration as long ago as 2300 B.C.E. Since then, localized independent efforts at drainage improvement have progressed to coordinated regional measures for control of surplus water. A catchment is the drainage area from which reservoirs, lakes, or rivers derive their water.

Land drainage

The four main methods used to drain land are open-channel drains, underground pipes, mole drainage, and pumping. In open-channel drains, or

▲ Big towns and cities need enormous drains and sewers to cope with the daily flow of water being discharged from homes and factories. These brick-lined sewers were built at the beginning of the 20th century and are regularly inspected for blockages, cracks, tree roots, and structural integrity.

protected by finely screened gravel or tarred paper to prevent any inflow of silt, which could cause a blockage.

Mole drainage entails molding drainage channels into the subsoil without an artificial lining. The system requires a stone-free clay soil and an even slope. Channels, parallel to the ground surface and about 2 ft. (61 cm) deep, 6 in. (15 cm) in diameter, and 3 to 5 yds. (2.7–4.6 m) apart, are made by a mole plow. This machine, invented in about 1800 B.C.E., has a vertical knife blade with a horizontal bullet-shaped bottom edge. It is the forerunner of a machine now capable of laying concrete drains in a mole channel, thus avoiding the need for digging and refilling trenches. The modern practice is to use mole channels in combination with pipe systems, the channels running at right angles to the pipes and feeding into the permeable material on top of the pipes.

Pumping water from the water table is carried out in areas where the groundwater level is so low that gravity drainage is not possible. The most common arrangement is for a pumping station to be used to abstract water from a low-lying area. The water is pumped to an embanked river that will carry it out to the sea.

Urban drainage

In towns and cities, drains are needed both for sewage and for the surface water that is collected from the many impermeable surfaces, such as roads and roofs.

There are three principal methods of urban drainage. In the combined system, a single main sewer under the street carries all the sewage and

ditches, excess water drains into a channel by gravity. They can be anything from small ditches, dug by hand, hydraulic excavators, or trenchers and often seen around the perimeters of fields, to large channels 15 ft. (4.6 m) or more deep, constructed by powered dragline excavators. They eventually feed into a river system, lake, or reservoir.

Underground pipes were developed from covered tiles, first used in Britain in the late 18th century and made by bending an ordinary clay tile into an inverted U cross section before baking it and laying it on a flat tile to produce a channel. By the mid-19th century, extruded cylindrical clay pipes were produced by machinery, and concrete pipes appeared a little later. Pipe sections range in length, depending on their diameter and use, but are normally 2 ft. (61 cm) or more in length.

Concrete and clay pipes have spigot joints—whereby a larger diameter lip is created at one end of the pipe so that the small end of the next pipe fits into it. This jointing system also provides some flexibility in case of ground subsidence. The pipes are placed in temporary trenches of varying depth, generally with a gradual fall towards the outlet. The trenches can be made using trenching machines or dug by hand, and there are special trenching machines that can be used to install lengths of plastic pipe.

When the pipe run has been inserted, gravel or permeable filler is placed on top of the pipes and finally the topsoil is replaced. Water can flow into the pipes at the joints, and these have to be

▲ Installing a septic tank. A four-person family will fill a tank like this in less than a month. In areas where discharge to soil is not permitted it must be emptied by a sewage truck and the sludge taken away for treatment at the local sewage works.

SEPTIC TANK

Rural areas without main drainage often rely on septic tanks, which afford rudimentary treatment to sewage. Sewage enters a number of chambers, which provide initial settlement to remove grit, allow bacteria to digest the organic components, and then return the cleaned effluent via a series of narrow pipes into the soil some distance underground.

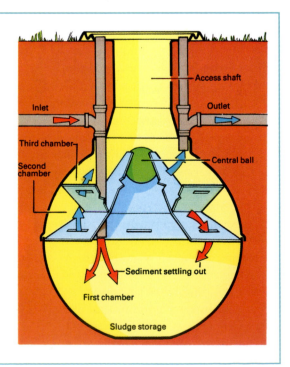

surplus surface water to a sewage treatment works. It is very expensive to have main sewers large enough to carry off all the rainfall that might occur in a heavy storm, and it would tax sewage treatment works to handle such large volumes. Therefore, it has been common practice in the past to provide storm-water overflows that discharge directly into rivers when the water level in the sewer is too high.

Although the amount of sewage relative to the amount of rainwater is low in these circumstances, and thus pollution is not usually a problem, because of increasing environmental standards, many systems are now incorporating either huge over-sized pipes to absorb the extra flows until they can be treated or large holding tanks in which the storm water can be contained until the storm is past. The overflow system is simple and cheap and is still used in rural areas where the amount of sewage is not high and main drainage is distant and therefore expensive to connect to. Overflows used to be common in seaside towns; sewage treatment works have since been built at many coastal locations to ensure that the effluent discharging to the sea is clean.

An alternative drainage method is the separate system, in which a main sewer under the street carries all the domestic sewage and industrial effluents to a sewage treatment works and a main drain carries all the surplus surface water into a river, lake, or reservoir. This method has largely been superseded by a partially separate system in which a main sewer under the street carries all the drainage from buildings (both sewage and the surface water from roofs) and a main drain carries all the surface water from the roads. Whichever system is used, rainwater from roofs is collected in a similar way.

Rainwater is drained into a gutter around the roof perimeter by the slope of the roof and is discharged through vertical downpipes into the drain system. Roads are built with a camber to drain surface water into roadside gutters. The surface water is then discharged at intervals through gullies into the drain system. On rural roads, surface water is often led straight into open roadside ditches or French drains, which are trenches filled with pebbles or large stones through which the water can easily percolate before seeping into the ground. Embankments are often drained by French drains.

A pipe network for urban drainage looks something like the branches of a tree—small lateral runs join household drainage systems to larger drains in the road, and these in turn join larger and larger drains until they reach main, or trunk, drains. These huge main drains are laid on a gradient and eventually feed either by gravity or,

▲ A trench-digging machine adapted for laying plastic pipe as it moves forward. Other types of piping can be fed into the ground by hand.

if a natural fall is not possible, by pumping into a sewage treatment works.

Drains vary in diameter from 4 in. (10 cm) or less for household purposes to several yards for main sewers, according to the amount of flow they are expected to carry. Small drains are usually constructed from cast iron, stoneware pipe, or increasingly in plastic, such as the 2 in. (5 cm) French drainage system. Some modern drainage pipes are made of rigid plastics, and both types can be fused together at the ends to create a smooth, waterproof joint.

As pipe size increases, precast concrete is used. Trenching methods similar to those for land drainage are used, but concrete foundations are usually provided to resist damage to the pipes by ground settlement. Also, the pipe joints are made watertight by sealing the spigot with cement or bituminous compounds. A round rubber gasket is often used, sandwiched between the spigot and the end of the next pipe to ensure the system remains relatively waterproof. Glass-reinforced plastic (GRP) can also be used for drainage, and such pipes can also be joined together to make a seamless whole.

If drains or sewers are particularly large or deep, tunneling methods may be used. Drains are laid on a gradient to provide the required flow to the point of discharge. For maintenance purposes, covered inspection chambers known as manholes are fitted at regular intervals, providing access from the road surface into the drain.

SEE ALSO:	Flood control • Land reclamation • Pipe and tube manufacture • Plumbing • Wastewater treatment

Dredger

Dredgers, also called dredges, are floating excavation machines used for keeping harbors, canals, and navigable waterways free from excessive accumulations of mud and silt. In modern times, several other functions of dredgers have developed, including supplying material for land reclamation, collecting gravel and sand for the construction industry, and mining diamonds, gold, tin, and other minerals from the inshore sea bed.

Early dredging involved the manually operated bag and spoon and manual or horse-drawn rakes. The horse-powered mud mills developed in the 17th century were the forerunners of the modern dredger, which developed rapidly during the 19th century with the application of steam power. The bucket dredger was the prime product of the 19th century, though grab, dipper, and suction dredges were also introduced. The 20th century has seen the steam engine superseded by diesel power with either direct-drive or

▼ This grab dredger, equipped with three multirope chains, can load a 35,000 cu. ft. (1,000 m³) hopper in three to four hours. It is particularly useful for excavating awkward corners in tight spaces such as docks.

electric transmission and by the considerable development of the suction dredger in particular. Dredging performance, efficiency, and accuracy have been much increased by engineering developments and more recently by the widespread application of electronic position-fixing and monitoring devices.

Bucket dredger

The bucket dredger was for many years the most common type, and many such machines are still in use today. It is essentially a chain-and-bucket conveyor, strung on a frame called a ladder, which is hydraulically raised and lowered at the appropriate angle to the seabed. The bucket dredger is usually not self-propelled and must be towed to the site by a tugboat. It is used in conjunction with hopper barges, which haul the dredged material out to sea to dump it. The bucket dredger is secured with a pattern of anchors (usually six) and can be maneuvered over its working area to a limited extent by pulling in one anchor cable and letting out another.

Bucket dredgers can handle a large range of seabed material but are restricted to relatively calm conditions. Their ability to cut into dry land has made them useful for excavating new dock basins and canals.

Grab dredger

The grab dredger is a vessel, normally self-propelled and fitted with its own hopper, carrying one or more rotating-jib cranes fitted with clamshell grabs. They are particularly useful for working into the corners of docks and, though working at anchor, use only light moorings as the dredging operations involve only lifting forces. When they are fairway dredging, they work by digging a series of holes into which spoil from the remaining high points is washed by wave action, resulting in an even channel depth.

Dipper dredger

The usual dipper dredger is a nonpropelled pontoon without a hopper, mounted with a mechanical box-shaped shovel fixed to a boom. The boom enables the shovel to swing round in a wide arc. As the scoop of this shovel is rigidly connected to the dredger, considerable leverage can be exerted against the material to be dredged, and hard material can thus be cleared. To counter this thrust, dipper dredges are normally anchored by means of spuds—pointed poles extending downward from the dredger to the river or seabed.

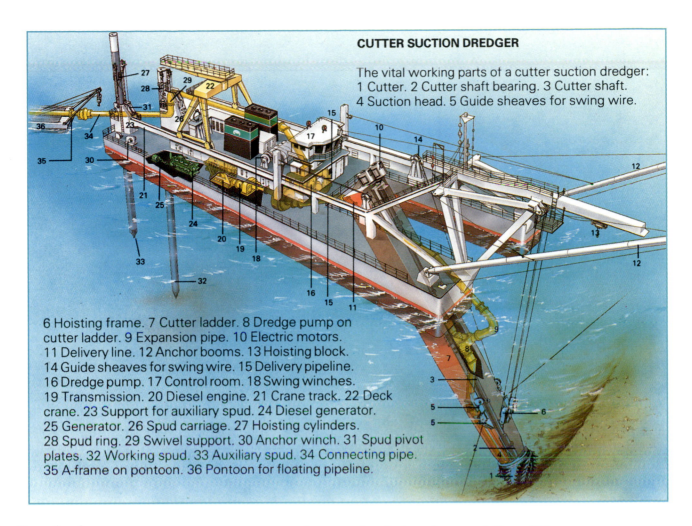

CUTTER SUCTION DREDGER

The vital working parts of a cutter suction dredger:
1 Cutter. 2 Cutter shaft bearing. 3 Cutter shaft.
4 Suction head. 5 Guide sheaves for swing wire.

6 Hoisting frame. 7 Cutter ladder. 8 Dredge pump on cutter ladder. 9 Expansion pipe. 10 Electric motors. 11 Delivery line. 12 Anchor booms. 13 Hoisting block. 14 Guide sheaves for swing wire. 15 Delivery pipeline. 16 Dredge pump. 17 Control room. 18 Swing winches. 19 Transmission. 20 Diesel engine. 21 Crane track. 22 Deck crane. 23 Support for auxiliary spud. 24 Diesel generator. 25 Generator. 26 Spud carriage. 27 Hoisting cylinders. 28 Spud ring. 29 Swivel support. 30 Anchor winch. 31 Spud pivot plates. 32 Working spud. 33 Auxiliary spud. 34 Connecting pipe. 35 A-frame on pontoon. 36 Pontoon for floating pipeline.

Suction dredgers

There are several types of suction dredgers, all making use of a centrifugal pump. The impeller of such a pump causes suction by its spinning action, which pulls water and solids up from the bottom through an airtight tube. The discharge of the tube is directed into the center of the spinning impeller, and the discharge vent of the pump is around the outside of the casing. Some dredgers have several pumps going at once. The tube can be made flexible with airtight fittings at the joints.

Where the material to be dredged is soft and granular, such as sand or gravel, no further refinements are needed, but for other applications, the suction device has been adapted for use with cutters, drag-arms, and scrapers (dustpans) to loosen the material or break it up. The sucking end of the suction tube is located near the mechanical device in order to collect the spoil as it is broken up.

The suction drag-arm vessel has a conventional sea-going hull, and the drag-arm is mounted underneath it. Hoppers for the spoil are also built into the hull. The cutterhead dredger has a revolving cutter at the end of a ladder—the cutter chops impacted material out of the bottom so that the suction device can handle it.

Some suction dredgers have spuds for stability in relatively shallow water; some have floating pipelines that can be extended some distance from the ship for dumping the spoil as soon as it is sucked up. Suction dredgers can be fitted with chutes in such a way that they deliver the spoil to waiting barges or dockside dump trucks. A suction dredger used in a land reclamation project can suck the spoil from the bottom and "shoot" the solids straight over a nearby embankment into the area being filled in. Water picked up along with the solids by the suction operation is allowed to spill out by means of overflow troughs, the solid material settling to the bottom of the trough or hopper.

The largest modern dredgers have hopper capacities of between 16,000 and 30,000 tons (14,500–27,000 tonnes). The building of Hong Kong's new airport at Chek Lap Kok was one of the most massive dredging operations of modern times. During construction, 70 percent of the world's dredging fleet was engaged in building the island on which the airport now stands.

SEE ALSO: Canal • Compressor and pump • Dam • Dock • Drainage • Flood control • Land reclamation • Lock, canal • Navigation • Quarrying • Ship • Siphon • Tanker

Drill

The electric drill is a portable drilling machine, powered by its own electric motor carried in the case. Apart from the motor, the essential components are the chuck, which holds the drill, and a simple gear train for gearing the speed of the motor down to a suitable speed for the drill.

The domestic electric drill usually takes the shape of a pistol, the pistol grip being a good example of ergonomic design, that is, correctly designed for easy usage. The power cord enters the case at the base of the grip, and the on-off switch is the trigger. Often an interlock is provided so that the trigger need not be held down continuously while using the drill. On larger, heavier models there are other handles on the case as well as the grip so that both hands can safely be used to bring pressure on the work. The other handle may be a simple bar extending from the case at the top, opposite the grip; it may be a stirrup at the back end of the case, opposite the chuck; or its position may be adjustable.

The chuck

The chuck is a three-jawed, self-centering device that protrudes from the transmission end of the case and holds the drill bit. Turning the outer sleeve of the chuck in a counter-clockwise direction opens the jaws; the other direction closes it, final tightening being achieved with the use of a key supplied with the drill.

The motor

Housed in the case is an electric motor of the series, or universal, type. The advantages of this type of motor are that it is suitable for use with either direct or alternating current and that it produces a high torque at low speeds: as one pushes harder while drilling, thus increasing the load, the speed decreases but the torque increases. The gear train reduces the speed to about 2,500 rpm. A disadvantage of this type of motor is that it provides interference with nearby radio and TV reception, but it can be overcome by fitting various chokes and capacitors to the motor circuitry.

Drill attachments

Drill bits are normally of the twist-drill type, having two helical grooves running from the twin cutting edges for about three-quarters of the length, the remainder being plain shank for inserting into the

▼ The chuck of the portable electric drill is tightened with the key provided. Drill bits can be changed easily to suit the material being drilled.

chuck. The capacity of electric drills ranges from ¼ in. (6.35 mm) to ½ in. (12.7 mm). Sizes larger than ½ in. are usually difficult to handle in a portable power tool.

An electric drill with a given capacity is designed to handle a drilling job of that size in drilling metal; a drill bit of a larger size, with a cut-down shank to fit the chuck, may be used with caution to drill wood or plastic. Caution is always necessary when drilling metal. Certain types of steel may need a very hard cutting edge, a specially ground angle on the cutting edge, lubrication while drilling, or all three. When drilling a hole all the way through a piece of metal, the pressure brought to bear must be carefully applied as the bit goes through, other-

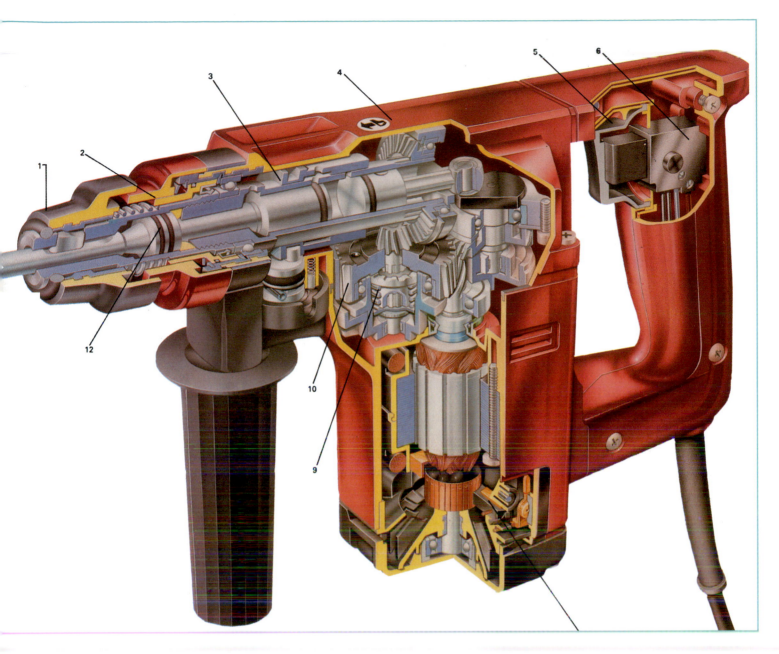

wise the emerging bit may "grab" the rough edge of the hole, giving the tool a severe wrench that can cause loss of control or snap off the bit itself.

Two-speed and percussion electric drills are also available. The first provides a lower alternative speed of about 900 rpm; the second gives a percussive effect combined with low speed and is designed for use on concrete and masonry. Because of the abrasive nature of concrete and masonry, drill bits with specially hardened cutting edges must be used—these are normally sold as masonry bits.

The versatility of the electric drill is extended by the availability of attachments designed to make use of the rotary motion, such as rotary files, sanding disks, hole saws, grindstones, and so on. An electric drill is often designed to be fitted to a bench- or table-mounted machine to turn it into a drill-press or a lathe attachment or for certain applications such as use with a jig.

▶ Drill bits need to be specially hardened to tackle masonry and brickwork. Cordless drills that can be recharged from mains electricity are becoming increasingly popular for household use and areas that are not close to an electricity supply. Although these drills reduce the risk of electric shocks, they do not have the power of an electric drill when penetrating a hard surface.

SEE ALSO:	ABRASIVE • BEARING AND BUSHING • GEAR • JACKHAMMER • MACHINE TOOL • PNEUMATIC TOOL • TOOL MANUFACTURE

Drilling Rig, Oil

The first producing oil well was drilled in Pennsylvania in 1859. Since then, over two million boreholes have been sunk worldwide. Many of these have failed to find commercial quantities of oil, as opposed to the exceptionally productive few. Drilling is a very expensive business, and a costly gamble too, hence the importance of preliminary geological surveys.

Offshore oil wells are more expensive than those on land, but they are not substantially different in operation. Most of the world's oil wells have so far been drilled on land, but now, partly because most of the likely land areas have already been explored, drilling at sea is increasingly important. Drilling for oil has been described as analogous to a dentist drilling a tooth with his patient the length of a football field away, thus giving an idea of the problems involved in controlling from the surface a drill at the bottom of a well up to 3 miles (5 km) deep.

The drill string and bit

Oil drilling is done by rotating a drilling bit to make a hole. The bit may be a fishtailed steel design for soft ground, but it is usually a rotary bit with hardened teeth. In very hard rock, diamond or tungsten carbide teeth are used, and it may take an hour to drill 1 ft. (30 cm). In softer rock, however, rates of about 100 yds. (90 m) per hour are possible. The bit is fixed to a "string" of drill pipes that rotate it as it bores the hole. Each length of pipe is normally 30 ft. (9 m) long and about 4½ or 5½ in. (11 or 14 cm) in diameter. The pipes are joined by heavy tapered threads.

The pipes situated just above the bit are heavier than those in the rest of the string. They are called drill collars and are used to put enough weight on the drill to force it into the ground while keeping the rest of the drill string in tension. The whole of the drill string may weigh several hundred tons, and if it were allowed to bear on the drill under compression, the string could easily break or jam in the hole. In fact, wells are designed so that most of the weight of the drill string is taken by the drilling equipment on the surface.

Rotary drilling

The most obvious part of the equipment on the surface is the derrick, looking rather like an electricity transmission tower and up to 200 ft. (60 m) high. Its height is needed to hoist lengths of drill pipe into place and to stack lengths of several drill pipes screwed together. The drill string is rotated

in the well through a rotating table at the base of the derrick driven at about 120 rpm by a powerful motor. This rotating table has a central hole, which is square or hexagonal in shape, through which a length of square or hexagonal cross-section special pipe known as a kelly, or grief stem, can slide and by which it can be turned. The kelly is the top section of the drill string and drives the rest of the string as it is turned by the rotary table. The drill string, consisting of the kelly, pipes, and bit, is suspended on a hook from the top of the derrick by cables and pulleys. As the bit cuts into the ground, the kelly slides through the hole in the rotary table. When the bit has descended almost the length of the kelly, the drill string is wedged in place, the kelly is disconnected, a new length of drill pipe is added to the string, the kelly is reconnected, and drilling begins again.

This operation will have to be carried out over 300 times in drilling a 10,000 ft. (3,000 m) well. Each time it is done, a team of workers has to carry out hard and exacting physical work in connecting and disconnecting pipes and wedges and taking new pipe out of the stack. Sheer hard work, as well as highly developed operating skill, is still a most essential part of oil drilling. As drilling continues, the drill itself becomes blunt, perhaps after only a few hours if it is in hard rock. Then the whole drill string has to be taken out of the hole so that the bit can be removed and a new one put on. This "round trip" can take up to a day to do. As the drill pipe comes up, it is unscrewed in lengths of three, not in single joints, to speed up operations.

During drilling, specially prepared mud, a complex colloidal suspension, usually in water, is

▲ The steel tower of the Magnus oil platform stands taller than the Eiffel Tower in France. After construction, it had to be towed over 350 miles (575 km) to the drilling site and positioned exactly over an area no bigger than a room in a house.

pumped down inside the drill pipes through a jet in the bit and back to the surface in the annular space between the drill pipe and the sides of the hole. This space exists because the diameter of the drill is always larger than the diameter of the drill pipe. The mud circulates through the well quite slowly and cools and lubricates the drill. It also flushes cuttings up to the surface, where they are separated from the mud, which is then reused. In returning to the surface, the mud coats the sides of the hole and helps to keep it from caving in. The mud also helps to control any flow of oil or gas from the well. The weight of the column of mud is generally greater than any likely pressure

of oil or gas, so the oil cannot get to the surface until the weight of mud is reduced. In early wells before mud was used, any oil or gas found under pressure shot at once to the surface, causing a gusher, which was both difficult to get under control and liable to catch fire.

While drilling, mud is invaluable in preserving the walls of the well and helping to prevent immediate caving in. Permanent protection is given as soon as possible by lining the hole with steel casing, which is fixed in position by forcing cement between the casing and the walls of the borehole. Casing consists of very strong thick-walled pipes, of slightly smaller diameter than the

▼ Drilling platforms are frequently situated many miles out at sea. Because they are so remote and drilling takes place 24 hours a day, they have to be self-contained and able to house the crew for months at a time. A helicopter pad is usually available for visitors and access in an emergency.

◀ An exploratory drilling rig. If the drilling mud appears to be disappearing below ground, this is a sign of porous rock and possibly oil, gas, or water.

drilling mud in the hole is insufficient to hold back any high-pressure gas, oil, or water that is encountered during the drilling process, this situation could result in the drilling mud being blown out of the hole. In such circumstances, the blowout preventer can be closed by a hydraulic control system to shut off the well entirely until the pressure can be relieved.

When oil is found, the first indication is usually from hydrocarbon analysis of the drilling mud returning to the surface. The oil is tested for quality and flow rate, and if this is satisfactory, production tubing is cemented in, and a Christmas Tree, so called because of the resemblance in shape of the complex of valves and tubing that makes it up to the familiar fir, is fixed at the well head.

Offshore drilling

Offshore drilling is being done in many parts of the world, but the North Sea is one of the most active areas. It is also the most difficult area so far explored, because of adverse weather conditions and the distance from the coast of most of the fields. Drilling has been going on for gas and oil in the North Sea since the mid 1960s, in comparatively shallow water. Intensive oil drilling is now being carried out in deeper water under more difficult circumstances. The whole of the North Sea is shallow compared with the oceans; much of it is between 100 ft. (30 m) and 650 ft. (200 m) deep. This is typical of the so-called continental shelf areas that make up about 10 percent of the world's undersea surface.

Types of marine platforms

To support the drilling rig, ancillary equipment and crew's quarters, some form of floating platform is needed. The first wells were drilled from converted ships, and these are still in use, but a limiting factor is their tendency to drag even the heaviest anchors during rough weather. Fixed, or self-contained, platforms are used in shallow water to a depth of about 100 ft. (30 m). Another type of rig is the self-elevating (jack-up) platform, which has an operational limit of 300 ft. (90 m) or so, because of bending stress in the leg supports. It can be towed into position and the legs jacked down until they stand on the sea bottom and then jacked further until the platform is well above the sea surface, clear of the highest waves. For greater water depths, semisubmersible rigs are used. They have several large hulls with long legs holding a platform above them, and the hulls are ballasted so as to sink about 65 ft. (20 m) below the surface of the water. As with jack-up rigs, the platform is still well above the water and clear of the waves. The rig may be held in place by multi-

borehole, that are screwed together and lowered into the well when the drill string is removed. The first string of casing is normally cemented after a few hundred feet of hole have been sunk. When the cement has hardened, drilling is resumed using a bit of smaller diameter than the one previously in use.

As the hole is deepened, successively narrower strings of casing are added, each new string passing through the string previously introduced and extending from the top of the borehole.

A blowout preventer (BOP) is fitted as soon as the first stage string of casing has been set. The BOP is really a large safety valve that is firmly fixed to the top of the casing. If the weight of the ple anchors or it may be dynamically positioned. In this method, multiple propulsion units on the rig respond to signals from a beacon on the sea bottom and keep the rig exactly in position in relation to the beacon, even in the worst weather.

At the hull level, a semisubmersible may be about 200 ft. (60 m) wide by 250 ft. (76 m) long, and its operating draft will be 60 to 90 ft (18–27 m). One rig could cost up to $50 million. Large semi-submersibles can drill to a depth of 33,000 ft. (10,000 m) in up to 1,000 ft. (300 m) of water. They can survive in winds of up to 136 mph (220 km/h) and in waves of up to 85 ft. (26 m).

Producing wells

After exploration rigs have been used to find oil, they are moved on to other areas for further exploration. In order to drill producing wells, production platforms are installed. These enormous steel or concrete platforms stand on the sea bottom and, by angling the borehole using a technique known as directional drilling, up to 30 producing wells can be drilled from each platform. Oil is treated on the platform to remove gas and water and is brought ashore by pipeline or by

tanker. The most recent offshore development has been the drilling of producing wells with sophisticated seabed well heads. Oil is taken from them to a floating production system mounted on an anchored tanker or a semisubmersible platform. In the mid 1980s, there were 57 subsea installations active worldwide, although some of these were satellite wells connected to existing fixed production platforms. Subsea techniques can show great savings compared with fixed platform systems, but they will probably only supplement rather than replace them.

Developments in drilling technology

Productivity of drilling platforms increased in the late 1990s with the introduction of the new technique of horizontal drilling. As the name suggests, the well is driven through the oil-bearing strata at a horizontal or shallow angle, which increases the wall area of the well in the productive rock. As a result, a horizontal well can produce as much oil as eight vertical or directionally drilled wells.

Another development has been the production of the turbine drill bit. In this, the circulating drilling mud is used to drive the drill bit via a turbine at the bottom of the drill string. By doing so, it eliminates the need for the whole of the drill string to rotate and so saves energy.

Oil recovery

Once the drill has reached the oil, pressure from dissolved natural gas or underground water causes it to rise up the borehole, where it can be pumped straight to a pipeline or a waiting tanker. Jack pumps or nodding donkeys are used at wells where the natural pressure is too low to force the oil out at a consistent rate. As the well becomes exhausted, a variety of methods are used to extract the last oil from the reservoir. These include pumping water or waste natural gas back into the rock to increase the reservoir pressure. Chemical flooding uses detergents to loosen oil trapped in pores in the rock that then rises up to the main oil layer. More viscous oil reserves can be made to flow freely by injecting steam, which heats and pushes the oil toward the borehole. Fire flooding combines steam flooding and gas injection. A fire is started at the lower margin of the reserve with the aid of pumped air. The heat and steam produced make the oil more mobile, and combustion gases, such as carbon dioxide, increase the pressure in the reservoir.

◄ The Magnus oil platform tower afloat over the target area. One bad storm at this stage could have written off 40,000 tons (36,000 tonnes) of steel.

SEE ALSO: ABRASIVE • DIAMOND • GAS INDUSTRY • LUBRICATION • OIL EXPLORATION AND PRODUCTION • PRESSURE

Drug and Alcohol Testing

Drug and alcohol testing encompasses a number of techniques for establishing whether a person has taken alcohol, narcotics, or other controlled substances. In the case of alcohol testing, the goal of the test might be to determine whether the amount of alcohol in a motorist's bloodstream exceeds the permitted concentration for a person in charge of a vehicle. Some parents use regular or random narcotics testing to discourage their children from experimenting with drugs, and some companies use narcotics testing to establish whether a current or potential employee has used narcotics in the recent past and might therefore be a liability in the workplace. National and international sports organizations require tests for controlled substances that promote athletic performance and give an unfair advantage to users.

Laboratory testing

The most reliable and precise forms of testing use techniques of analytical chemistry to determine the presence and concentrations of substances in samples of blood, hair, saliva, or urine. Such techniques include gas chromatography (GC), gas chromatography in combination with mass spectrometry (GC-MS), and high-performance liquid chromatography (HPLC). These tests sometimes indicate the presence of the controlled substance itself, other times they measure the concentrations of metabolites—substances that form as the body breaks down a controlled substance.

The results of testing must be interpreted with great care. The levels of controlled substances and their metabolites depend on how much of a substance was taken, when it was taken, and how it was taken—orally or intravenously, for example. The interpretation of metabolite concentrations is particularly complex, since a given metabolite might derive from a number of substances, not all of them controlled. The poppy seeds on a bagel contain enough morphinelike substances to form metabolites that could suggest heroin use, for example, so that a metabolite that forms only from diamorphine (heroin) must be detected to confirm a positive result.

The abuse of certain substances is difficult to detect directly. One such substance is erythropoietin (EPO), which boosts stamina by increasing the red blood cell count. EPO is a natural hormone, so the presence of EPO or its metabolites in blood does not necessarily imply the malicious use of EPO to enhance performance in endurance

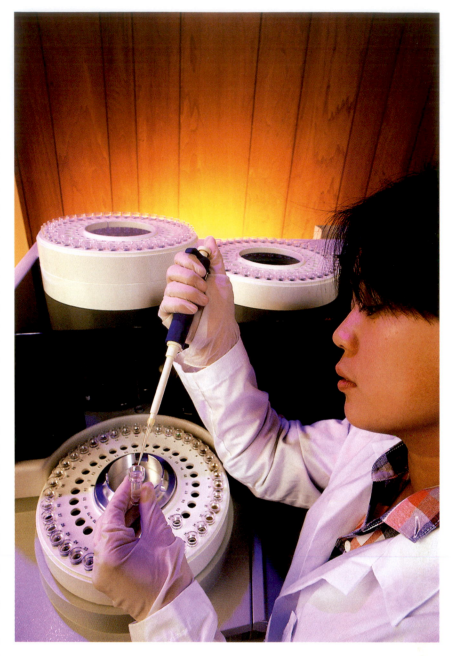

▲ Urine tests are the most common method of identification for a wide range of drugs, such as anabolic steroids, cocaine, and amphetamines, as they are easily traceable.

events, such as long-distance cycling. In August 2000, the International Olympics Committee ratified a test that identifies EPO abuse by detecting the levels of five substances in blood that indicate recent bursts of increased rates of red blood cell formation consistent with EPO abuse.

Portable drug-testing kits

Parents sometimes wish to test their children for drug abuse. Home drug-testing kits are cheaper than full-scale laboratory analysis and offer the advantage of confidentiality. Such tests indicate the presence of controlled substances and their metabolites as color changes on test strips. The color changes develop—if at all—within a few minutes of applying drops of urine to the test strip. Such strips can detect cocaine (including crack), methamphetamine (crystal meth), opiates, PCP, and THC from cannabis.

Portable alcohol detectors

Traffic police use a number of portable alcohol detectors to determine whether motorists have been drinking and, if so, whether the amount drunk has caused a blood-alcohol concentration (BAC) greater than the allowed limit; similar tests are also used on employees in high-risk occupations, such as aircraft pilots, operators of nuclear plants, ships' captains, and railroad engineers. Portable detectors measure the concentration of alcohol in breath, which is related to the BAC, to determine whether more accurate tests using blood or urine samples are necessary.

Inflatable-bag breathalyzers

The cheapest but least accurate of the portable breath analyzers is the inflatable-bag breathalyzer. A breathalyzer kit consists of a mouthpiece, a sealed transparent glass tube containing a mixture of chemicals, and an inflatable bag. For use, the ends of the tube are broken off, the mouthpiece attached to one end, and the bag to the other. The test subject is instructed to take a deep breath and blow through the tube until the bag is fully inflated. The bag controls the sample size, so the amount of alcohol in the sample is converted into a concentration. Any alcohol in the breath is

◀ Creatine is a substance that occurs naturally in the muscles of the body but which is increasingly being taken as a supplement by athletes and bodybuilders to help increase muscle mass and thus enhance performance. Drug-testing authorities are finding it difficult to assess whether the levels of substances like creatine found in the urine of athletes are a result of natural processes or are due to a supplementary intake of dietary nutrients.

oxidized by the chemicals in the tube, which change color as they react. The amount of alcohol in the breath determines how far down the tube the color change extends, so it is possible to estimate roughly the amount of alcohol exhaled and, therefore, the BAC.

Inflatable-bag devices are of limited accuracy, however. When they were the most common roadside alcohol test, a significant percentage of drivers who had failed the breathalyzer test were subsequently found to be below the legal limit in more accurate laboratory tests for body alcohol using either blood or urine samples.

Infrared detectors

Infrared alcohol detectors estimate the concentration of alcohol in breath using a beam of infrared light, filters, and a photocell detector. Infrared light causes most types of molecules to vibrate, and a given type of molecule has a "fingerprint" of infrared frequencies that it absorbs as its vibration becomes more intense.

Filters in an infrared alcohol detector select frequencies of infrared light that are strongly absorbed by alcohol molecules but that pass straight through other common substances in breath without being absorbed. A sample of breath in a chamber absorbs those frequencies to an extent that depends on the concentration of alcohol in the breath and the length of the beam's path through the sample chamber. The voltage generated in the photocell by the infrared light that falls on it therefore decreases with increasing alcohol concentration. A microprocessor uses the photocell's output voltage to calculate a value for the concentration of alcohol in a subject's breath.

Provided certain precautions are taken when the test is administered, it is possible to deduce a test subject's blood-alcohol concentration from the breath-alcohol level, since a close relationship exists between the two concentrations. The accuracy of infrared alcohol detectors is witnessed by the much lower incidence of false-positive results when compared with inflatable-bag detectors.

▲ A fuel-cell detector in operation. A green light indicates that the device is ready for measurement, and it remains green if no alcohol is detected or if the level of alcohol is well below the acceptable limit after the subject has blown into the mouthpiece (white tube at top). A red light indicates an alcohol reading in excess of the legal limit, and a yellow light indicates a borderline result.

Fuel-cell detectors

While infrared detectors are much more accurate than inflatable-bag detectors, they are costly and relatively inaccurate at low concentrations of alcohol. An alternative electronic device that is cheaper and more sensitive is based on fuel cells. A fuel cell consists of an absorbent material soaked with electrolyte and sandwiched between two platinum black electrodes. Hydrogen-containing compounds react at one electrode, while oxygen reacts at the other; the products of the reaction include oxidation products and an amount of electrical energy that depends on the amount of hydrogen-containing material used by the cell.

When a subject exhales through the sampler of a fuel-cell device, a small piston draws a fixed volume of the subject's breath into a chamber next to the fuel cell. Immediately, alcohol in the sample starts to be consumed by the fuel cell, which produces an electrical current in a circuit that links the two electrodes through a resistor. The oxidation products of alcohol (ethanol, C_2H_5OH) are thought to be acetic acid (CH_3COOH) and water (H_2O). The current rises to a peak and then gradually diminishes as the alcohol is consumed. Eventually, the current falls to zero as the last of the alcohol is consumed. A microprocessor integrates the current output of the cell, which is the equivalent of measuring the area under a graph of current against time. The value so obtained is directly related to the amount of alcohol in the sample and, therefore, to the BAC.

Fuel-cell devices have several advantages over other types of alcohol detectors. They are compact and robust, which makes them ideal for portable applications. They are highly sensitive and accurate and highly specific to alcohol against other compounds that commonly occur in breath. For this reason, they can be relied on to give alcohol measurements for use in legal evidence.

SEE ALSO: Alcohol • Biochemistry • Chemistry, analytical • Fuel cell • Oxidation and reduction

Dry Cleaning

◀ Dry cleaning machinery used for cleaning extremely dirty industrial clothing. It uses perchloroethylene, the most commonly used cleaning solvent.

Dry cleaning, like so many other benefits of modern living, was discovered by accident. The discovery was made by a French dyeworks owner, Jean-Baptiste Jolly, in Paris in 1825, as a result of a simple accident. A maid in the Jolly household upset a kerosene lamp on a tablecloth. Jolly was amazed to discover that the area over which the kerosene had spilled was so clear that it showed up the dirtiness of the rest of the cloth. Operating from his dyeworks, he offered this new discovery as dry cleaning to distinguish it from the soap-and-water process previously used.

At the time of the discovery of the dry cleaning process, all garments were made from natural fibers such as wool, cotton, and so on, that swelled when immersed in water and shrank on drying. The French public realized the value of dry cleaning when they found that garments could be totally immersed in the inert solvent and thoroughly cleaned without distortion through shrinkage. By using the new cleaning process, dirt ingrained over many years was gently floated away. Dry cleaning spread to other countries where it was at first known as French Cleaning because of its origin. As it developed into an industry, the first crude solvent, kerosene, was replaced by benzine (an aliphatic petroleum hydrocarbon not to be confused with the aromatic compound, benzene, spelled with an "e") and later by thinner (a volatile liquid used to dilute paint), which is still used in many countries as a cleaning solvent. In the United States, a controlled-quality thinner known as Stoddard solvent is widely used.

Benzine has a flash point of 32°F (0°C), and the fire risk involved reduced its suitability as a cleaning solvent; thinner in its controlled form as Stoddard solvent has a flash point of 100°F (38°C) and is very much safer. The flash point is described as the temperature at which a solvent gives off enough vapor to ignite immediately upon contact with a small flame.

Solvents used today

When the dry cleaning industry moved out of its factory-based environment into local shopping areas, a nonflammable solvent was required. The first of these to be established was trichloroethylene ($CCl_2=CHCl$), a powerful solvent and an efficient cleaner. The introduction of clothing made from triacetate rayon, which could be affected by this solvent, caused a general change to perchloroethylene ($CCl_2=CCl_2$), which is suitable for most garments brought to the dry cleaner. Known as perc, it quickly became established and is still the most widely used solvent in automatic dry cleaning machines as displayed in on-the-spot unit cleaners. Perc is a clear, colorless liquid with a sharp, sweet odor that does not cause dyed fabrics to bleed. It can be recycled and reused, making it a cost-effective solution for dry cleaning, but it is toxic to humans and the environment.

Fashion fabrics are subject to continuous change; some of the new fabrics and trimmings on sale are heat sensitive and some are sensitive even to perchloroethylene. This class of fabrics can be handled in a fluorinated solvent in the Freon range (once used widely as refrigerants), called solvent 113. It will dry at a low, safe temperature and, being a gentle solvent, is suitable for delicate fabrics. There is a further fluorinated hydrocarbon solvent, solvent 11, used in some European countries, that has a low-temperature drying facility similar to 113, but its solvency power is near to that of perchloroethylene. Concerns about the effect these volatile chemicals have on the ozone layer are leading to increasing restrictions on their use in the European Union and the United States, and investigations are underway into alternative methods of cleaning clothes.

Dry cleaning process

In response to the public demand for a cleaning service conveniently sited in the local shopping area, the machine manufacturers began to develop self-contained machines that would complete the whole dry cleaning operation as sequential processes (cleaning, drying, aerating, and so on), producing the garments ready for inspection, spotting (stain removal), and finishing.

Perc is a very suitable solvent for use in such automatic machines. Its strength of 90 on the Kauri-Butanol scale (an indication of solvency power) is adequate for cleaning without being too severe. The action of the solvent is to dissolve

DRY CLEANING MACHINE

Professional dry cleaning machines are enclosed units linked to solvent-recovery systems. Articles to be cleaned are put in the perforated drum in the cleaning cylinder. After cleaning and solvent rinsing, clothes are spun to remove excess solvent and dried. Used solvent is filtered and purified by distillation.

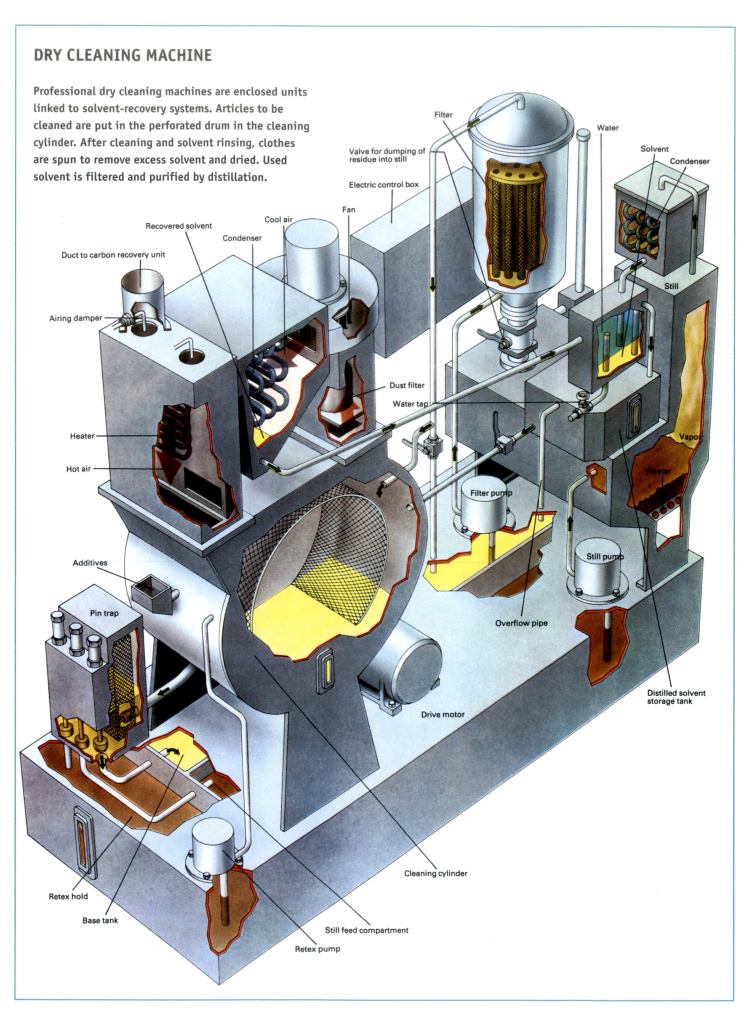

Recovered solvent

Condenser

Cool air

Fan

Filter

Water

Solvent

Condenser

Valve for dumping of residue into still

Electric control box

Duct to carbon recovery unit

Airing damper

Still

Heater

Hot air

Dust filter

Water tap

Vapor

Heater

Filter pump

Additives

Still pump

Pin trap

Overflow pipe

Distilled solvent storage tank

Drive motor

Retex hold

Base tank

Cleaning cylinder

Still feed compartment

Retex pump

grease, and dry cleaning works because most of the soiling on the garments is composed of dirt particles associated with oily matter, by which the particles become attached to the fabric. The solvent dissolves the grease, and thus the dirt particles are loosened. This process is assisted by the agitation of the perforated rotating drum in which the articles are placed until all the dirt is removed. Not all the dirt on garments can be removed by the solvent, and a small percentage of water-carrying detergents is added to the solvent to remove water-soluble dirt, such as food and beverage stains. After cleaning and solvent rinsing, the garments are spun at high speed to extract excess solvent, followed by a drying process in which the clothes are gently tumbled in a stream of warm air.

The used solvent is then filtered to remove the solid dirt particles, followed by distillation to remove the soluble contaminants; thus the solvent is continuously purified for reuse. Perc distills easily in a simple vessel similar in operation to a kettle—unlike thinner, which requires distillation in a vacuum. A simple water-cooled condenser transforms the vapor into liquid solvent. Garments (especially woolen ones) hold small amounts of water; this comes off during drying and distillation. The purpose of the water separator is to act as a settling tank, and it is constructed to take advantage of the wide difference in specific gravity between the solvent and the water. Because the unwanted water is lighter than the solvent and does not mix with it, it rises to the top and can be drained off before the solvent passes to the storage tank. The solvent from the drying section is similarly passed through the water separator.

After cleaning and drying is complete, the air in the machine still has some solvent content. Before the garments are unloaded, this solvent-laden air is exhausted to a carbon solvent recovery tower, which adsorbs (attracts to the surface of a solid) the solvent vapor in the same manner as the activated charcoal in a gas mask adsorbs poisonous vapors. Even this vapor is recovered.

Additives to provide water repellency, mothproofing, and so on can be included in the process. They are added in small amounts to the solvent as part of a one-stage or, more frequently, two-stage cycle. Here the bulk of the dirt is removed by the first washing, and the second solvent wash provides the additive treatment. The most common of such additives is retexturing.

To help the public and dry cleaners through the difficulties of identifying fabrics and suitable cleaning treatment, clothes are frequently labeled with advice in the form of symbols.

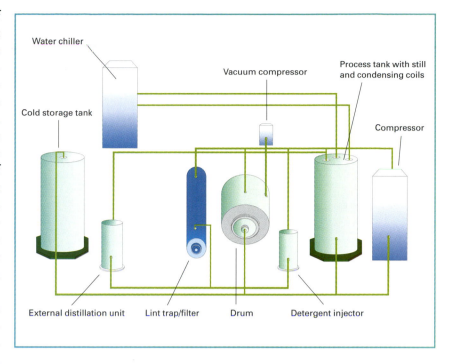

Water chiller

Cold storage tank

Vacuum compressor

Process tank with still and condensing coils

Compressor

External distillation unit   Lint trap/filter   Drum   Detergent injector

▲ Supercritical carbon dioxide could offer a safe and less environmentally hazardous method of dry cleaning in the future. Researchers at Los Alamos National Laboratory found that, under pressure, carbon dioxide acts like a liquid and washes the dirt out of fabrics. When it is allowed to return to the gaseous state the solids drop out and can be collected. The carbon dioxide can be repressurized and used over and over again.

New cleaning methods

Since the dangers of solvents to the human body and the environment became apparent, there has been much research to find alternative methods of cleaning fabrics without damaging them. One method that is gaining commercial acceptance is wet cleaning, which uses water as the solvent. Unlike home laundry, this is a professional service that uses computer-controlled machines and specially formulated detergents and additives. Tests using wet cleaning have shown it to be suitable for silks, linens, woolens, leather, and suede—often with superior results to dry cleaning.

Another method undergoing commercial trials uses a synthetic petroleum solvent process. Although the synthetic petroleum has a much reduced fire risk than ordinary petroleum and modifications have been made to the cleaning process to reduce the risk of flashing, some local fire regulations in the United States prohibit its use as a cleaning solvent.

Liquid carbon dioxide may prove to be an even better cleaning solvent. At 800 to 1,000 lbs. per square inch, carbon dioxide liquefies and can lift dirt out of clothing. When the pressure is released, the carbon dioxide becomes gaseous again and the dirt drops out of the solution for collection. By repressurizing the carbon dioxide, it can be used for further cleaning cycles.

Two more methods are under development. One process uses glycol ethers; the other is a water-based process using pulses of ultrasound.

SEE ALSO: DETERGENT MANUFACTURE • DISTILLATION AND SUBLIMATION • HYDROCARBON • ULTRASONICS • VAPOR PRESSURE

Dyeing Process

◄ These leather-dyeing pits at Fez, Morocco, are used to color vegetable-tanned goatskins. The crimson dye is extracted from local berries.

The efforts of humans to make themselves and their surroundings more colorful date from pre-historic times. People painted their bodies, either for adornment or for ritual purposes, long before they learned to make cloth from animal and veg-etable fibers. Experiments over the course of thousands of years taught them how to obtain colors from all kinds of sources, including ani-mals, plants, and even the soil and rocks.

While mixtures of finely ground minerals with oils or fats were useful as paints for the body and for decorative work, their application to textiles was much less satisfactory. Because they were insoluble in water, the colored particles in such paints did not penetrate the fibers of textiles. Also, since the adhesion of paints to the surface of the fibers was poor, they tended to flake off.

True dyeing, and not merely surface staining, depends on the ability of a dye to gain access to the interior of the fiber and stay there. To pene-trate fibers, a dye must be soluble—generally in water—even if only during the actual dyeing process. Once inside a fiber, dye particles stay fixed either because of a strong chemical affinity

▶ Filter presses (right) remove undissolved dye particles from dye solutions to prevent uneven dyeing. They consist of several sheets of fibrous filter material held apart by spacing frames. Crude dye solution is pumped in at one end and drains from the other, leaving any solid particles trapped on the filters.

for the dyed fiber or because of a final stage in the dyeing process that converts the dye into water-insoluble particles that are unable to escape the narrow pores of fibers during washing.

Until the mid-19th century, the only available coloring agents were natural dyes, whose colors were far from vivid. Furthermore, few of those dyes were fast to light and washing, so they soon faded through the action of sunlight or washing.

Early synthetic dyes

The first synthetic dye was made in 1856 by William Perkin, an English chemist who was attempting to convert aniline from coal tar into quinine, an important antimalarial medicine. By accident, he made an intense purple dye he later called mauveine. The almost-immediate success of aniline initiated an era of intensive chemical research in the industrial countries of Europe. This activity produced thousands of synthetic dyes derived from aniline, benzene, toluene, naphthalene, and other components of coal tar, generically known as aniline dyes.

The first synthetic dyes were more brilliant than any of the natural dyes, and their fastness to light and washing was excellent when used to dye animal fibers, such as wool and silk. However, the same dyes were less than satisfactory for fibers of vegetable origin, such as cotton and linen, because aniline dyes have little or no chemical affinity for cellulose-based fibers, so they wash out too easily—even in cold water.

The problem of poor fastness with cellulose fibers was largely remedied by mordanting—a process that had long been used to fix natural dyes. In mordanting, a dye is fixed in a fiber by treatment with solutions of metal salts, often in combination with tannic acid. The treatment

forms insoluble metal of the dyes that become fixed in the fine capillary spaces of the fibers and can no longer be washed out.

Because of their brilliance and high color yield, aniline dyes are still in use for coloring short-lived articles, such as cheap paper, but they no longer find much application in textiles.

Azo dyes

In 1858, a German chemist named Johann Gries discovered a reaction that joins certain aromatic molecules through an azo linkage—a double-nitrogen bridge (–N=N–). The combination of two aromatic rings attached to an azo linkage gives rise to molecules that absorb visible light, making them potentially useful as dyes. Nevertheless, it took until 1876 to develop the first useful azo dye, chrysoidine.

By careful selection of the starting materials, a variety of functional groups can be included in an azo compound. These chemical groups influence the chemical properties and color of the dye. Most azo dyes have intense orange, red, or yellow colors; a few are blue or green.

Water-soluble azo dyes that contain acidic functional groups are known as acid dyes. They have a strong chemical affinity for the amide groups of proteins, which are the basis of all animal fibers. This affinity makes them extremely stable dyes for such textiles as wool and silk.

Acidic azo dyes have no chemical affinity for cellulosic fibers. Instead, such fibers as cotton and linen can be colored using completely insoluble azo dyes in a process called ingrain dyeing. In this process, Gries's azo-coupling reaction happens in the fiber itself. One water-soluble component of the azo dye is soaked into the textile, then the presoaked textile is squeezed or spun to remove the excess solution. When the fiber is dipped into a solution of the other component of the dye, the two components react to form the dye. Where the components react within a fiber, the insoluble dye that results stays trapped within the fiber and cannot be washed away, so the dye is fast.

Vat dyes

The vat-dyeing process is based on the same principle as ingrain dyeing using azo dyes: a soluble precursor of a dye soaks into fibers where it is converted to an insoluble dye that remains fast in the dyed fibers. Like ingrain dyeing, vat dyeing is mainly used for cellulosic fibers.

Vat dyes include the well-known natural dye indigo, which has been in use for thousands of years. Indigo is now synthesized for dyeing, but its use is confined mainly to dyeing traditional nonfading blue denim (blue jeans) material.

◄ These reactors are used to manufacture azo dyes. The products of the chemical reaction are emptied into barrows and taken for drying, grinding, and packaging in other departments of the plant.

Most modern vat dyes are anthraquinones—derivatives of anthracene—or similar high-molecular-weight organic compounds. They are water-insoluble but can be converted into soluble "leuco" derivatives by chemical reduction. After dyeing, exposure to air or immersion in oxidizing chemical baths converts the leuco form into an insoluble dye that is firmly embedded in the fiber.

Sulfur dyes

The sulfur dyes are soluble in the presence of sodium sulfide, which is inactivated after dyeing so that the once more insoluble dye is held in the cellulosic fiber. Though these dyes are not as brilliant and light-fast as the vat dyes, they are fast when washed. The blacks and browns are mainly used.

Reactive dyes

The most recently developed dyes, the reactive dyes, are also very fast on cellulosic fibers and are produced by introducing a highly reactive group into soluble azo or anthracene dyes. This group combines chemically with cellulose. Reactive dyes compete strongly with vat dyes because of their brilliance, fastness, and ease of application.

Disperse dyes

The dyes mentioned so far are intended mainly for natural fibers. At the start of the 20th century, the first semisynthetic fibers came into production. These were the rayons and acetates—both produced by chemically digesting cotton linters

or wood pulp and then reconstituting fibers by further chemical treatment and spinning. The dyes used for cotton worked well for rayon, since it is essentially cellulose, as is cotton. Acetate fibers, which are cellulose modified using acetic anhydride, proved difficult to dye in this way, however, and the disperse dyes were developed in the 1920s for use with this fiber.

Disperse dyes are water-insoluble azo and anthraquinone dyes that dissolve in acetate fibers at elevated temperatures. They are prepared as fine dispersions, stabilized in water by surfactants similar to detergents. The fiber or textile is soaked in dye dispersion at around 175 to 185°F (80–85°C). At this temperature, acetate fibers swell and become porous, allowing the dispersed dye to penetrate them. When the fiber cools, it closes around the dye particles, making them fast.

Dyes for synthetic fibers

The main synthetic fibers are acrylics, nylons, and polyesters. Acrylics contain acid groups, so base-functional azo and other dyes are used. Nylons have amide groups similar to those of the proteins in animal fibers, so acid dyes are used.

Polyesters have the least potential for chemical affinity, so disperse dyes are used. Polyesters are less receptive to dyes than are acetates, however, so higher temperatures, elevated pressure, and solvents called carriers must be used.

Dyeing methods

The process of dyeing is dynamic: under the conditions of dyeing, dye molecules constantly move between the dye solution and the fibers. Since a good dye has an affinity for a fiber, it will tend to migrate from the solution onto the fiber, and this migration must be uniform if an even coloring is to be achieved. For this reason, either the material or the dye liquor must be kept moving to ensure a regular flow through the material. Localized regions where dye liquor becomes "spent"—depleted in dye—must be returned from the surface of the fiber for intimate remixing with the main body of the liquor to promote a steady fall in dye concentration in the bath.

The textile material may be dyed as loose fiber, yarn, or woven or knitted fabric, the form depending on subsequent processing. Single-color fabrics may be dyed after knitting or weaving, for example, whereas a multicolored fabric might be made using previously dyed yarn.

The type of machine used for dyeing depends on the form of the material that is to be dyed. Loose fibers can be dyed by compressing them into perforated containers through which the dye liquor is pumped. Yarns can be wound onto perforated tubes from which the liquor passes into the body of the yarn package. Similarly, woven fabrics can be dyed after rolling them onto perforated beams from which the dye liquor issues.

▲ A commercial silkscreen press prints a three-color design onto fabric. Each color is applied using a separate screen; the vessel containing the paste of dye and thickener for the green screen is visible at bottom right.

Most dyeing machines operate at elevated temperatures to increase the affinity between dye and material and to increase the speed at which dye molecules penetrate fibers. With polyester fibers, maximum affinity occurs well above the boiling point of water (212°F, 100°C), so a pressurized dyeing vessel must be used to prevent the water in the dye liquor from boiling off.

In pigment dyeing, affinity between dye and fiber is of no consequence. Organic or inorganic water-insoluble colorants of the type used in paints and lacquers are prepared in the form of fine aqueous suspensions. A water-dispersed resin that becomes insoluble on heating is added. After coating with the water-based dispersion of pigment and resin, the material is rapidly heated to around 250°F (120°C) in an oven. The high temperature drives off the water and hardens the resin, which adheres to the fiber and retains the pigment. Although the fibers are colored only on the surface, the method is useful for coloring impermeable fibers that have little or no chemical reactivity—glass fiber is a prime example.

FACT FILE

- *In Egypt, archaeologists found linen mummy wrappings, dating from 2000 B.C.E., dyed blue with extracts from indigo and woad plants. Other early Egyptian dyes included yellows and reds derived from the safflower, or dyers' thistle.*

- *Optical brighteners are fluorescent compounds that function by absorbing invisible ultraviolet radiation and emitting in the blue part of the spectrum. These additives, which are included in washing powders, are used to enhance the brilliance of white fabrics and overcome yellowing in some other brightly colored fabrics.*

- *In the preparation of Tyrian purple, the shell of the whelklike* Murex brandaris—*a mollusk from the eastern Mediterranean—had to be broken and a small sac removed by hand. A single pound (454 g) of the dyestuff required sacs from more than 3,500,000 shellfish, making the dye enormously expensive. Roman emperors, who wore purple togas and slippers, forbade others to wear purple-dyed garments, and in the Byzantine Empire only royal workshops were allowed to make purple cloth.*

Fabric printing

Fabric printing is a form of dyeing in which only certain parts of the surface of a fabric are colored or several colors are brought onto the fabric alongside one another in a pattern. The dyes are the same as those used in dyeing, but they are formulated into pastes that contain a high concentration of dye with a thickening agent, such as starch, to prevent the printed pattern from running. These pastes are applied by means of screen stencils or engraved metal rollers. A separate screen or roller is required for each color. After printing, the cloth is dried and then steamed to induce diffusion of the dyes into the fiber. Finally the thickener is washed out and the cloth dried once more.

Dye fastness

Modern dyed and printed textiles are expected to have colorfastness properties that were unattainable using older dyes. The fastness properties of principal interest to consumers are light and washfastness; others include specific resistances to perspiration, acids, and ironing.

Washfastness can be evaluated using prolonged washing under defined conditions, comparing dyed samples with standard panels of material before and after washing. Accelerated testing for lightfastness is performed using equipment that exposes test specimens to intense visible and ultraviolet radiations similar to those in sunlight. The test samples are exposed to this irradiation together with a standard panel of known lightfastness as a control. The specimens are checked for changes in shade at regular intervals. In this way, the lightfastness of a new dye compound or a particular dye batch can be established within hours as against the several weeks or even months needed with daylight testing.

Lightfastness is assessed on a scale of 0 to 8. A rating of 8 means that a dyed material will retain its shade until the material is worn out and has served its purpose. A large number of modern high-quality dyes have a lightfastness of 8, and the vat dyes are notably strong in this respect as well as in other fastness properties. Nevertheless, dye chemists constantly endeavor to synthesize new dyes that have maximum fastness ratings on all types of natural and synthetic fibers.

▲ Bundles of dyed yarn being removed from a dyeing vat to a drier. During the dyeing process, hot dye liquor issues from the perforated drum at the center of the vat, passes through the packed yarn, then drains through the perforated outer drum.

SEE ALSO: ANILINE AND AZO DYES • CHEMISTRY, ORGANIC • FIBER, NATURAL • FIBER, SYNTHETIC • LEATHER • PAINT

Dynamics

Mechanics is the study of moving bodies. It is traditionally divided into two parts, kinematics, which is concerned with the description of motion, and dynamics, which seeks to understand how the motion of objects is affected by the forces that the objects exert on each other. Kinematics makes use of concepts like mass, force, energy, and momentum to explain how objects influence the motion of each other. These influences are explained using the laws of motion, which explain how to identify the forces acting in any situation from their effects.

Engineers tend to treat the study of situations in which there is no motion as a separate science of "statics." Knowledge of statics is needed to design dams that will not burst and bridges that do not collapse. The principles of statics, however, are simply the laws of motion used in dynamics applied in situations where all of the force acting on each part of every object are in balance, so one can think of statics as simply a specialized part of dynamics.

History

In the 17th century, Sir Isaac Newton formulated three laws of motion based on his observation of the action of forces on objects. Newton and later scientists used these laws with spectacular success in their explanations and analysis of many types of motions, from the motions of planets around the Sun to the behavior of dust particles.

The discovery of Neptune in the mid-19th century was a notably successful application of dynamics. A dynamical analysis of the Solar System had shown that the observed motions of the known planets were at variance with what was predicted theoretically. It was then realized that the existence of an eighth planet was necessary, as the deviations could be explained only if there was a distant planet whose gravitational attraction was influencing the orbits of the known planets. Independent calculations by Leverrier in France and Adams in Britain predicted where to look for the eighth planet, its size, and some details of its orbit around the Sun. Then in 1846, the planet was located within a couple of degrees of the calculated position by Johann Galle in Berlin.

While Newtonian mechanics succeeds in describing the motions of most objects, it is inadequate for subatomic particles. Their properties can be described only through the theories of quantum mechanics.

Scalar and vector quantities

The properties that bodies exhibit because they are moving are called dynamical variables. Among the dynamical variables are speed, velocity, acceleration, momentum, and energy.

Speed is defined as distance traveled per unit time and is a scalar quantity, meaning that it has a magnitude expressed only in units of speed such as miles per hour or meters per second. Many dynamical variables, however, are vector quantities, which means that they must be assigned a direction in space as well as a magnitude.

Velocity, for example, is defined as speed in a particular direction and is a vector quantity. Thus, two automobiles may have the same speed if they cover the same distance in the same time but will only have the same velocity if they are traveling in the same direction (that is, in parallel paths). Momentum is also a vector quantity because it is defined as mass multiplied by velocity, and the direction of the resulting vector is the same as the velocity involved in its calculation.

The momentum of a body can be considered as a measure of how difficult it is to bring it to

30 mph (48 km/h)

▼ By pitching with topspin, a baseball can be made to curve downward in flight, because the stitches on the ball's surface drag air around the ball, creating an area of low pressure below it. The downward force of this low pressure accelerates the baseball downward faster than gravity alone, often fooling the batter.

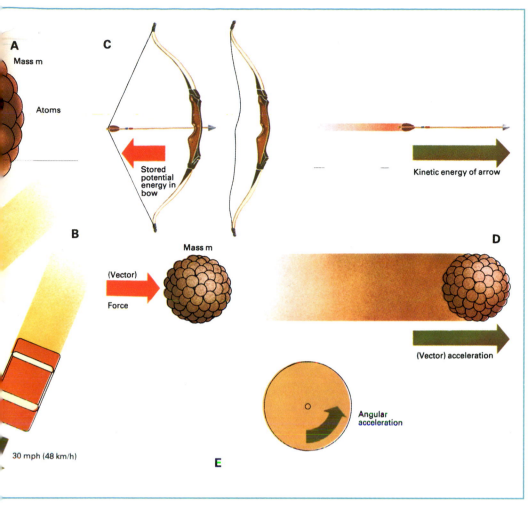

A Mass m

Atoms

C

Stored potential energy in bow

Kinetic energy of arrow

B

Mass m

(Vector)

Force

D

(Vector) acceleration

Angular acceleration

E

30 mph (48 km/h)

through turbines that convert some of the kinetic energy of moving water into electrical energy. In the process, the water is slowed down, that is, it yields part of its energy associated with its motion. The brakes of a moving vehicle cause it to slow down by converting some of the kinetic energy of the vehicle into heat, which is dissipated to the air.

Potential energy is the form of energy that a body possesses by virtue of its position in a force field or by its being compressed or stretched out of its normal shape. For example, a ball held above the ground has the potential to fall to the ground in Earth's gravitational field. While falling, some of its potential energy converts into kinetic energy as the ball gains speed. An archer's bow acquires potential energy when the string is drawn back. When the arrow is released, this potential energy is converted into kinetic energy as the arrow gains speed.

Both potential and kinetic energy are forms of stored energy—the former is stored by virtue of the position of an object, the latter by virtue of its motion. Work, on the other hand, is the amount of energy transferred to or from a body. It is, for example, the amount of energy imparted to a body when a force acts on it.

Power is another important dynamical variable, since it is the rate at which energy is transferred in time—the rate of doing work. Energy, work, and power are all scalar quantities, since they cannot be associated with a specific direction. Given an appropriate mechanism for doing work, energy can be harnessed to cause motion in any direction, for example.

rest. Consider two moving bodies, one with twice the mass but half the speed of the other. They are equally difficult to stop because the greater mass of the slower body compensates for the greater speed of the lesser mass. Provided they are moving in the same direction, the two bodies have exactly the same values of momentum.

Newton's first law observes that the momentum of a body in motion will change only if a force acts on that body, so a stationary object will not start to move unless a force acts on it, nor will a moving body change its speed or direction of motion. Newton's second law states that the rate (and direction) of the change of a body's momentum directly depends on the size (and direction) of the force that acts on it. Newton's third law—that two objects exert an equal and opposite force on one another (action and reaction)—helps calculate the forces that cause changes in motion.

Energy, work, and power

When a body is moving, it possesses a form of energy called kinetic energy. This energy may be harnessed and put to a useful purpose. Hydroelectric power stations do just that with the energy of moving water. The water passes

▲ Some of the basic concepts of dynamics. Mass (A) is the amount of matter in an object. Speed (B) is the rate at which an object covers distance, whereas velocity is the speed of an object in a stated direction. While two cars have the same speed in different directions, their velocities are also different. The potential energy stored in an archer's bow (C) is converted to the kinetic energy of the arrow when it is released. The action of a force on a mass causes it to accelerate (D); in a similar way, the action of a torque on a body causes angular acceleration (E).

Rotary motion

With linear motion, the force acting on a body is equal to the mass of the body times its acceleration (Newton's laws). Acceleration is the rate of change of velocity with time. With a rotating body, a similar relationship exists between the twisting force, or torque (from the Latin *torquere*, "to twist"), and angular acceleration; torque is equal to the moment of inertia of a body (inertia is resistance to being moved) multiplied by angular acceleration.

SEE ALSO: BALLISTICS • ENERGY, MASS, AND WEIGHT • INERTIA • NEWTON'S LAWS • PHYSICS • QUANTUM THEORY • STATIC MECHANICS

Earth

Earth is one of nine planets that orbit a very average yellow star called the Sun. The Sun and its entourage of planets, collectively known as the Solar System, are located toward the outer edge of a great spiral whirlpool of stars—a hundred thousand million of them in all—called the Milky Way galaxy. The Milky Way is just one galaxy among billions of others, all of which are rushing away from each other in the aftermath of the Big Bang, in which, it is theorized, the Universe was born some 12 billion years ago.

Earth makes one revolution around the Sun every 365¼ days, an interval of time called the year. Its orbit is slightly elliptical, at an average distance of 93 million miles (150 million km) from the Sun. Light takes just over eight minutes to cover this distance, and so, if the Sun were to switch off or suddenly brighten, it would take that long before life on Earth noticed the difference.

As it orbits the Sun, Earth spins rapidly about an axis through its north and south poles. It makes one revolution in just under 24 hours, an interval called the day. Earth is not a perfect sphere— it has a diameter at the equator of 7,930 miles (12,780 km), 25 miles (41 km) greater than its polar diameter, the distance between the north and south poles. The difference arises from the combined pull of the Sun's gravity and the spinning effect, which makes the equator bulge slightly and flattens the poles.

Earth does not spin vertically on its axis. The plane of Earth's equator is tilted at 23½ degrees to the plane of its orbit around the Sun, causing regions of Earth to experience changes in the amount of sunlight received during the year, known as seasons. Seasons occur because the Sun's rays strike the ground at a more vertical angle, and therefore have a greater heating effect, at one point in Earth's orbit than at the opposite point six months later. For example, summer occurs in the Northern Hemisphere at a point in Earth's orbit when the Northern Hemisphere is tilted toward the Sun and the Southern Hemisphere is tilted away to an equivalent degree.

Gravitational influences

The Sun's gravity pulls on the equatorial bulge of Earth and causes Earth's axis to gradually change its direction in space, a process known as precession. Polaris, the star currently above Earth's north pole, just happens to be where Earth's axis points today. The axis pointed in a different direction in the past, and the Egyptians, for instance, called a different star the pole star. The spin axis

▲ Volcanic eruptions provide scientists with an insight into the internal processes beneath Earth's crust.

sweeps out the surface of an imaginary cone, with a half angle of 23½ degrees once every 26,000 years. This path, however, wobbles in and out owing to the gravitational pull of the Moon as it orbits Earth.

Both the Moon and the Sun raise tides in Earth's oceans. The Moon's tides are about three times as high as the Sun's because of its close proximity to Earth. Tides arise because the Moon's gravity pulls the oceans on the side facing it more strongly than on the side opposite it. This causes twin bulges to occur on opposite sides of the planet that follow the orbit of the Moon. Because Earth spins rapidly, the Moon lags slightly behind this tidal bulge and acts as a brake on Earth's rotation. The effect is small and lengthens the day by just 16 seconds every million years. Nevertheless, the effect is discernible in the fossil record. Growth rings of ancient corals indicate to palaeontologists that 500 million years ago the length of a day was much shorter at just 21 hours.

The average density of Earth, found simply by dividing its total mass by its volume, is 3.2 oz./cu. in. (5.5 g/cm³). However, geologists know that Earth's crust is made mostly of silicates, which have a much lower density of about 1.6 oz./cu. in. (2.7 g/cm³). This discrepancy implies that there must be denser material at the center of the planet. Geologists say that the interior of Earth is differentiated into a number of different layers.

Structure of Earth

The internal structure of Earth has been determined by seismological studies. Earthquakes generate shock waves, which propagate as they pass through Earth. These waves are bounced back, or reflected, to the surface when they encounter boundaries where the density of rock changes abruptly. They may have their direction changed or be absorbed completely by some rocks. By observing the arrival times and properties of seismic waves arriving at measuring stations all about the globe, geophysicists are able to piece together a picture of Earth's interior, despite the fact that they can never penetrate deep below its surface with their instruments.

Earth has a thin outer skin rather like the skin of an apple. This skin is called the lithosphere, and includes the continental and ocean crusts that lie on top of it. The lithosphere consists of comparatively lightweight rock and varies in thickness from 62 miles (100 km) under large mountain ranges to as little as 3 miles (5 km) under the oceans. Temperatures of the rocks increase from an ambient surface temperature to about 2000°F (1100°C) at the base of the lithosphere.

Beneath the lithosphere is the mantle, the upper portion of which is molten. The mantle is some 1,740 miles (2,800 km) thick and within it temperatures rise from 2000°F (1100°C) to about 6690°F (3700°C) at the edge of Earth's core. The core, like the mantle, has a solid interior and a molten exterior. It consists of an iron sphere calculated to be roughly 2,175 miles (3,500 km) in diameter, where temperatures peak at about 7770°F (4300°C). It is the movement of the liquid core that gives rise to Earth's magnetic field.

INSIDE EARTH

Nobody can say for certain what lies beneath Earth's surface, but scientists have been able to make assumptions about its likely structure from the information obtained by observing earthquakes. Seismologists studying shock waves passing through Earth have detected three levels of major discontinuity that deflect waves at different angles, depending on how far through Earth the shock waves travel. Just below the crust lies a partially molten rocky material called the mantle. Farther in is believed to lie a layer of liquid iron, moving around a solid iron core. Expansion of the inner core may provide a possible explanation for plate movement.

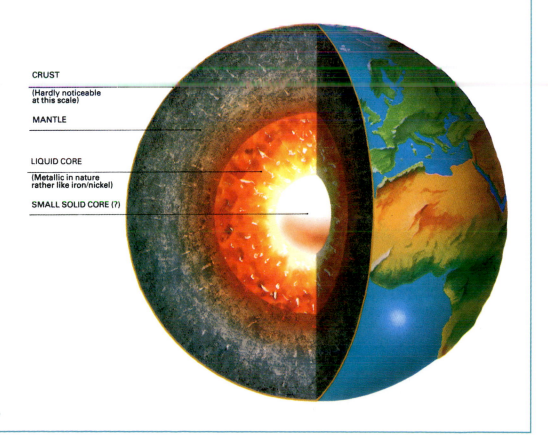

CRUST
(Hardly noticeable at this scale)

MANTLE

LIQUID CORE
(Metallic in nature rather like iron/nickel)

SMALL SOLID CORE (?)

Age of Earth

Earth's age has been determined from the radioactive dating of rocks. Elements that are radioactive gradually transmute into other elements, sometimes over geological time periods. The ratio of the abundance of the original element to the decay product changes with time. It is a clock set ticking when a rock first solidifies, and geologists can read the age of a rock by measuring the rate at which particles are emitted.

The oldest rocks found on the surface of Earth are thought to be about 3.8 billion years old. Any older rocks have not survived but have been remelted and incorporated into younger rocks. However, dating of meteorites from space has shown them all to be between 4.5 to 4.7 billion years old. Therefore, it is generally believed that the first objects solidified to form the Solar System about 4.6 billion years ago, and so this is also the age of Earth. Earth and the other planets formed from a pancake of gas and dust left over from the formation of the Sun.

The differentiation of the interior of Earth suggests that at one time, shortly after its formation perhaps, Earth was completely molten. This state would have allowed material to separate out and, in particular, the heaviest material—iron—to sink to the core. This idea presents a problem for modern theories of the origin of Earth. They require Earth to have accumulated over a period of about a hundred million years from the accretion of many small asteroids made of iron and stone. Imagine a large lump of clay at which many smaller lumps are thrown and stick; Earth, according to the most widely held theories, grew in a similar manner.

Unfortunately, this process could not have heated Earth's core above 2190°F (1200°C), well below even its present value, because the impacting bodies would have released their energy close to the surface of a forming planet, where it would

▲ An artist's impression of the formation of the Solar System. Matter in the original nebula clumped together in a rotating disk, which, over a period of about 50 million years, accreted into planet-size spheres.

be easily radiated away into space as heat.

Luckily, there is another source of heat that can explain how Earth melted and save the accretion theory of the origin of Earth—the natural radioactivity of rocks, particularly rocks containing the elements uranium, thorium, and potassium-40. The particles emitted in the decay of these elements heat up their surroundings. Because the heat released in this way does not leak out of the interior easily, it can be calculated that within a few hundred million years of the formation of Earth, the temperature of the interior had reached the melting point of iron. Once molten, the iron would have gravitated to the center to form the small solid core the planet has today.

The core makes up roughly one-third the mass of Earth, and the accumulation of such a large mass at the center would have released an enormous amount of gravitational energy as heat, enough to raise the central temperature to above 7590°F (4200°C) and melt the entire Earth. The lighter, more buoyant, rocks would quite naturally float to the surface, eventually cooling to form the crust.

This drastic heating of Earth about four billion years ago would have led to a considerable outgassing of gases, such as methane and ammonia, and of water vapor previously locked up inside rocks. Some of these gases formed the atmosphere, but some of the water vapor liquified and collected in hollows on the surface. Over many millions of years, these hollows also collected water precipating out of the atmosphere as rain, which leached salts out of the continental crust, making the growing oceans salty.

Plate tectonics

The surface of Earth—the crust plus lithosphere—is divided into more than a dozen large rafts, or plates, that float on the molten upper mantle. The continents and the oceans are carried on the backs of these plates, the continental crust riding higher, because it is lighter, than the much thinner oceanic crust. This picture of Earth's surface was arrived at only in the 1960s and 1970s. This revolution in geological thinking is known as plate tectonics. It is now known that the map of the world we take for granted is slowly changing as continents drift and smash into each other and new oceans are formed. In particular, 200 million years ago all the land mass of Earth was clumped together in a single supercontinent now known as Pangaea. The continents we see today were formed, according to the theory, as Pangaea broke up and the pieces moved in different directions.

Convection currents in the upper mantle are believed to provide the motive force for the movement of plates. Convection currents occur when hot and therefore light liquid wells up from the base of the upper mantle to be replaced by colder, heavier liquid coming down. A circulating current is established. Plates separate at rifts in the thin ocean floor. Here, molten rock, or lava, from the upper mantle squeezes out to fill the void. In this way, new ocean floor is continually being created in a process known as seafloor spreading. The Atlantic Ocean is growing in this way, and Europe and America are consequently moving apart at a rate of about one inch a year.

Plates can be destroyed when they collide perpendicularly. These collisions can occur between two oceanic plates, two continental plates, or an oceanic and a continental plate. In the latter, the denser oceanic crust of one plate plunges under the lighter continental crust of another, melting as it is consumed by the mantle beneath. The overriding plate crumples upward and forms mountain ranges and volcanoes while the over-ridden plate buckles under the tremendous pressure and forms a deep ocean trench. The area where one plate slides under another is known as a subduction zone. Two oceanic plates meeting act in a similar way, forming arcs of volcanic islands and very deep ocean trenches, such as the Mariana Trench near the Philippines. One of the more visible consequences of plate tectonics occurs when two continental plates meet. Because continental rocks are very light, the surface crust resists downward motion and instead buckles upward or sideways. The Himalayas were formed when the Eurasian plate met the Indian plate and created the highest mountains in the world.

When plates slide parallel to each other, they tend to slip in a series of jolts as contact stresses are built up then relieved. Such jolts can lead to quite devastating shallow earthquakes, as residents along the San Andreas fault well know.

Atmosphere

Earth has an atmosphere that is composed of roughly one-fifth oxygen and four-fifths nitrogen. The atmosphere is responsible for ironing out the extremes of temperature that would arise on an airless world, such as the Moon or Mercury. Sunlight falls more directly on the equator than on the poles and is particularly strong in the summer. Fortunately, this uneven heating leads to a planetwide circulation of the atmosphere. On a nonrotating world, hot air at the equator would tend to well up and flow toward the poles to be replaced by cool air flowing near ground level from the poles. The net result would be to warm the poles and cool the equator. The situation is slightly more complicated on Earth because the planet rotates quite rapidly around its north–south axis.

On Earth, air rises at the equator and tries to flow directly to the poles. However, at the equator the air is rotating at nearly 1,000 miles (1,600 km) per hour. As it moves to higher latitudes, an air mass also moves closer to Earth's rotational axis, and like a spinning skater raising her arms closer to her spin axis, it speeds up in the same direction as the rotating Earth. So high-latitude winds flowing toward the poles blow from the west (westerly), with the sense of Earth's rotation.

An Earthbound observer, unaware that Earth was spinning, would be puzzled by the tendency of air masses to be deflected in this way. It would be necessary to conclude that a force was responsible. This fictitious force, often used in discussions of atmospheric circulation, is called the Coriolis force. This is the same force that is used

▼ A view of Kanchenjunga from India. The Himalayas were formed when the Tibetan plateau was forced up as India and Asia collided. All the mountains in the Himalayas are getting higher every year as the plates continue to squeeze together. Evidence that they were once at sea level comes from water-laid sedimentary rocks found high up the peaks.

to account for the deflection of a missile initially launched in a northerly direction. It also accounts for why air flow around a low-pressure region is cyclonic—counterclockwise in the Northern Hemisphere and clockwise in the Southern Hemisphere—and anticyclonic near a high-pressure region.

The circulation in the atmosphere is more complicated than described, but nevertheless, the Coriolis force is an important concept for making sense of the wind systems on the planet. The large-scale ocean currents, familiar to mariners, are driven primarily by the winds. The oceans and other large bodies of water play a key role in regulating Earth's weather and climate. Almost 70 percent of Earth's surface is covered by water, at an average depth of 2.3 miles (3.7 km). Land temperatures change faster than those of water. Winds that have picked up heat from traveling over land masses cool as they pass over large bodies of water. When they hit warm land again, water vapor precipitates out, providing a source of fresh water for organisms to live on.

The biosphere

The most important of Earth's realms must be the biosphere. It penetrates the lithosphere, oceans, and atmosphere and is defined as the realm of life. There is good evidence that as long as 3.5 billion years ago single-cell organisms existed on Earth. Thinly layered deposits of limestone rock called stromatolites are known to be the fossilized reefs of algae dating from this early period. Life played an important part in creating the atmosphere Earth has today, expiring oxygen in the process of photosynthesis. Another theory suggests the biosphere regulates itself, adjusting oceans and atmosphere to protect and further life. As far as is known, Earth is the only planet in the Solar System on which life has arisen. As yet it is impossible to tell whether there may be life elsewhere in the Universe.

▲ Life on Earth may well have originated from single-cell blue-green algae growing in pools of warm water, as found today in areas of thermal upwelling, such as these geysers near Black Rock, Nevada.

SEE ALSO: AIR • ASTROPHYSICS • EARTHQUAKE • GEOLOGY • GEOPHYSICS • GRAVITY • LIFE • PLANETARY SCIENCE • PLATE TECTONICS • SEISMOLOGY • SOLAR SYSTEM • TIDE • WATER

Earthmoving Machinery

Earthmoving is an key part of most construction, landscaping, quarrying, and civil engineering projects. It encompasses the excavation of trenches for underground cables and pipes, the preparation of holes for foundations, and the creation of even surfaces for roadways and railroads.

The Industrial Revolution of the late 18th century started a rapid growth in earthmoving operations, as large tracts of land were cleared and leveled for factory construction, and canal, rail, and road networks flourished. At first, poorly paid manual laborers cleared and excavated land using picks, shovels, and carts. Then in 1835, a U.S. engineer, William Otis, invented a steam-powered excavator with cables that maneuvered a shovel at the end of a boom. Otis's shovel was first used to excavate cuttings for railroads in Maryland, then to dig canals in Canada; in both cases, the steam-powered shovel proved an invaluable aid in boosting productivity. The use of steam-powered earthmoving machines became widespread as the 19th century progressed.

Around the start of the 20th century, internal combustion engines started to replace steam engines as the source of tractive and lifting power for earthmoving machines. From the 1930s, hydraulics were used to deliver power from an engine to cutting and digging tools, removing the need for cumbersome cables and thereby increasing the efficiency of earthmoving machines.

Types of earthmoving operations

The most basic earthmoving operations are the breaking, removal, and redistribution of soil and rubble. For roadbuilding, topsoil is dug out to an even level and layers of concrete and aggregate are deposited on the new surface. For construction, troughs and shafts are cut to make room for foundations and sometimes a basement. For pipes and cables, a level-bottomed trench is first cut and the topsoil temporarily stored alongside the trench while the pipes or cables are laid. The topsoil is then replaced and compacted. In strip mining, earthmoving machines remove the overburden—soil and rubble that covers the mineral or ore—move it to storage, and then replace and landscape the overburden when extraction is complete. Finally, earthmoving machines can be used in combination with bioremediation or with incinerators and washers to remove or destroy soil contaminants such as dioxins or oil.

Two considerations are important for all types of earthmoving. First, earth becomes less dense and compact when broken into, since the excavation process shears the earth layers and allows air into the soil. When the soil is replaced, it must be compacted to remove entrained air and form a stable surface. The second consideration is the water content of soil, which can not only cause landslip but also places a strain on motors, tires, and tracks as machinery struggles to get a grip.

▲ The tracks of this bulldozer allow it to get enough grip to push a heavy load even in the rough terrain of a quarry.

BIG MUSKIE (1969–1999)

Officially a Model 4250-W Bucyrus-Erie dragline, *Big Muskie* was the largest ever machine to walk—or rather shuffle—on Earth's surface. Instead of wheels, *Big Muskie* had two cam-driven sleds that would lift her bulk and move it forward before setting her down and dragging themselves on to take another step. In this manner, *Big Muskie* could move at a maximum speed of 0.1 mph (0.2 km/h) around the Central Ohio Coal Company's strip mine near Cumberland, Ohio.

When *Big Muskie* was dedicated on May 22, 1969, she had taken three

Big Muskie's hull contained electric winches that could lift up to 325 tons (295 tonnes) in a 5,940 cu. ft. (168 m³) scoop hung from and pulled by 5 in. (13 cm) thick cables. The motors to run

Air filters

A-frame

Support cables

Mast

Hoist ropes

Press tubula

Tippi

Walkways

Hoist winch

Drag winch

Electric motors

Swing rack

Revolving frame

Tub (base)

Drag ropes

Operator's cab

Rotate mechanism

Cam-and-slide walking mechanism

years to build and cost $25 million. No other Model 4250-W would be built.

The statistics of *Big Muskie* are very impressive. The main body of the machine was 151 ft. (46 m) wide—as broad as an eight-lane highway—and 160 ft. (49 m) tall. With the boom down, the machine reached 487 ft. (148 m) in length. The unladen weight of the machine was 13,500 tons (12,245 tonnes).

the machine had a power demand equivalent to 27,500 homes.

For more than 20 years, *Big Muskie* would strip an hourly total of up to 19,500 tons (17,700 tonnes) of rock and soil, uncovering a coal seam 100 to 150 ft. (30–46 m) below the surface. Teams of bulldozers would then excavate the coal and load it into trucks for transport to a power station at Relief, Ohio.

In 1991, a drop in demand for Ohio's high-sulfur coal led to the closure of the Cumberland mine. *Big Muskie* remained a tourist attraction until 1999, when the Surface Mining Reclamation Act called for her removal. Despite widespread protests, *Big Muskie*'s boom dropped for the last time on May 20, 1999—two days before her 30th birthday—when the scrappers' high explosives cut through her cables.

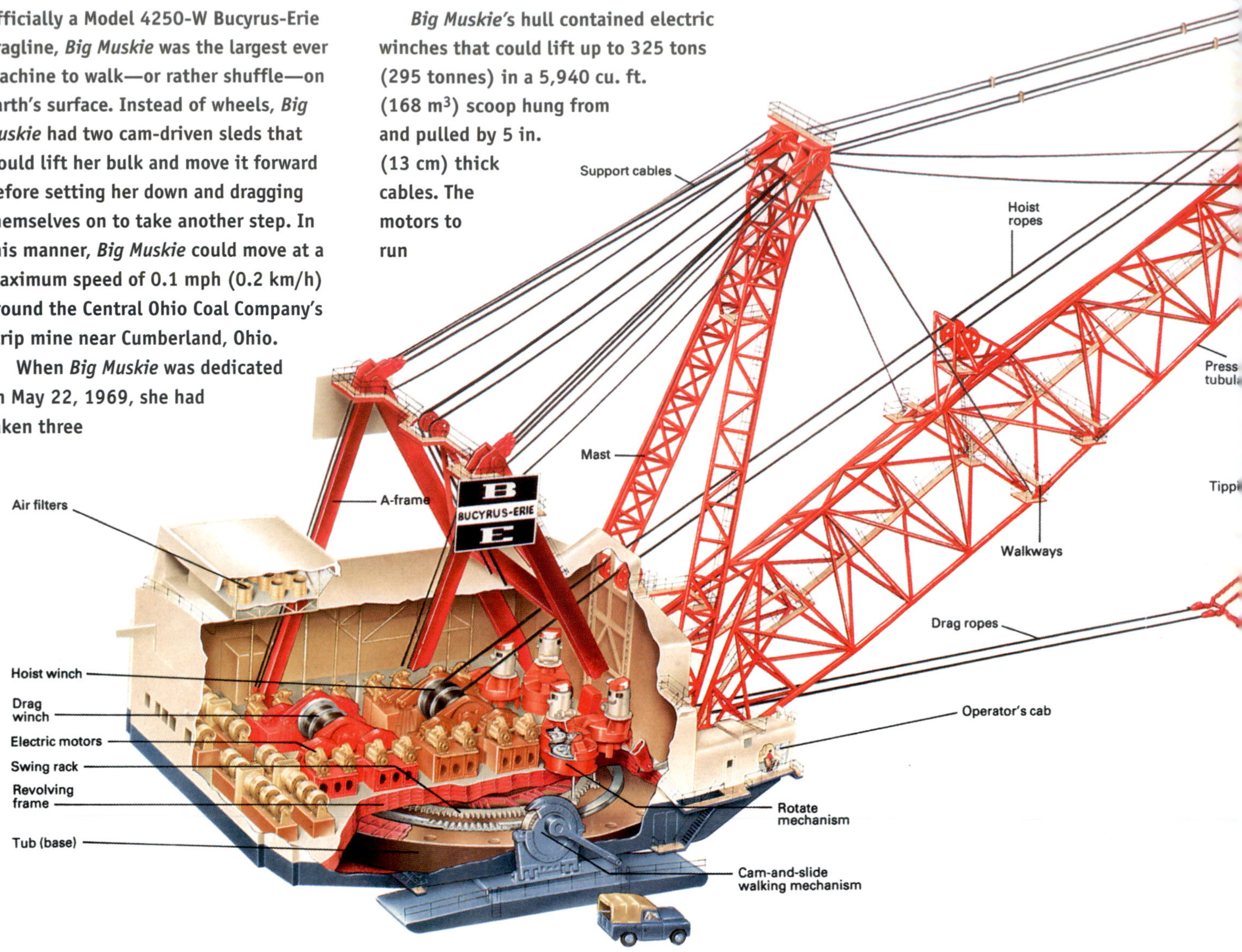

Developments in machinery designs

From the first steam-powered shovels to the most modern equipment, there has been a steady increase in the power-to-weight ratio of earthmoving machinery. The greatest increases occurred as a result of the change from steam to internal combustion engines and even electric power. Also, improved designs, materials, and engineering tolerances have contributed to improved power-to-weight ratios. A second trend in machinery design has been an increasing specialization of equipment according to the individual requirements of civil engineering tasks and catering for differences in types of soils, rocks, and artificial surfaces, such as concrete.

The tractive systems of earthmoving machinery have also been a focus of developments over the years. Diggers have to move to maintain the best position from which to excavate, while dump trucks often have to carry excavated material across rough terrain, for example. The first mobile steam shovels ran on track-mounted rails similar to railroad tracks that not only allowed the machine to move but also provided a stable platform on soft earth. Other machines used continuous tracks similar to those of military tanks to spread their weight. Bars across each pad of the continuous track enabled tracked machines to be used for haulage work. For decades, crawler tractors with high-grade steel tracks were the only option for high-power earthmovers.

In the 1980s, developments in heavy-duty tires and multiwheel-drive transmissions made wheeled earthmoving machines a viable alternative to tracked machines for some applications. Nevertheless, tracks still predominate on machines that draw or push tools rather than support heavy weights, such as loaded buckets.

Excavation

Of all the stages in the basic earthmoving cycle—cutting, lifting, transport, dumping, and consolidation—it is cutting that has the greatest demand for power. The type of equipment used for cutting depends on the volume of earth to be moved. For all but the largest-volume projects, machines with boom-mounted buckets or shovels tend to be used. Such machines suit a wide variety of applications, but they lose valuable productive time by lifting, slewing, and dumping between cuts.

High-volume cutting operations call for continuous production using cutting buckets mounted around the edges of massive wheels. The excavated material is carried away continuously by conveyor systems. Large multibucket wheel excavators are used for quarrying and mineral extraction, where the properties of the material to be cut are fairly consistent and easy to cater for with purpose-built cutting wheels. Elsewhere, cutting wheels are used to prepare shallow trenches without sharp turns for pipe-laying machines to install long stretches of pipelines for the transport of gas, water, or oil.

Large-scale machinery

Major earthmoving machinery—typically in the 200 to 1,000 horsepower (150–750 kW) power range—is used for large-scale schemes such as dam or highway construction projects or stone

and mineral extraction. Such equipment includes single- or dual-purpose machines that are tailored to shifting large volumes rather than to precision work where a fine-tolerance finish is the aim.

Projects such as major highway schemes often require the excavation of earth in one location and its removal for compaction in another part of the project. In undulating terrain, the level of a road surface is generally chosen so that the spoil produced by excavating cuttings through higher ground matches the demand for fill material for embankments across valleys, gullies, and water courses. Coordinated fleets of excavators and dump trucks then perform a continuous cutting-and-removal operation, sometimes moving earth over several miles. Where the earth is dumped, it must be consolidated by compactors—weighted trucks whose wheels or rollers apply pressure to drive excess air out of freshly deposited soil, leaving a stable solid mass of topsoil.

Scrapers (graders)

Scrapers are machines that both excavate and transport earth; also called graders, they are most useful for soft topsoils. At the heart of all scrapers is a box scraper—a metal container whose front end has an opening at the bottom above a blade that projects from the underside of the box. As the scraper moves forward, it cuts a slice of earth 4 to 6 in. (10–15 cm) deep from the topsoil. The cut earth pushes back into the box, and when the box is full, the blade lifts so that the load of spoil can be transported to where it is needed. In some cases, the box scraper trails behind a towing tractor. Otherwise, it may have a single diesel engine cantilevered forward of the towing axle, sometimes with a second engine to power the rear wheels. In particularly soft ground, a crawler tractor can provide massive extra force by applying full power to the shunting block on the back of the scraper to achieve a full box.

Draglines

Particularly soft earth can be removed by a dragline excavator. A dragline excavator has a large cutting bucket suspended from the end of a boom. The operator first lowers the bucket mouth down where earth is to be removed, then a second cable—the dragline—pulls the bucket across the surface. The weight of the bucket and the pull of the dragline make a blade at the mouth of the bucket dig into the topsoil, filling the bucket as it moves. When the bucket is full, its contents are tipped by lifting and inverting the bucket over a waiting dump truck. Dragline excavators are particularly useful in strip mining, where they remove the overburden or topsoil.

Bucket

Clamshell grabs

Clamshell-grab excavators are useful for digging deep shafts in soft earth. The clamshell grab is a form of bucket, hinged at the top, that swings open as it is lowered into the earth. The weight of the open grab drives it into the surface, where its jaws close to trap the cut soil. The suspension cable then pulls the grab up, and operating cables open it over a dump truck to empty its contents.

Hydraulic excavators

Heavy clays and soils with excessive water content require more concentrated cutting force than can be achieved using scrapers, draglines, or clamshell grabs. In such cases, a hydraulic excavator is the preferred machine. Descended from the original steam shovels, hydraulic excavators have a toothed bucket mounted on hinges at the end of a cable-operated boom. The boom positions the bucket at the cutting face, where powerful hydraulic rams drive it into the hard earth. After the cut, the excavator swings round on its base to tip the contents of the bucket.

Backhoes

Backhoes are used for similar types of earth as hydraulic excavators, but they have a different action. Instead of being mounted on a boom, the cutting bucket of a backhoe is fitted to a hydraulic arm that pivots in two places. Hydraulic rams first extend the arm and raise the bucket to the top of the cutting face, then they draw the bucket down and toward the power unit in a clawing motion.

The action of backhoe excavators makes them suitable for digging at vertical faces and for digging trenches. Backhoes can operate in relatively confined spaces and can even excavate the earth between their tracks, making backhoes ideal for digging trenches. Another advantage of the clawing action is that the whole weight of the machine assists in cutting, while the same force would topple a similar-sized hydraulic excavator.

Front-end loaders

One of the most versatile excavators is the front-end loader. This type of machine, originally developed for mineral extraction, has a cutting bucket hinged at the end of two hydraulically operated arms that protrude from the front of a wheeled or tracked power unit. The advantage of the wheel loader over the hydraulic excavator is in the former's flexibility and ability to feed conveyors or dump trucks without having constant stoppages to relocate for maximum efficiency.

Multipurpose machines

The backhoe loader, or 180-degree excavator, is a multipurpose earthmoving machine that has both a front-end loader bucket and a backhoe. Both tools are mounted on a wheeled or tracked power unit that can be stabilized for backhoe operations by raising the machine on hydraulic outriggers.

The backhoe loader started its career in the late 1950s as a tool for cutting trenches for the installation of utilities and foundations, as well as for moving spoil from the excavation site and

▼ A hydraulic excavator loads quarried material into a dump truck. For efficient working, the number of dump trucks must suit the production rate of the excavators.

moving building material to the point of construction. Such machines are designed for more precise work than the bulk earthmoving machines described above, and they reduce the number of machines required to fulfil all the groundbreaking and earthmoving requirements of a small-to-medium sized construction site. Their versatility is extended by such devices as jackhammer attachments for the backhoe arm and pile-driver rigs.

Bulldozers

Bulldozers developed in the 1920s from crawler tractors—powerful, reliable, and economical tractive units that ran on tracks to have good adhesion on soft ground. The bulldozer's tool is a vertically curved blade, somewhat wider than the track base of the power unit, that can be raised or lowered on arms that extend from the front of the power unit. While winched cables changed the elevation of the blade on early bulldozers, hydraulic rams that act through the arms are now used. Typical bulldozers weigh from 6 to 40 tons (5–36 tonnes) and they have engines that produce from 50 to 700 horsepower (37–520 kW). The tracks are usually of such a size that the bulldozer exerts less downward pressure than a human foot.

When the blade is horizontal, it simply pushes the load in front of the bulldozer, the vertical curve of the blade helping the load to roll along. If the blade is raised slightly, it leaves behind an even layer of the material in front of the blade, so a pile of gravel can be evenly spread, for example. Lowered slightly, the blade can cut an even layer from the ground in front of it and is used for clearing vegetation and providing an even surface.

Some bulldozers, called angledozers, have their blades set on an angle so that they discharge material to one side. Angledozers are useful for removing surface debris and topsoil.

Because of their great tractive power, bulldozers and angledozers spend much of their time hauling trailer appliances. Such appliances include compaction rollers and box scrapers.

Recent developments

While the basic forms of earthmoving machines have changed little in the past decades, the conditions in the operator's cabin have improved drastically. The introduction of electronic controls and measures to abate noise, vibration, and heat buildup have all helped reduce operator fatigue.

Laser guidance helps earthmoving machines to cut to more precise levels along more exact lines. Satellite guidance allows earthmoving machines to be operated remotely in large-scale schemes or potentially hazardous environments.

SEE ALSO: BUILDING TECHNIQUES • CONVEYOR • MINING TECHNIQUES • QUARRYING • ROAD CONSTRUCTION

Earthquake

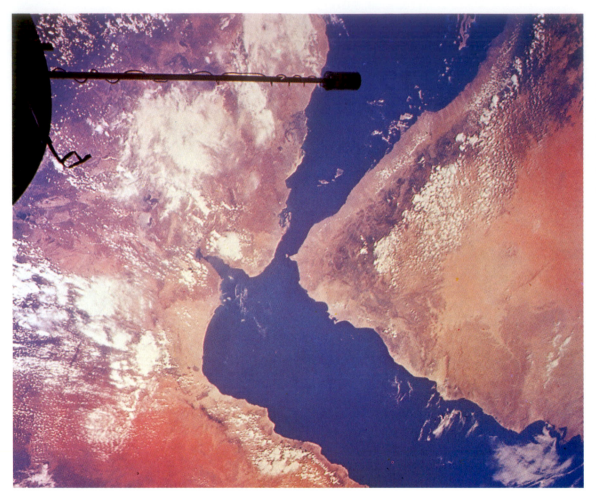

Earthquakes are some of the world's most dramatic natural phenomena. An earthquake is a vibration in Earth's crust that results from a release of energy generated by volcanic eruptions, man-made explosions, or more usually, a dislocation in rocks deep under the surface. The ground heaves and sways, rocks about, and even splits open. Movement may last for only a few seconds, or at the most a few minutes, but the aftermath can be one of total destruction of property and great loss of life.

Certain areas of the world are recognized as earthquake belts. The most notable are around the edge of the Pacific Ocean and across central Asia, extending toward the Mediterranean. Other areas of the world suffer only minor tremors that are barely noticeable—Britain, for example.

Within the earthquake belts, earthquakes may strike at almost any place and at any time, although some places seem to exhibit some kind of pattern. San Francisco's San Andreas fault is probably the most famous earthquake zone and seems prone to a major earthquake every 70 to 80 years. Though there have been a number of earthquakes in the area since the major event of 1906, it is now overdue for another, and many people are worried at the prospect. San Francisco is not the only city that has been almost wiped out by earthquakes: Tokyo, Lisbon, Guatemala City and Managua have all been victims.

Earth movements

Earthquakes are ground movements caused by shock waves. The geological forces at work in the Earth are beyond comprehension, strong enough to move entire continents. The mechanism behind earthquakes was suggested by the German

▼ The location of an epicenter is found by plotting its distance from three recording stations. The units calculate the range of the epicenter and this is used as the radius of an overlapping circle plotted around each station.

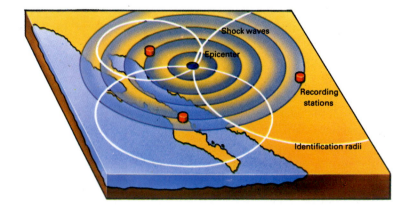

geophysicist Alfred Wegener in the early 20th century, when he postulated that the continents were moving across Earth's surface on giant plates. It took the scientific establishment some 50 years to embrace Wegener's theories, but now his explanation of the makeup of the continents is almost unanimously accepted by scientists.

Earthquakes and plates

Earthquakes occur along the boundaries of plates, whether they are moving toward or away from each other. Differential forces result in slow elastic deformation of the rocks. These stresses can continue building up strain in Earth's crust until rocks break and movement takes place along the fracture until the strain in the rock is partly or wholly relieved. The sudden movement and release of energy causes the shock waves that form an earthquake. This explanation of earthquakes is called the Elastic Rebound Theory.

Although most earthquakes happen at the edges of plates, they can also occur within continents along fault lines. A fault is a fracture in the crust where two or more blocks of the crust have slipped with respect to each other. In normal faults, the overlying block moves down the dip of the fault plane as a result of pulling or tension. Reverse, or thrust, faults occur when the crust is squeezed and one block rides up the dip of the fault plane. Lateral, or strike-slip, faults happen as a result of two blocks moving horizontally past each other, either because of tension or compression. This is the main process in the San Andreas fault.

Most earthquakes originate in the crust or the upper mantle at a point called the focus. Earthquakes are classified into three types according to the depth from the focus to the surface. Shallow earthquakes occur up to 43½ miles (70 km) below the surface, and intermediate between 43½ and 186 miles (70–300 km). The deepest-seated earthquakes have been measured at a depth of 435 miles (700 km), though these are still comparatively shallow given that the distance from Earth's surface to its core is 3,960 miles (6,370 km).

From the initial disturbance, a complex pattern of shock waves radiates outward through the rock and softer surface layers. They are reflected and refracted at discontinuities in these layers and at the ground surface so that, at any one point, they combine to form a complex shaking motion with vertical, horizontal, and torsional components. The point on the surface immediately above the focus is called the epicenter and is where the strongest shaking is usually felt. Even when the main build-up of pressure has been relieved, the area may experience to feel smaller aftershocks for weeks or months afterward as the ground settles into its new positions and smaller stresses that arise as a result of the main movement are eased.

Effects of earthquakes

Earthquakes are characterized by their destructiveness, but the largest magnitude earthquakes do not necessarily cause the most intense surface effects. Areas that have sand, clay, or other waterlogged, unconsolidated strata lying beneath them will suffer more than those supported by granite or basalt. When these sediments are shaken, they lose their strength and liquefy, causing subsidence in the layers above. Landslides triggered by the shaking can do more damage than the earthquake itself. Earthquakes beneath the ocean floor can sometimes create large destructive waves called tsunamis that can devastate coastal areas many hundreds of miles away.

Building techniques

Given the nature of earthquakes, there is obviously nothing that can be done to stop them. Instead, millions of dollars are being spent worldwide to minimize the effect of earthquakes.

Building techniques have been a focus of attention. Buildings are designed so that little or no damage will occur in a moderate earthquake, but with the knowledge that considerable damage will probably occur during a very strong shock. The design approach concentrates on the survival of the building's structure so that there will be no serious loss of life.

Initially, the energy put into a building is nearly all converted into shaking the building itself. The amount of energy that can be absorbed depends on the structure's natural damping, which is normally fairly low for modern buildings. Brittle materials, such as masonry, unreinforced concrete, and brickwork have only a limited capacity to

▼ Taken from 20,000 ft. (6,100 m), this infrared photograph of California shows vegetation as a false red color. The San Andreas fault runs diagonally across the picture from top left to bottom right.

absorb energy. However, well-constructed steel-framed and steel-reinforced concrete buildings tend to perform well in earthquake conditions.

Ideally, structures erected in earthquake-prone areas should combine very stiff concrete walls with a flexible framing system. A drawback when constructing this kind of building is that bolted connections have serious limitations, because the joints are almost entirely brittle in nature. The designer must ensure that the main steelwork has been designed so that stresses on the bolts are minimized.

Predicting earthquakes

While the major earthquake zones in the world are known, predicting where and when an earthquake will happen can only be based on estimates of probability. To do this, scientists can study the history of earthquakes in a particular area and set up strain gauges to measure the build-up of pressure in the crust. By collecting data on how much strain accumulates in a particular section of the fault in a year, how long it has been since the last earthquake in the section, and how much strain was released, scientist can calculate how long it will take for the strain to build to a level where an earthquake will result. So far, the San Andreas fault is the only earthquake zone in the United States subject to such intensive monitoring.

▲ This building in Kobe, Japan, shows the effects of the severe earthquake that shook the city in January 1995. Kobe is built on alluvial soils that liquefied when the earthquake happened. Many traditionally built houses were destroyed, though many new office buildings survived because they were built to resist lateral shaking movements. Fires from ruptured gas pipes added to the damage—with over 2,000 breaks in the water supply system hampering firefighting efforts, many were simply left to burn.

FACT FILE

■ *Measurements taken at the time of the Chilean earthquake of May 1960 indicated a series of "free oscillations" of the entire planet, which in effect vibrated like a giant bell. These measurements were made with a new seismograph that is capable of measuring strains and recording earth movements that occur with a frequency as low as an hour per vibration.*

■ *With the growing likelihood of a major earthquake on the San Andreas fault, monitoring is increasing in southern California. To measure radon and thoron gases, monitors are attached to boreholes drilled up to 200 ft. (60 m) deep in the rock. The equipment includes microcomputers that regulate the bubbling of air through groundwater in the boreholes.*

SEE ALSO: BUILDING TECHNIQUES • EARTH • ELASTICITY • GEOLOGY • GEOPHYSICS • PLATE TECTONICS • RADIOACTIVITY • SEISMOLOGY • SKYSCRAPER • TSUNAMI

Eclipse

An eclipse occurs when one celestial body passes in front of another, wholly or partially obscuring it. A solar eclipse, for example, occurs when the Moon passes across the disk of the Sun. Stars can also be eclipsed when they pass behind the Moon or one of the planets; this type of eclipse is known as an occultation.

During a solar eclipse, the shadow of the Moon falls on Earth. Anyone located inside this cone-shaped shadow will witness the Sun disappear completely. This phenomenon is known as a total solar eclipse and is one of the most dramatic of all astronomical events. The sudden disappearance of the Sun during the day terrified ancient peoples, understandably so.

Total solar eclipses are rare. They can be seen from a given spot on Earth only once every 300 years on average. Nevertheless, it can be calculated that there is one visible somewhere in the world about every eighteen months.

Total solar eclipses can occur because of a remarkable astronomical coincidence. Although the Sun is in reality some 400 times the diameter of the Moon, it is also about 400 times as far away. Consequently the Sun and the Moon appear the same size in the sky. However, because the Moon's orbit is tilted at about 5 degrees to Earth's orbit around the Sun, the Moon's shadow usually misses Earth, making a solar eclipse a rare event. Similarly, lunar eclipses are not as frequent as might be expected, because the Moon usually passes above or below Earth's shadow. Eclipses can therefore be seen only when Earth, the Moon, and the Sun are directly in line.

The corona

During a total solar eclipse, the Sun's corona can be seen, apparently sprouting from the black disk of the Moon. The corona is a shroud of extremely hot gas, at a temperature of millions of degrees, which extends out many solar diameters from the Sun's visible disk. The gas is so tenuous that its light is normally swamped out by the fierce light of the Sun—except, that is, during a total eclipse. Then, an extensive white halo is seen, sometimes with great streamers of gas flowing away from the equator.

Astronomers do not have to wait, though, for a total solar eclipse to observe the corona. With an instrument called a coronagraph, they can arrange for the image of the Sun's disk to be blocked out by a round black disk and so create an artificial eclipse. From this, astronomers can take measurements of the corona, observe the huge

jets of gas that flare out from the surface of the Sun, and measure the brightness of stars usually hidden by the Sun's light.

The region of Earth's surface from which a total solar eclipse can be seen is never more than 170 miles (275 km) across and is known as the path of totality. The period of totality can last as long as 7½ minutes in any one place along the path but usually averages 2½ minutes. The region of darkest shadow cast by the Moon is known as the umbra. Surrounding this region is a lightly shadowed ring called the penumbra in which a partial solar eclipse can be seen. Here, the Sun is only slightly dimmed as the Moon takes a bite out of its disk. Often, though, the tip of the Moon's shadow cone does not reach Earth, and a ring of sunlight surrounds the darkened Moon. This phenomenon is known to astronomers as an annular eclipse.

Lunar eclipse

There is one other arrangement of Earth, Sun, and Moon that also results in an eclipse. This is the lunar eclipse, which occurs when Earth passes between the Sun and the Moon and casts a shadow on the lunar surface. In order for a lunar

▲ This picture, taken during an eclipse in India, shows the full extent of the Sun's corona and radiating streamers stretching 200 miles (320 km) into space. This outer layer of gases (brown and blue regions) is normally invisible owing to the brightness of the Sun. It can be seen only during a total eclipse or when astronomers use a coronagraph to create an artificial eclipse.

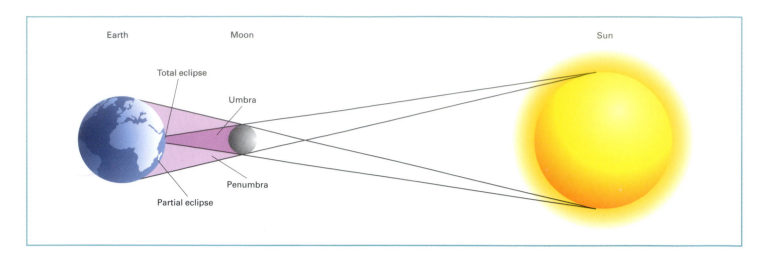

eclipse to happen, geometry requires that the Sun be setting as the Moon rises on the opposite horizon. The Moon rises already shadowed. The edge of the shadow is curved, providing direct evidence that the Earth is round, not flat.

Eclipses elsewhere in the Solar System enabled the first accurate determination of the speed of light, back in 1675. These eclipses were eclipses of Jupiter's four largest moons, discovered when the Italian astronomer Galileo first turned a telescope on the planet in 1610. All four

▲ An eclipse occurs when the Moon is in line with Earth and the Sun. Areas directly beneath the darkest part of the Moon's shadow experience a total eclipse, whereas regions covered by the penumbra see only a partial eclipse.

◀ A lunar eclipse shot by time-lapse photography, showing the shadow cast by Earth on the Moon as it rises.

disappeared behind Jupiter at some point in each orbit. With the aid of the newly invented pendulum clock, it was possible to time the interval between successive eclipses for each moon. For example, astronomers found that the moon Io went into Jupiter's shadow every 1¾ days.

However, there was a mystery. When Earth and Jupiter were on opposite sides of the Sun, the eclipses came 22 minutes later than they did when Earth and Jupiter were on the same side and therefore closest together. The Danish astronomer Olaus Roemer solved the puzzle. He realized that the delay was due to the finite speed of light. The 22 minutes, he reasoned, was the extra time taken for light from the eclipse to cross Earth's orbit. Believing that Earth's orbit was 174 million miles (278 million km) across, he concluded that light must travel at 130,000 miles per second (208 million km/s), a quite remarkable result for his time. The true value is 186,000 miles per second (299 million m/s).

Stellar occultation

An eclipse of a star by a planet is an event eagerly sought by astronomers. If the planet has an atmosphere, then the starlight will not be cut off abruptly but will instead dim in a more complicated way. From the variation in light, known as a light curve, information on the composition and structure of the atmosphere can be gleaned.

Stellar occultation revealed the rings around Uranus in 1977. A star was observed to dim repeatedly as it was occulted by each of Uranus's narrow, dark rings. Close observation of Neptune suggested this planet also had a ring structure, a fact confirmed when the *Voyager 2* probe flew past it in 1989.

SEE ALSO: ASTRONOMY • ASTROPHYSICS • LIGHT AND OPTICS • PLANETARY SCIENCE • RELATIVITY • SOLAR SYSTEM • SPACE PROBE • TELESCOPE, OPTICAL • TIDE • TIME

Ejection Seat

Toward the end of World War II, emergency parachute escapes from military aircraft were becoming increasingly difficult, and the introduction of jet-powered aircraft, with their vastly increased speed, virtually eliminated the possibility of a successful "over the side" bailout.

In 1944, James Martin, an aeronautical engineer, was invited by the Ministry of Aircraft Production in Britain to investigate the practicability of providing fighter aircraft with a means of assisted escape for the pilot in an emergency.

After investigating alternative schemes, it soon became apparent that this goal could be best achieved by forced ejection of the pilot's seat, with the pilot sitting in it, and that the most effective way of forcing ejection would be by an explosive charge. After ejection, the pilot would fall away from the seat and open a parachute by pulling a rip cord in the usual way. This solution also fitted in with the requirement of the British Air Staff at that time that any ejection system "utilize existing safety equipment."

Operation

When an ejection seat is operated in an emergency, the seat, complete with the occupant, carrying a parachute and a pack of survival aids, is ejected from the aircraft by an ejection gun. The ejection gun is secured to the aircraft vertically behind the back of the seat and is powerful enough to hurl the seat well clear of the aircraft even at high speed.

Some seats are fitted with a rocket motor underneath the seat in addition to the ejection gun to increase the height attained by the seat. The rocket is fired as the seat leaves the aircraft, and the combined force of the gun and the rocket will propel the seat and occupant to a height of about 300 ft. (91 m), which is high enough to allow a parachute to open fully, even if the ejection is made from ground level with the aircraft stationary. This feature is a decided asset when installed in modern vertical takeoff and short takeoff aircraft.

To commence ejection, the pilot pulls a handle located between the knees or pulls a screen down over his or her face, starting the ejection sequence while also protecting the face from the air blast. This action jettisons or fractures the cockpit canopy and fires the primary cartridge in the ejection gun, which unlocks the seat and ejects it from the aircraft. If a rocket motor is fitted, it is fired as the ejection gun tubes separate, thus continuing the thrust imparted by the ejection gun.

After the seat has left the aircraft, a drogue (small parachute) attached to the top of the seat is deployed. To ensure quick and positive deployment of the drogue, it is pulled out of its container at the top of the seat with some force by a heavy bullet fired from a drogue gun. The object of the drogue is to stabilize the seat and slow it down to a speed at which the occupant's parachute can be opened without fear of its bursting.

When the drogue has slowed the seat sufficiently, a barostatically controlled (pressure-sensitive) time release unit releases the drogue from the top of the seat, transferring its pull to the canopy of the occupant's parachute, pulling it out of its pack. Simultaneously, the time-release unit releases the occupant's safety harness from the seat, and the occupant is pulled clear by the opening parachute to make a normal parachute descent while the seat falls free without causing the pilot any obstruction.

Should the ejection take place above 10,000 ft. (3,048 m), the action of the time-release unit is delayed by the barostat control, which responds to atmospheric pressure in a similar way to an

▲ Some ejection seat mechanisms fracture the canopy using a detonating cord rather than by blowing off the canopy, enabling the pilot to eject more quickly. Ejection seats can also be used in stationary aircraft, as the rockets under the seat blast the pilot to a sufficient height for a safe parachute landing.

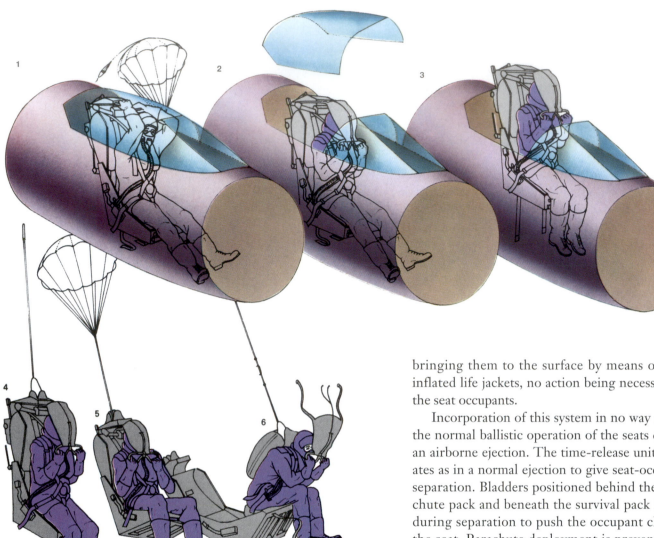

aneroid altimeter or barometer (atmospheric pressure falls as the altitude increases). By delaying the opening of the main parachute until this height, the seat and its occupant, stabilized by the drogue, descend quickly through the cold, rarefied upper atmosphere. The seat incorporates a built-in oxygen supply for the occupant to breathe, which is turned on automatically during ejection. This entire sequence is automatically controlled from the time the pilot operates the seat until landing by parachute, but in the unlikely event of the mechanism failing, the pilot can intervene and open the parachute by a manual rip cord.

Underwater ejection

An underwater escape system has been designed to provide automatic escape from submerged aircraft, even though the occupants may be unconscious. Ejection seats fitted with this underwater system are capable of ejecting occupants from the aircraft, separating them from their seats, and

▲ Operation of an ejector seat. (1) The face screen is pulled down to trigger the ejection mechanism. (2) The canopy is ejected. (3) The seat begins to eject and the drogue gun is primed. (4) The drogue gun fires, releasing the drogue from its container. (5) The drogues stabilize the seat and reduce its forward speed. (6) The time-release unit operates, pulling out the main parachute and freeing the pilot from his seat to land safely.

bringing them to the surface by means of fully inflated life jackets, no action being necessary by the seat occupants.

Incorporation of this system in no way affects the normal ballistic operation of the seats during an airborne ejection. The time-release unit operates as in a normal ejection to give seat-occupant separation. Bladders positioned behind the parachute pack and beneath the survival pack inflate during separation to push the occupant clear of the seat. Parachute deployment is prevented by severance of the parachute withdrawal line by a guillotine as the occupant leaves the seat. After separation from the seat, the occupant rises to the surface aided by a life jacket that is inflated by pressure from a carbon dioxide cylinder mounted on the life jacket and actuated by air pressure from the air cylinder.

Survival aids

In addition to the parachute, a pilot has a pack containing a variety of aids to assist survival. If the pilot comes down in a lake or the sea, a rubber life raft is used in addition to the normal life jacket. Of the other survival aids, the most important is a radio beacon that sends out a distress signal enabling search aircraft and ships to locate the pilot. Signaling equipment, protective clothing, food, and fishing equipment are also supplied.

The ejection seat is one of the most important parts of a modern military aircraft, and the Martin-Baker seat alone has saved nearly 7,000 lives since the start of manufacture.

 SEE ALSO: AIRCRAFT DESIGN • PARACHUTE • ROCKET AND SPACE PROPULSION • V/STOL AIRCRAFT

Elasticity

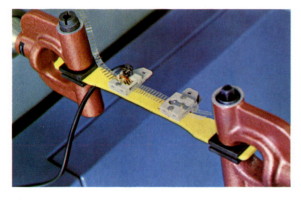

Elasticity is the ability of a substance or object to deform in response to an applied force and to return to its original dimensions when that force has been removed. All solids, liquids, and gases are elastic to some extent, but only gases are truly elastic under all conditions—no matter how far a sample of gas is compressed or expanded, it will always have the same volume at a given pressure, provided it returns to the temperature it had before the expansion or compression. Liquids are elastic within certain limits, but a bulk of liquid can fragment at low pressure, as happens when the thread of mercury breaks in a thermometer. The deformation and fracture of solid materials can be catastrophic if those materials form part of a structure or device, one of the reasons why studies of elasticity, deformation, and fracture generally concentrate on the solid state.

When the length of a solid material along a certain dimension is plotted against the magnitude of a tensile force along that dimension, part of the plot will be a straight line. That part of the plot is called the elastic region, and it represents conditions under which a solid expands in proportion to the size of the force applied to it. Beyond a certain point—the elastic limit—the solid no longer behaves in an elastic manner. For example, a large stretching force may permanently change the shape of a solid through a process known as plastic deformation, or plastic flow. Increasing the stretching force yet further will eventually cause the solid to fracture.

Hooke's law

Robert Hooke was the first scientist to study the elasticity of solids in depth. One of his conclusions—now known as Hooke's law—states that the change in length of a given body is proportional to the force acting on that body, provided its elastic limit is not exceeded. In more precise terms, the stress on an object is proportional to the strain on that object.

Strain, stress, and elastic modulus

The strain and stress cited in Hooke's law are concepts that help apply the law to a material in general, regardless of the shape of sample. A steel wire hung from a beam will extend by a certain amount if a weight is hung from it. If the same weight hangs from a similar wire of twice the length, the second wire will stretch by twice as much as the first wire, thus showing that the extension is proportional to the length of the wire. The strain—extension per unit length—is the same for both wires, so using strain in Hooke's law makes the length of the sample irrelevant.

If a weight is hung from two wires of different cross-sectional areas, the extension of the thicker wire will be less than that of the thinner wire in proportion to the ratio of their cross-sectional areas. For this reason, stress—force per unit cross-sectional area—is used to make Hooke's law applicable to samples of any cross section. Dividing strain by stress gives a constant value for any material within its elastic limit, and this constant is called the elastic modulus, or Young's modulus.

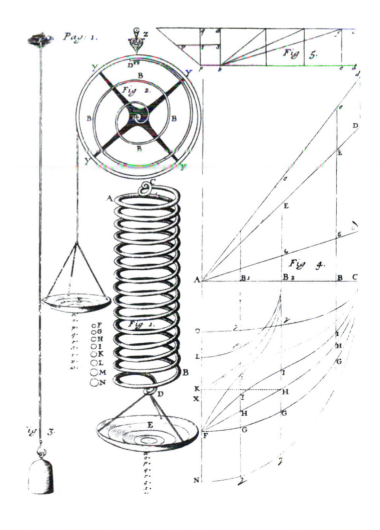

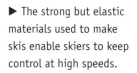

▶ The lower two samples have been subjected to strain testing—their original dimensions were identical to those of the upper sample. The middle sample has become longer and narrower, and there is some necking to the left of the center of the shaft. In the bottom sample, necking proceeded until the sample failed.

▶ The strong but elastic materials used to make skis enable skiers to keep control at high speeds.

Compression

The effects of compressive forces on solids are slightly different to those of tensile forces, since long, thin samples tend to buckle or fold under compression. If a sturdy block of a material is compressed, however, it will suffer a compressive strain that is proportional to the pressure placed on it. Pressure is simply a compressive stress and has the same units as tensile stress. When the stress and strain are plotted for such a sample, the modulus is the same as that for stretching.

Shear stress and strain

Another type of elasticity applies to substances that are made to bend. The elastic modulus in this case is the shear modulus, otherwise known as the rigidity modulus or torsion modulus.

If, for example, one end of a steel rod is firmly fixed to a horizontal base and a horizontal force applied to the top surface (that is, a shear force), the rod will bend, or lean over slightly. In this case, the rod changes not in size but in shape: it distorts. This shearing force produces a shear stress in the steel, which is the force divided by the area over which the force acts (that is, the top surface of the rod, which is therefore its cross-sectional area). The shear strain is a measure of the distortion of the rod and is determined from the angle of lean. The shear modulus is calculated from the ratio of shear stress to shear strain.

Shear modulus is used to calculate the degree of yield when, for example, a horizontal beam is loaded with weights. Shear modulus is important when choosing girder sizes for buildings.

Bulk modulus

When considering the change in volume of a solid or liquid under pressure, the bulk modulus is used, defined as the ratio of pressure (stress) to the relative change in volume (volumetric strain). The bulk modulus is particularly useful for liquids, which have a definite volume but no fixed shape. It is an important factor to consider, for example, in hydraulic systems.

Different types of materials

A highly elastic material, such as rubber, will suffer a great deal of strain before it reaches its elastic limit. It then has a relatively small range of plastic flow before it snaps. A brittle material, such as glass, can withstand little tensile strain before it fractures. Tough steel has a large Young's modulus, so it can withstand great tensile stress.

SEE ALSO: BUILDING TECHNIQUES • HYDRAULICS • PRESSURE • TENSILE STRUCTURE

Electret

An electret is an insulating material (or dielectric) that retains an electrostatic charge for many years and as such can be considered the electrostatic equivalent of a permanent magnet. Thus, while the magnet is a permanent source of external magnetic field, the electret is a permanent source of electric field. Electrets are usually produced in sheet or film form with one surface positively charged and the other negatively charged.

The analogy between magnets and electrets can be taken further, because both lose their effects when heated. Furthermore, a magnet will retain its magnetization longer if the magnetic path is short-circuited between the north and south poles with a bridge of iron, and similarly, an electret will retain its charge longer if the two surfaces are electrically short-circuited by sandwiching them between two connected metal plates, or keepers.

Electrical polarization

When an electret is formed, the material is said to be polarized—meaning that the positive and negative charges have been orientated in a pre-ferred direction. Electrets are called real-charge electrets or dipolar-charge electrets, depending on the method of preparation.

In dipolar-charge electrets the charges are arranged in positive–negative pairs and aligned in the same direction throughout the material. Here the arrangement is the same as the dipoles created in a dielectric material of a capacitor, but no external electrical field is needed to keep them aligned.

In a real-charge electret, external charges are trapped near each surface of the electret, so that one surface bears a permanent positive charge and the other surface a compensating negative electric charge.

Forming electrets

The earliest electrets were formed by a Japanese scientist, Eguchi, in 1919. He found that, if a high voltage was applied to two electrodes immersed in a molten mixture of waxes and resins and the mixture was then solidified with the voltage on, the material between the electrodes retained some permanent frozen polarization. This technique is known as the thermoelectret forming process and has been extended to include forming from materials requiring only elevated temperatures (not necessarily to the molten state). Indeed, in some cases no thermal treat-ment is required at all.

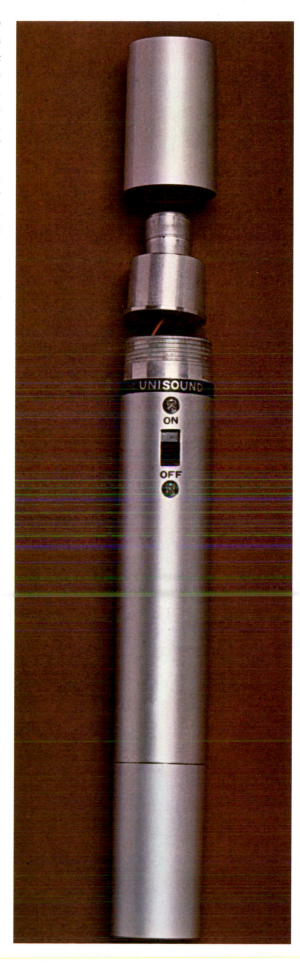

◀ This compact electret microphone contains an electret transducer connected to a small high-input impedance high-gain amplifier with battery.

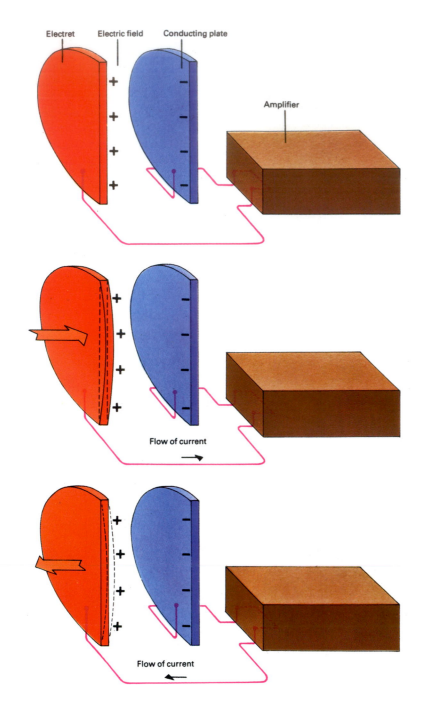

The most common material used for early work was carnauba wax, a hard yellow Brazilian wax used in furniture polishes and cosmetics. Electrets have been formed in this way from materials including Plexiglas, ice, shellac, and anthracene, and many other solid dielectrics (insulators) can be polarized in the same manner.

Recent interest has centered on the production of real-charge electrets, where, in essence, the effect is simply the ability of some materials to retain surface electrostatic charge for a considerable period. This renewed interest coincided with the advent of pure polymers in flexible-film form. They retain charge for long periods and, because of their very good insulating properties and roll-film form, permit simpler continuous charging techniques such as knife-edge corona charging

▲ In a microphone and amplifier circuit, the electret material and metal marker plate are connected as shown. When the electret is moved toward the conducting marker plate, an induced current flows through the amplifier, which in turn produces a voltage.

and electron-beam charging. Electrets of this type have been made from polyethylene, polypropylene, polystyrene, polycarbonate, fluorocarbon (including PTFE—Teflon), and many other polymer films.

Uses of electrets

One of the earliest uses of carnauba thermoelectrets was by the Japanese in the microphones of some of their field telephones during World War II. At the same time, United States and British patents were taken out for their use in equipment such as microphones, loudspeakers, electrometers, and voltmeters.

With the development of suitable polymer films, the interest in electrets for microphone use was renewed in the 1960s. The polymer-film electret can form the flexible diaphragm of a condenser microphone without the need of an external polarizing voltage. When a sound wave makes the charged diaphragm plate vibrate, the voltage across the plates changes and creates a signal that can be transmitted to a recording device. Such microphones have the advantage of wide, flat frequency responses, low distortion, insensitivity to shock and noise, low cost, and light weight, and they can be made extremely small (less than 0.2 in., 0.5 cm, in diameter and thickness).

Other forms of electret foil transducers have been used for ultrasonic detectors (up to 10^8 Hz), seismic detectors (down to 10^{-3} Hz on Apollo missions), and all frequencies between, including record player pickups, hearing aids, and earphones. Another application is in pushbutton keys for such devices as telephones and electronic calculators. It is estimated by one authority that ten million electret transducers are produced annually in Japan alone.

Electret transducers

Although the need for battery power may be a disadvantage, electret microphones enjoy many advantages over other types; their power requirements are simpler than those of capacitor microphones, their low moving mass makes them less susceptible to vibration and handling noise than moving-coil designs and offers a smooth frequency response, and perhaps as important, they can easily be fitted into a diverse range of housings. Cellular and cordless telephones, modems and other computer peripherals, voice-controlled toys, and even microphones on board space probes are typical applications.

SEE ALSO: ELECTRONICS • MICROPHONE • POLARIZATION • POLYMER AND POLYMERIZATION • TRANSDUCER AND SENSOR

Electrical Engineering

Electrical engineering uses electricity in practical applications. Many of these applications also draw on expertise from other disciplines, such as aeronautical, hydraulic, and mechanical engineering, and sometimes materials science and theoretical physics. The scale of electrical engineering covers an enormous range: from microcircuitry in computers, where distances are measured in microns, to power systems that span whole continents. This article presents some of the recent advances and current research in electrical engineering.

Advances in electric motors

The electric motor is a mainstay of electrical engineering. In its most basic form, it has changed little for well over a century: a motor consists of coils, called windings, wrapped around a rotor—a shaft that rotates between magnets. Currents in the coils produce magnetic dipoles that interact with the magnetic field to produce a turning force that spins the rotor. The windings of the motor are fed with electricity one after another through a commutator—a set of contacts at one end of the rotor. The commutator contacts slip between two feeder contacts, called brushes, and this action is a major cause of mechanical wear and eventual motor failure.

A new type of motor eliminates the need for a commutator—and avoids the risk of its failure—by using electronic switches to feed current to the appropriate winding at any given rotor position. Commutatorless motors are more reliable than their conventional counterparts, and they operate efficiently over greater ranges of speed and load.

The use of electronic switching also revolutionized a less conventional motor: the reluctance motor. This type of motor has a cog-shaped soft-iron rotor wheel. Fixed coils around the edge of the wheel are fed with current in sequence to provide a rotating magnetic field that drags the rotor around. In 1842, Robert Davidson of Aberdeen, Scotland, used a reluctance motor to provide traction for a primitive battery-powered locomotive. However, Davidson's motor used a rotating commutator to switch power between the coils of the motor, and the resulting loss of mechanical energy made his motor too inefficient to gain widespread acceptance. Electronic switching eliminates these losses, resulting in compact motors that are efficient and easily controlled. In the 1980s, switched reluctance motors acquired acceptance as drives for flexible-cycle washing machines, high-speed machine tools, and lightweight, easily controlled traction motors.

▲ The five-car *MLX01* high-speed magnetic-levitation train is a recent triumph of electrical engineering. In April 1999, this train attained a top speed of 343 mph (552 km/h) in trials on the Yamanashi Maglev Test Line, in Japan.

Magnetic micromotors

In 1991, the Japanese Toshiba company developed a reluctance motor with a potentially wide range of applications owing to its microscopically small size. The Toshiba micromotor measured less than 0.03 in. (0.8 mm) in diameter.

A variety of reluctance micromotors have been built since the Toshiba model. Their rotors are typically 0.004 to 0.006 in. (0.1–0.15mm) in diameter, with coils fixed in rings some 1.5 times the diameter of the rotor. Such motors have maximum speeds of around 150,000 rpm, can operate continuously at 20,000 rpm for a day or more, and produce more than 1×10^{-9} Nm of torque. The high rotor speed would necessitate a miniature transmission for many applications; nevertheless, it is thought that micromotors will one day be used to remove plaque from the inner walls of clogged arteries in human beings, for example.

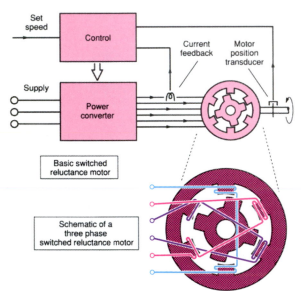

▼ The introduction of electronic switching in the late 20th century revived interest in reluctance motors. This type of motor was invented in the 1840s but abandoned owing to a lack of efficiency caused by the commutators used in the original design. A reluctance motor (top left) is considerably smaller than a conventional motor of equivalent power (top right). The main reason for the compactness of reluctance motors is the small diameter of the rotor (bottom left) which turns between windings in a cage (bottom right). The diagram at left shows schematically the circuits and components of a reluctance motor that runs from a three-phase AC supply.

Superconducting devices

For many decades, electrical engineers have been developing applications of superconductors—materials that lose all electrical resistance at low temperatures—with the intention of reducing energy losses and increasing the efficiency of electromagnets and electrical machinery.

When wound into coils that are well insulated and cooled with liquid helium, superconductors, such as niobium–titanium alloys, can be used to make extremely powerful electromagnets, because coils of such materials can carry extremely large currents without suffering the energy losses and overheating that would happen were a conventional conductor to be used. With careful design, superconducting electromagnets can produce magnetic field strengths four to ten times stronger than those achieved using conventional electromagnets.

To date, the most widespread use of superconducting electromagnets has been in nuclear magnetic resonance (NMR) spectrometers, which are used for scientific analysis, and in the closely related magnetic-resonance imaging (MRI) body scanners used for diagnostic tests in hospitals. Both types of equipment require extremely strong magnetic fields in order to function effectively.

More experimental applications include high-flux magnets for containing plasma at extremely high temperatures in nuclear fusion experiments, and superconducting coils in prototype electricity generators. General Electric has successfully tested a 20 megawatt generator that used superconducting coils. The generator was half the size of a conventional machine of the same power output, yet more efficient.

The applications of superconductors have long been limited by the requirement of extremely low temperatures for materials to behave as superconductors—close to absolute zero (– 460°F, –273°C) for the first known examples. Such temperatures could be achieved only by cooling with liquid helium, which boils at –452°F (–269°C). Ceramic materials have since been formulated that superconduct at –218°F (–139°C)—a temperature that is easily achieved using readily available liquid nitrogen—and it is hoped that materials scientists will eventually develop superconductors that will function at room temperature and not need to be cooled.

Maglev vehicles

Electrical engineers have been developing maglev (magnetic-levitation) vehicles since the early 1960s. Magnetic fields support, propel, and brake such vehicles, so they have no physical contact with their tracks. The absence of wheel-to-rail contact eliminates rolling friction and wheel noise, thereby improving passenger comfort and causing less environmental impact than a conventional high-speed train. Also, because the heavier part of the drive mechanism is built into the track, maglev vehicles are lightweight and require significantly less energy than conventional trains to accelerate to high speeds and to climb gradients. The power required to lift such a vehicle is a mere 1.5 kW/ton (1.7 kW/tonne)—the same consumption as 15 (17) 100-watt lamps. A so-called transformer coupling supplies onboard current demand through the gap between the track and the vehicle without physical contact, so no overhead or third-rail current collector is necessary.

Numerous "short-hop" maglev links exist already—typically as transports to ferry people between airport terminals—but the potential for scheduled high-speed intercity passenger services is yet to be fully exploited. However, a number of test schemes for high-speed intercity systems are approaching fruition around the world. The German Transrapid system is one such project. It uses conventional electromagnets that are attracted upward toward twin steel guide rails, which also provide lateral guidance. Speeds of 240 mph (400 km/h) have been achieved on the Emden test track in Germany. Another system, developed at the Miyakazi Maglev Test Center in Japan, uses superconducting electromagnets to provide lift and drive. This system has reached vehicle speeds of around 340 mph (550 km/h) on test tracks at Yamanashi and has even been tested on two trains passing one another at a relative speed of 600 mph (966 km/h). Both types of systems require good magnetic shielding, otherwise stray magnetic fields could damage passengers' credit cards, watches, and other magnetizable objects and could even stop cardiac pacemakers.

The first commercial long-distance services are due to start in the early decades of the 21st century. In 1996, the German federal government approved a 176 mile (284 km) Transrapid link between Berlin and Hamburg, but this is unlikely to meet its completion date of 2005. Instead, the first Transrapid system will probably be built in China. The first long-distance maglev in the United States could be a Transrapid link between Las Vegas and the California–Nevada state line, but no construction schedule has been decided. Japan has plans to install a Tokyo–Osaka link.

► The *Yamato I* of the Ship and Ocean Foundation of Japan cruises around Kobe Harbor, near Osaka. Its magneto-hydrodynamic propulsion system has no moving parts.

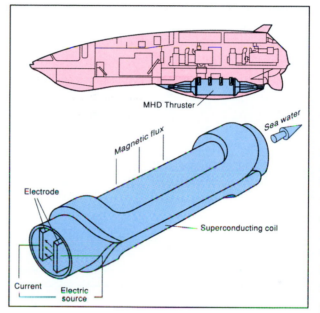

MHD Thruster

Magnetic flux

Sea water

Electrode

Superconducting coil

Current

Electric source

◄ The two MHD turbines of the *Yamato I* are in the underbelly of the vessel below the waterline (top right). Each turbine has a pair of superconducting electromagnets that produces a vertical magnetic flux within it. This flux interacts with an electrical current that flows between electrodes at the sides of the tubes, forcing water through the tube to generate thrust.

Magnetohydrodynamic propulsion

Magnetohydrodynamics, or MHD, is an effect whereby a current-carrying liquid experiences a force in a magnetic field. The origin of the effect is exactly the same as that which causes a force in the wires of an electric motor's windings: the interaction between an electric current and a magnetic field at right angles to that current produces a force that acts at right angles to both the electric current and the magnetic field.

In 1992, the Ship and Ocean Foundation of Japan launched a boat that uses MHD for propulsion. Called *Yamato I*, it is 100 ft. (30 m) long, weighs 180 tons (163 tonnes), and can carry seven passengers. The boat cruises at a modest six knots (7 mph, 11 km/h), but it is believed that much bigger boats will be able to cruise at 100 knots (115 mph, 185 km/h) using MHD propulsion.

The principle of operation is simple. Sea water can flow freely through two tubes running along the length of the boat below the waterline. Superconducting coils above and below each tube produce a magnetic flux in a vertical plane through those tubes. Electric current is passed through the water at right angles to both the flow and the magnetic field. A force is exerted on the water that propels it through the tube and out through the nozzles, giving forward thrust. Water flows smoothly through MHD turbines, which cause neither the turbulence nor the vibration associated with conventional propeller drives.

Electricity and the environment

The effective use of electrical power contributes to environmental protection in a number of ways. Fossil fuels can be burned efficiently in power stations, producing more useful energy per unit weight than they would in factory furnaces or internal combustion engines, for example. This fact and the fact that an increasing amount of energy derives from "free" renewable sources are two of the reasons why the U.S. Department of Energy predicts an increase in energy consumption of only 4.4 percent in the first decade of the 21st century. The gross domestic product—an indicator of commercial activity—is forecast to increase by 9.5 percent in the same period.

Electricity produces no pollution where it is used, and power stations that burn fossil fuels can be equipped to control pollution far more effectively than can smaller fossil-fuel-burning engines and turbines. As a result, electric vehicles have long been seen as the best option for reducing transport-related pollution. While electric streetcars and trains follow fixed routes and can be catered to by their own power-supply networks, electric cars and trucks must carry their own power supplies in order to be able to move with the same freedom as a gasoline or diesel vehicle.

▲ Volvo's hybrid-drive concept car of the late 1980s combined electric traction with a diesel-powered generator unit that could be used to recharge the car's battery on long journeys.

Some electric vehicles are supplied by onboard batteries, but they have the disadvantages of poor acceleration, low maximum speeds, and limited ranges between stops for recharging. Other prototype electric vehicles use fuel cells that convert hydrogen-containing fuels into water as they produce electricity. These suffer from the weight of their fuel-storage equipment and the potential risks of highly inflammable fuels.

In the late 1980s, Volvo produced a hybrid-drive concept car that compromised between the advantages and disadvantages of diesel and electric cars. Hybrid-drive cars run on electricity alone with no exhaust emissions on short runs, while on longer runs, the diesel turbine can be used to recharge the power plant as the car is moving, thus giving a longer range.

Plasma-arc incineration

As well as helping to reduce the amount of pollution produced, electricity can be used to actively destroy pollutants to prevent them from harming the environment. Since 1991, Nufarm, an Australian herbicide manufacturer, has been using plasma-arc technology to destroy waste products at its manufacturing plants. An electric arc, struck between copper electrodes, creates a plasma whose temperature is between 18,000 and 27,000°F (10,000–15,000°C)—around twice as hot as the surface of the Sun. This temperature is sufficient to decompose even chemicals such as dioxins, which are extremely toxic and difficult to destroy in conventional incinerators. Since the waste is destroyed as it forms in the plant, the risks of storage and disposal are avoided.

◀ The superconducting windings of this prototype electricity generator, built by General Electric, were cooled to −452°F (−271°C) during extensive trials in which it produced over 20,000 kilovolt-amperes—more than twice the power output of a conventional generator of the same size.

SEE ALSO:	Automobile • Electricity • Electric motor • Linear motor • Low-emission road vehicle • Magnetohydrodynamics

Index

i